THE EARTH STORY
IN THE NEW
TESTAMENT

The Earth Bible, 5

THE EARTH STORY IN THE NEW TESTAMENT

edited by
Norman C. Habel
and Vicky Balabanski

SHEFFIELD ACADEMIC PRESS
A Continuum imprint
LONDON • NEW YORK

THE
PILGRIM
PRESS
Cleveland

Copyright © 2002 Sheffield Academic Press
A Continuum imprint

Published by Sheffield Academic Press Ltd
The Tower Building, 11 York Road, London SE1 7NX
370 Lexington Avenue, New York NY 10017-6550

www.SheffieldAcademicPress.com
www.continuumbooks.com

Published in the USA and Canada (only) by
The Pilgrim Press
700 Prospect Avenue East
Cleveland, Ohio 44115-1100
USA

USA and Canada only
ISBN 0-8298-1501-5

British Library Cataloguing-in-Publication Data
A catalogue record for this book is available from the British Library

Typeset by Sheffield Academic Press
Printed on acid-free paper in Great Britain by MPG Books Ltd, Bodmin, Cornwall

ISBN 0-8264-6060-7

Contents

Foreword

Archbishop Desmond Tutu

Planet Earth is in crisis. More and more life systems are being threatened. Scientists estimate that at least half, and perhaps as many as 80 per cent, of the world's animal and plant species are found in the rainforests. The rainforests are the lungs of the planet, producing much of the oxygen that humans and other oxygen-dependent creatures need to survive. The rainforests, alas, are still being destroyed at an alarming rate.

Resolving the ecological crisis of our planet, however, is no longer a problem we can leave to the scientists. Just as we are all part of the problem, so we are all also part of the solution. We all need to come to terms with the forces that have created this crisis and the resources within our traditions that can motivate us to resolve the crisis. One of those traditions is our biblical heritage.

It is significant, therefore, that the Earth Bible Project has chosen to take the Earth crisis seriously and to re-read our biblical heritage in the light of this crisis. The Earth Bible Team has listened closely to ecologists and developed a set of principles to re-read the biblical text from an ecojustice perspective. The concern of Earth Bible writers is not to defend the biblical text blindly, but to identify those passages which may have contributed to the crisis and to uncover those traditions which have valued Earth but been suppressed.

I commend the Earth Bible Team for including representative writers from around the globe, including the Southern hemisphere. I commend the team for confronting the biblical tradition honestly and openly in dialogue with ecologists. And, in particular, I commend the writers for daring to read the biblical text afresh from the perspective of Earth. Feminists have forced us to confront the patriarchal orientation of much of the biblical text. Earth Bible writers are now confronting us with the anthropocentric nature of much of the biblical text. We now ask: does the text devalue Earth by making the self-interest of humans its dominant concern?

I recommend you read the Earth Bible series with a critical but empathetic eye. As a critical reader you will want to assess whether writers make their case for their interpretation of the text in terms of the principles employed. As an empathetic reader, however, you will need to identify with Earth and the suffering Earth community as you read the text.

I hope that the promise of 'peace on Earth' will be advanced by this laudable project as scholars probe our heritage to understand and assist in resolving the crisis of our planet.

Editorial Preface

Norman C. Habel

I am writing this Preface at a time when a number of seminary communities are celebrating the centenary of the birth of the illustrious
Alttestamentler, Gerhard von Rad. The insights of this great scholar are
numerous. I was struck again by the approach he enunciated at the
beginning of his volume *Wisdom in Israel*. He writes:

> We are therefore left with no alternative but to use, to begin with, the
> terms with which we are familiar. In what follows, therefore, frequent use
> will be made of 'orders', of an 'inner law' of creation, of a 'secular
> understanding of the world' etc. (1972: 6).

Though it may be disputed whether von Rad's approach to wisdom
literature is close to an ecological reading, this critical approach has a
radically different orientation to the *Heilsgeschichte* hermeneutic usually
identified with von Rad. Biblical scholars, following the lead of von Rad,
continue to search for the tools necessary to 'read' the text in legitimate
new ways. The approach of the Earth Bible Series represents another
way in the journey of contemporary hermeneutics.

In the interests of continuing the dialogue about this approach, we
have included in this volume a number of papers that are more open-
ended and reflect dimensions of the dialogue itself. The paper of the
Earth Bible Team is a series of reflections on the state of play of
ecojustice hermeneutics and is designed to further the debate. My paper
on John 1 is not intended to be definitive, but, as the title suggests,
extends a challenge to scholars exploring texts included in the Christian
Bible and written after the beginning of the first century CE, known as
the Christian Scriptures (also known as the New Testament or Second
Testament).[1] I am inviting scholars to consider whether this classic text—

---

1. Although the debate about an appropriate and inclusive term for the texts
written after the beginning of the first century CE—and included in the Bible used by
many Christians—is still ongoing, we have decided to use 'Christian Scriptures'
instead of the term 'New Testament' where appropriate. However, where authors
have chosen to use the term 'Second Testament' to describe these texts, we have

located at the beginning of one of the Gospels in the Christian Scriptures — is Earth-friendly. Vicky Balabanski and Elaine Wainwright have offered an initial set of responses to this challenge.

Another example of this dialogical approach is found in the paper by Elmer Flor from Brazil. Not only does his work raise significant questions about the Cosmic Christ texts that informed colonial conquests of countries like Brazil, but he has provoked me to take the discussion a step further. At pivotal points in the paper, ecojustice questions arising from the paper are presented for further research and analysis.

The articles in this volume of the Earth Bible Series do not attempt to deal with the large number of texts in the Christian Scriptures that pose problems when read from the perspective of Earth. Seven articles on texts from the Christian Scriptures appear already in the first volume. An article on Romans 8 by Marie Turner appears in the third volume. This volume, however, does include representative articles on texts from the Gospels, Acts, the Pauline Epistles, the book of Hebrews and the book of Revelation.

These articles also reflect differing approaches and styles. While each article interacts with one or more of the ecojustice principles, some are more technical exegetical works and others more contextually reflective. The analyses by Alan Cadwallader exhibit a high level of appreciation of the ancient Graeco-Roman world of the text. This leads to a surprisingly fresh reading of Hebrews 11 revealing that the 'heavenly home' of believers is not equivalent to heaven as a home above, but is rather a new way of relating with Earth. Similarly, Barbara Rossing's grasp of the role of the Roman Empire in destroying the environment leads to a new understanding of Earth in Revelation 12.

Insights into the role and voice of Earth in several passages is facilitated by an exploration of the immediate context and specific connections with traditions relating to the Hebrew Scriptures. The question Michael Trainor poses in his investigation of Stephen's speech in Acts 7 can only be fully appreciated in the light of the cosmology reflected in key passages from the Hebrew Scriptures. Adrian Leske, by studying the prophetic imagery of key parts of Second Isaiah, enables a richer appreciation of the natural world discussed in Mt. 6.25-34.

In several articles, the contemporary context also plays a key role in

deferred to their choice as this term seems not to have the exclusivity of the older and more familiar term 'New Testament'. Our intention in making this choice is to avoid offending any biblical scholars. If our choice of terminology is nevertheless offensive to any reader of the Earth Bible Series, please accept our apologies, as this was not our intention.

focusing on how Earth or components of Earth are valued in the text. For Oyeronke Olajubu, reflection on the nature and value of water in the Yorubu culture enables her to discern new dimensions in the healing narrative of John 9. Elmer Flor's acute consciousness of how the beliefs of the Church are complicit agents in the colonial conquest of Brazil helps him to appreciate the dilemma of how to interpret the relationship of the Cosmic Christ to the natural world in Ephesians 1.

Writers continue to interact with the ecojustice principles of the Earth Bible Project in various ways. William Loader reads the preface of Mark's Gospel with a view to hearing the voices of Earth in the wilderness, from the sky and with the animals. Anne Elvey dares to confront the probability that the text of Lk. 12.13-34 presents an over-evaluation of humans in relation to the natural world.

The articles by Harry Maier and Keith Dyer are both written against the background of how popular understandings of apocalyptic have influenced readings of texts such as Revelation 22 and Mark 13 respectively. The task they undertake is to reread the text in the light of the principle of interconnectedness, using Earth as partner in the process. Dyer even articulates (somewhat tongue in cheek) a set of six popular biblicist apocalyptic principles that stand in diametric opposition to the six ecojustice principles of the Earth Bible Project.

My thanks to all contributors in *The Earth Story in the New Testament*, including Denis Edwards who has supported the Earth Bible Project since 1998 when, at a conference on Religion and the Environment, the Earth Bible Project and a Contextual Ecotheology Project were initiated. One result of the Contextual Ecotheology Project, under Denis's leadership, is a well-crafted and highly relevant volume entitled *Earth Revealing/Earth Healing: Ecology and Christian Theology* (Collegeville, MN: Liturgical Press, 2000).

My thanks also to the core members of the team—Vicky Balabanski, Charles Biggs, Duncan Reid, Marie Turner, Peter Trudinger, Michael Trainor, Alan Cadwallader and Shirley Wurst (who continues to be the indispensable team editor formatting articles to make them consistent).

I remain grateful to those who have supported the project in various ways, whether with funds, in kind or in person. The project is now located in the Centre for Theology, Science and Culture associated with the Adelaide College of Divinity and Flinders University of South Australia. The body whose financial support has underwritten the project to date is the Charles Strong Memorial Trust. This trust is named after Charles Strong, the founder of the Australian Church that operated from 1885 to 1955. The trust promotes the sympathetic study of all religions and fosters dialogue between religion and other disciplines.

This project is the result of a dialogue between religions, especially Christianity, and ecology. Continuing supporters of this project include Flinders University and the Adelaide College of Divinity.

A special word is in order about the logo for this series. The artist who worked with me in developing this logo and drafted its final form is Jasmine Corowa. Jasmine is a young Indigenous Australian whose art reflects traditional Aboriginal techniques of communication. Her father, Dennis Corowa, is one of the Rainbow Spirit Elders whom I supported in their publication *Rainbow Spirit Theology.* I was privileged to edit a set of Jasmine's paintings, published in 2000 by The Liturgical Press and entitled *The Rainbow Spirit in Creation: A Reading of Genesis 1.*

The logo is a symbol of Earth. The land dots are in Earth colours forming that maze of shimmering life we call Earth community. The white dots of the sky rise above Earth. The surface of the land/Earth is an open book. This is a double symbol: not only is the land/Earth read like a book (as Australian Aboriginal peoples do) — when we read The Book we do so from beneath, from Earth.

I appreciate the continued commitment of Sheffield Academic Press and The Pilgrim Press. I want to express my personal gratitude to the publishers David Clines and Philip Davies who have made the academic component of the Earth Bible Project possible. The staff of Sheffield Academic Press also deserve commendation for their professionalism and patience.

Preface

Denis Edwards

It is a joy for me as a theologian to be invited to offer a few words by way of preface to Volume 5 of the Earth Bible Project. It would be hard to overstate the importance of this project. My own conviction is that there is no more urgent task for biblical scholars than the work undertaken in these volumes.

My generation bears responsibility for the loss of much of the abundance and diversity of life on Earth and faces the prospect of an increasingly impoverished planet. I believe that this state of affairs calls for a new commitment to Earth from people of every age group, every country and every occupation—from parents, farmers, lawyers, business people, architects, teachers, gardeners, writers, artists, politicians, builders, cooks, engineers and biblical scholars. We need all the resources of the human community focused on the issue of the health of our planet and committed to its healing. This task will require a long-term and sustained resolve.

Those of us who work in theology and in biblical studies have a humble but fundamental role to play in this process. For many people, religious convictions matter. For them, religion is something that shapes and underpins their view of the world. Theologians and biblical scholars are required to ask critical questions about the way that particular biblical and theological texts, images, ideas and symbols function. Do they reinforce an unthinking anthropocentrism? Do they function to support exploitative attitudes? Or do they function to communicate and sustain a love and respect for Earth creatures in all their diversity?

I would argue that Christians have nothing to fear and much to gain from such a critical stance towards the tradition. At its deepest level, Christian theology is a theology of ongoing creation. Things exist in all their diversity because God enables them to be and to become within an evolving universe. The greatest thinkers of the biblical and theological tradition have understood the diversity of creatures as the self-expression of a God who transcends every creature, and who is most fittingly represented by the abundance and fecundity of the diverse creatures that make up our universe. They have understood that God loves each creature, delighting in its uniqueness and specificity and holds each in a redemptive embrace. They believe that in the life and death of Jesus of Nazareth, God is with the world of creatures in the most radical way possible, bringing healing and hope. His resurrection is the promise and the beginning of eschatological communion in the Trinitarian God for the whole of creation.

I believe that Aldo Leopold captured something central to the Christian understanding of God when he said: 'God likes to hear birds sing and to see flowers grow.' A fearlessly critical assessment of our tradition can only be a gift to a theology that seeks to be faithful to such a God.

It seems clear that we Christians are called to rethink every aspect of our theology in the light of the ecological issues we face. This involves not just honest criticism of what leads towards attitudes destructive of Earth and Earth creatures, but even more importantly the creative development of what leads to liberation and Earth healing. Rosemary Radford Ruether has said, in *Women Healing Earth* 1996, that we need to be 'less dogmatic and more creative' about what is good and bad, useful and unusable in our traditions. She suggests that we avoid the extremes of smug self-satisfaction on the one hand and rejection of one's tradition as toxic waste on the other. What is needed is the sustained effort to bring to the fore the liberating and life-respecting dimensions of our own traditions.

It has been a great privilege to work in Adelaide with scholars who share these convictions. It has been wonderful to collaborate over the last few years with a team of theologians working on ecotheology, a collaboration that has borne fruit in the publication of the book *Earth Revealing/Earth Healing* by The Liturgical Press. But those of us working away in systematic theology have been much encouraged by the enormous creativity of our colleagues in biblical studies that has resulted in the five volumes of the Earth Bible Series. The Earth Bible Series is a truly substantial contribution to the work of ecological theology, involving scholars with different specialities from many parts of the world. The ecojustice readings of biblical texts that it offers will be foundational for all of us who are trying to contribute to an authentically ecological Christian theology.

Abbreviations

AB	Anchor Bible
ABD	David Noel Freedman (ed.), *The Anchor Bible Dictionary* (New York: Doubleday, 1992)
ANRW	Hildegard Temporini and Wolfgang Haase (eds.), *Aufstieg und Niedergang der römischen Welt: Geschichte und Kultur Roms im Spiegel der neueren Forschung* (Berlin: W. de Gruyter, 1972–)
BAGD	Walter Bauer, William F. Arndt, F. William Gingrich and Frederick W. Danker, *A Greek–English Lexicon of the New Testament and Other Early Christian Literature* (Chicago: University of Chicago Press, 3rd edn, 2000)
BARev	*Biblical Archaeology Review*
BBR	*Bulletin of Biblical Research*
BETL	Bibliotheca ephemeridum theologicarum lovaniensium
Bib	*Biblica*
BibInt	*Biblical Interpretation: A Journal of Contemporary Approaches*
BibSem	The Bible Seminar
BibTod	*Bible Today*
BMCRE	British Museum Coins of the Roman Empire
BTB	*Biblical Theology Bulletin*
CurTM	*Currents in Theology and Mission*
ETL	*Ephemerides theologicae lovanienses*
HTR	*Harvard Theological Review*
HUCA	*Hebrew Union College Annual*
IB	*Interpreter's Bible*
ICC	International Critical Commentary
JBL	*Journal of Biblical Literature*
JNES	*Journal of Near Eastern Studies*
JRS	*Journal of Roman Studies*
JRT	*Journal of Religious Thought*
JSNTSup	*Journal for the Study of the New Testament*, Supplement Series
LD	Lectio divina
NCBC	New Century Bible Commentary
NICNT	New International Commentary on the New Testament

NIGTC	The New International Greek Testament Commentary
NovT	*Novum Testamentum*
NRSV	New Revised Standard Version
OTP	James Charlesworth (ed.), *Old Testament Pseudepigrapha*
RevExp	*Review and Expositor*
SBLSP	SBL Seminar Papers
SBT	Studies in Biblical Theology
SNTSMS	Society for New Testament Studies Monograph Series
SNTW	Studies in the New Testament and its World
TDNT	Gerhard Kittel and Gerhard Friedrich (eds.), *Theological Dictionary of the New Testament* (trans. Geoffrey W. Bromiley; 10 vols.; Grand Rapids: Eerdmans, 1964–)
WBC	Word Biblical Commentary
WUNT	Wissenschaftliche Untersuchungen zum Neuen Testament
ZNW	*Zeitschrift für die neutestamentliche Wissenschaft*
ZPE	*Zeitschrift für Papyrologie und Epigraphik*

List of Contributors

Vicky Balabanski, a member of the Earth Bible Team, is a Lecturer in New Testament at Parkin Wesley College, Adelaide College of Divinity, Flinders University of South Australia. She has recently published *Eschatology in the Making: Mark, Matthew and the Didache* and *That We May Not Lose the Way*. Her current research is on the Jewish Queen, Alexandra Salome.

Alan Cadwallader, a member of the Earth Bible Team, lectures in New Testament in the School of Theology, Flinders University of South Australia. His earliest publication was a contribution to an environmental assessment of human impact on part of Australia's coastline (1976). More recently he has edited *AIDS: The Church as Enemy and Friend* (1992) and penned *Jesus in Paul* for the Australian Biblical Project (1998). He celebrates in the crisp morning air and evening gully breezes of the Adelaide hills.

Keith Dyer is Professor of New Testament, Whitley College, Melbourne, Victoria. His recent publications include *The Prophecy on the Mount. Mark 13 and the Gathering of the New Community* (1988) and 'But concerning that day...' (Mk. 13.32) in *Prophetic and Apocalyptic Eschatology in Mark 13* (1999). His current research is in the Gospel of Mark, the book of Revelation, and Paul and politics.

Denis Edwards is senior lecturer in systematic theology at the Adelaide College of Divinity and Flinders University of South Australia. He is the author of *Jesus the Wisdom of God: An Ecological Theology* (1995) and *The God of Evolution: A Trinitarian Theology* (1999). His current research project involves developing an ecological theology of the Holy Spirit.

Anne Elvey is an Honorary Research Associate in the Centre for Women's Studies and Gender Research at Monash University; in 1999 she completed a PhD entitled 'Gestations of the Sacred: Ecological Feminist Readings from the Gospel of Luke'. Anne has published 'Leaf

Litter: Thinking the Divine from the Perspective of Earth', in *What's God Got To Do with it?* and 'To Bear the Other: Toward a Passionate Compassion (an Ecological Feminist Reading of Lk. 10.25-37)', in *Women Scholars in Religion and Theology 1* (2001). Her current research interests are on the intersection between senses of genealogy and senses of place in biblical literature and in contemporary Australia.

Elmer Flor is a Brazilian Lutheran Professor who recently received a Doctorate in Theology from the University of South Africa (Pretoria). His thesis was on 'Amen in Old Testament Liturgical Texts: Its Meaning and Later Development as a Plea for Ecumenical Understanding' (May 2001). He is presently undertaking a research project on the bio-ethical worth of water in biblical time and its relevance for the preservation of the hydric resources of Brazilian rivers.

Norman C. Habel, the Chief Editor of the Earth Bible Project, is Professorial Fellow at Flinders University of South Australia and Adelaide College of Divinity. His major works include a commentary on *Job* in the Old Testament Library, *The Land Is Mine: Six Biblical Land Ideologies* and *Reconciliation: Searching for Australia's Soul.* His current research extends to ecoliturgical and ecojustice writings for the wider community.

Adrian Leske is Professor of Religion Studies at the Concordia University College of Alberta. His published writings include 'Context and Meaning of Zech. 9.9', (2000) and 'Matthew' in *The International Bible Commentary: A Catholic and Ecumenical Commentary for the Twenty-First Century* (1998). Other relevant research involves 'Isaiah and Matthew: The Prophetic Influence in the First Gospel—a Report on Current Research', in *Jesus and the Suffering Servant: Isaiah 53 and Christian Origins.*

Harry Maier is an Associate Professor of New Testament Studies Fellow of Green College, University of British Columbia, Canada. Two of his recent publications include *Remembering Apocalypse: Autobiographical and Exegetical Studies in the Book of Revelation at the End of Christendom* (2002) and 'Staging the Gaze: Early Christian Apocalypses and Narrative Self-Representation' (1997). He is pursuing research in colonial studies and Christology in the first two centuries of the Common Era and the use of the New Testament in post-New Testament early Christianity.

Oyeronke Olajubu is Senior Lecturer in the Department of Old Testament, University of South Africa. She has published a number papers, including 'Polluting your Ground? Woman as Pollutant in Yehud: A Reading from a Globalised Africa', and 'Esther and Northern Sotho Stories: An African–South African Woman's Commentary' (2001). She is currently engaged in contextual re-readings of the Hebrew Bible from a bosadi (African–South African womanhood) perspective. Her 1996 doctoral thesis was titled Proverbs 31.10-31 in a South African Context: A Bosadi (Womanhood) Approach.

Barbara Rossing is Associate Professor of New Testament at the Lutheran School of Theology in Chicago. Her publications include 'River of Life in God's New Jerusalem: An Ecological Vision for Earth's Future' (1998), and *The Choice between Two Cities: Shore, Bride, and Empire in the Apocalypse* (1999). Her research in recent years has focused on the policies of the Roman Empire, especially in relation to the environment.

Michael Trainor, a member of the Earth Bible Team, is Senior Lecturer in the School of Theology at Flinders University of South Australia. His major publications include *Jesus in Luke's Gospel, According to Luke: Insights for Contemporary Pastoral Practice,* and *2001: Quest for Home: The Household in Mark's Community.* His current research is in hermeneutics, Gospel study in the light of social scientific perspectives and the intersection of archaeology and biblical research, with particular interest in ancient Colossae.

Desmond Tutu is former Archbishop of Capetown, South Africa, and is currently Archbishop Emeritus of the same city. Two of his major publications include *The Rainbow People of God* and *No Future Without Forgiveness.*

Elaine Wainwright is a Lecturer in Biblical Studies and Feminist Theology in the Brisbane College of Theology, and Adjunct Fellow in the School of Theology at Griffith University, Queensland. Her publications include *Towards a Feminist Critical Reading of the Gospel according to Matthew,* and *Shall We Look for Another? A Feminist Re-reading of the Matthean Jesus.* Her current research is on the genderisation of healing in the Graeco-Roman world.

Six Ecojustice Principles

1. *The Principle of Intrinsic Worth*
The universe, Earth and all its components have intrinsic worth/value.

2. *The Principle of Interconnectedness*
Earth is a community of interconnected living things that are mutually dependent on each other for life and survival.

3. *The Principle of Voice*
Earth is a subject capable of raising its voice in celebration and against injustice.

4. *The Principle of Purpose*
The universe, Earth and all its components are part of a dynamic cosmic design within which each piece has a place in the overall goal of that design.

5. *The Principle of Mutual Custodianship*
Earth is a balanced and diverse domain in which responsible custodians can function as partners, rather than rulers, to sustain a balanced and diverse Earth community.

6. *The Principle of Resistance*
Earth and its components not only suffer from injustices at the hands of humans, but actively resist them in the struggle for justice.

The principles listed here are basic to the approach of writers in the Earth Bible Project seeking to read the biblical text from the perspective of Earth. For an elaboration of these principles see Earth Bible Team 2000b: 38-53.

Ecojustice Hermeneutics: Reflections and Challenges

The Earth Bible Team

With this, the fifth and final volume in this Earth Bible Series, it is timely to reflect on how the approach and principles of ecojustice hermeneutics outlined at the beginning of this series have been appropriated by the various writers in the series, and to survey some of the tasks and challenges that remain for Earth-centred readings. The basic outline of this approach and the ecojustice principles were introduced in the initial volume of the series (Habel 2000c: 24-37; Earth Bible Team 2000b: 38-53).

However, the understandings of team members and writers in the volumes have developed as the series progressed. The writers in the Earth Bible Series were invited to adapt, and have adapted, the approach to fit particular circumstances or texts, and they have selected and focused on ecojustice principles that were most pertinent to the passages on which they were focusing. The diverse contexts of writers from around the world have also had an impact on the way texts have been read from the perspective of Earth.

This essay, then, summarizes the state of play in the development of an ecojustice hermeneutic. Despite how far we have come, much more remains to be done.

Suspicion and Retrieval

As outlined in the opening volume of the Earth Bible Series, the ecojustice approach of the Earth Bible Team embraces a hermeneutic of suspicion and retrieval (2000b: 39). We suspect that biblical texts, written by humans to meet human circumstances, will reflect human interests at the expense of the non-human Earth community. We suspect that many texts will therefore be overtly anthropocentric. And even where texts are theocentric, they are likely to be more concerned about God's relationship with humanity than with the fate of creation — the Earth community seen as a whole — as such.

Is this fair? The ancient writers of the biblical texts, living over nineteen centuries ago, could not be expected to have a contemporary understanding of the planet as an intricate interconnected and intrinsically valued biosphere. We could not expect a biblical writer to assume a biocentric perspective. True!

Before we appropriate any of the biblical tradition in support of ecotheology or ecoethics, however, we need to explore the attitude to the natural world reflected in the text. A given biblical tradition may not incorporate the range of insights and discoveries reflected in current ecological thought, but the story of Earth — along with the story of God and the people of God — is one of the three grand narratives of the biblical tradition and the voice of Earth in that narrative, we would argue, still deserves to be heard.

Does an ecojustice approach bypass a serious analysis of the social and cultural background of the biblical text? Far from it! Each writer is expected to begin with close examination of the text in its original social and cultural context, as far as that is possible. Our concern, however, is also to identify attitudes, beliefs and factors in that time-and-place context that reflect living relationships with the natural world. The cosmology imbedded in the text is vital information for our understanding of the text. Given this information, we are in a position to ask second-level questions about whether the text is consistent, or in conflict, with whichever of the six ecojustice principles may be considered relevant.

A consideration of the social and cultural context should, where possible, also explore evidence of attitudes or action in relation to the environment as it was understood in that context. For example, Barbara Rossing's research, which lies behind her article in this volume, has exposed the exploitation of natural resources — including the sea — by the Roman Empire. These findings shed entirely new light on the social context of the book of Revelation (Rossing 1998).

Even after exploring the social, religious and cultural context of a passage, there is a general reluctance on the part of many writers to discern those components of the text in context that are forcefully anthropocentric, embrace injustice towards Earth, devalue creation or depict God as actively destroying components of Earth. One clear exception to this trend is Anne Elvey's study of Lk. 12.13-34: she recognizes a devaluation of the other-than-human nature in the providence of God described in this text. As Elvey demonstrates, this text suggests that those who seek the *basileia* (Kingdom) need not bother about material interests on Earth because they have a greater treasure in heaven.

Is the Earth Bible approach merely a cover for a superficial attempt to 'retrieve' an ecofriendly dimension behind the text? Certainly not! We recognize, with Keith Dyer, that some passages clearly 'resist retrieval'.

This especially applies to passages with apocalyptic components such as 2 Pet. 3.12 and Mark 13.

The situation, however, extends well beyond isolated apocalyptic passages. The entire book of Ezekiel, for example, portrays YHWH as a jealous deity who repeatedly brings devastation upon the lands of Earth, not to effect repentance, but to vindicate the divine name. The image of YHWH battering the natural places of Earth is boldly exposed by Kalinda Rose Stevenson in her article in Volume 4 (Habel 2001b: 158-71). The Ezekiel Seminar at the 2001 Annual Conference of the Society of Biblical Literature tackled just this issue, using a revised version of her paper and another by Norman Habel entitled 'The Silence of the Lands'.

Heavenism and Earth

One of the issues frequently tackled by Earth Bible writers is the relationship between heaven and Earth in key biblical texts. The difficulty arises partly from the diversity of meaning of the term 'heaven' in these texts and in the prior conditioning of Western interpreters to the concept of heaven. The perceived relationship of heaven and Earth influences whether or not Earth is seen to be devalued by the writer and whether a particular kind of connection is made between them. Here the principles of intrinsic worth and interconnectedness are intimately involved.

The term rendered 'heaven' — *shamayim* in Hebrew and *ouranos* in Greek — is used in at least three distinct senses. The first refers to the skies as the upper portion of the physical universe, the firmament that spans Earth. As Habel (2000b: 41) demonstrates, this is clearly the intent of Gen. 1.1-8. The second refers to the locus in or above the skies where God reigns (Pss. 2.4; 8.2). As the psalmist says, 'YHWH's throne is in heaven' (Ps. 11.4; cf. Acts 7.55-56). The term 'heaven' also seems to be used to refer to the spiritual world of God without being associated with a particular locus in the cosmos. In some contexts, 'heaven' is a euphemism for God — John the Baptist seems to speak of the 'kingdom of heaven' being 'near' as a circumlocution for God being near (Mt. 3.2).

Western thought has tended to redefine heaven and Earth as a dualism — heaven is the realm of God and therefore holy, superior, eternal; whereas Earth is the domain of mortals, corrupt and inferior (Earth Bible Team 2000b: 40-41). This heritage of Western thought seems to have combined with popular Christianity to create a widespread belief that in this paper we will designate 'heavenism'.

'Heavenism' is the belief that heaven, as God's home, is also the true home of Christians, the place where they are destined to dwell for eternity. Heaven is holy, free of troubles and eternal. Earth, by contrast, is only a temporary 'stopping place' for humans en route to heaven. Christians are aliens and pilgrims in a corrupt and barren land called Earth. The purpose of life is not to redeem Earth, but to prepare for heaven, to be ready for the day of judgment. Heaven is therefore a realm far superior to Earth. Heaven is eternal; Earth is disposable. Heaven is blessed, the 'golden shore' and goal of the Christian's journey. Earth is cursed and 'very evil', a land of great trials and tribulations that must be endured (Habel 1998: 33-34).

This heritage of dualism, whether in its popular — or more sophisticated philosophical — form, is likely to condition our 'from a Western perspective' reading of biblical texts; this may be true whether we are located in the West, or in countries whose readings have been influenced by Western traditions. The task of the Earth Bible interpreter is therefore to discern whether there is a dualistic view of heaven and Earth in the text, and if there is, what form it assumes. Does it have the same parameters as the version we Western interpreters have inherited? Michael Trainor, in his article in this volume, recognizes that the writer of Luke–Acts is operating in a context of a heaven–Earth dualism. But that dualism is interpreted in terms of the biblical heritage of the Hebrew Scriptures. In that context heaven is God's throne and Earth is God's footstool (Acts 7.49). But as in his earlier analysis of Lk. 2.14 (2000), Trainor asks whether Earth, in spite of its 'subordinate' position in the cosmos, may not also be chosen by God as an agent of peace.

Alan Cadwallader, in his second article in this volume, argues that the very text of the Christian Scriptures' book of Hebrews, which is regularly cited as the biblical basis for heavenism, has been read in terms of a later Western dualism that is not inherent in the text. In the political and social context of Roman displacement of Jewish Christians, 'the heavenly country is not another place elevated and removed. Rather it is a description of a way of engaging the Earth'.

A number of writers in this volume speak of a new connectedness being established between heaven and Earth. Bill Loader suggests this in his article in connection with the account of the heavens being 'torn open' for the dove to descend and the voice from heaven to be heard (Mk 1.10-11). In his study, Elmer Flor suggests that in Ephesians 1 the 'gathering up of all things in him, in heaven and in Earth' involves a reconnecting of the rent world through the cosmic Christ. Adrian Leske's analysis of Matthew 6 is concerned with bringing the Earth community into greater harmony with heaven.

However, from the perspective of the ecojustice principles of this project, we may pose a challenge to our own writers. Is this connectedness more than theological or spiritual? And if so, does it have a genuine ecological dimension in which intricate interconnections of the biotic and non-biotic components of the universe are implied? Have we so spiritualized the domain of heaven that we miss the very material stuff of that domain in the various biblical cosmologies? A challenge for future writers is to continue attempts to extend the principle of inter-connectedness to embrace domains beyond those which ecologists and biologists discern as interacting as part of the balance of nature.

Principle of Purpose

One of the Earth Bible Project ecojustice principles that has been some-what ignored by most writers is the principle of purpose. This principle asserts that Earth and life on Earth is not an accidental by-product in a sequence of cosmic events. Rather, the universe, Earth and all its com-ponents are part of a dynamic design within which each piece has a place in the overall goal of that design. Integral to the ecological para-digm is the concept of an Earth which functions according to an in-built design—a pattern of mysterious ecological balancing acts, many of which are beyond human conception and understanding. The scope of this design is still being explored, let alone its detail. David Suzuki and Amanda O'Connell observe in their recent book *The Sacred Balance:*

> Each discovery reveals the magnitude of our ignorance; far from filling in the picture, these discoveries show us just how much remains to be learned. The total knowledge base currently accumulated by scientists is still so limited that it can rarely be prescriptive; it is almost impossible to generate scientifically based policies or solutions for managing our surroundings we know so little. It is as if we are standing in a cave holding a candle; the light barely penetrates the darkness and we have no idea where the cave walls are let alone how many more caves there are beyond (1997: 19-20).

The principle of purpose as a biological force is endorsed by writers such as Charles Birch (1990). He rejects the old philosophical argument from design (Birch 1990: 60), which asserts there must be some sort of overall designer or demiurge that has planned everything in blueprint and now puts it into action. Nor is there some kind of external deter-mination of everything that happens. This perspective would imply a hierarchical structure of reality, replete with the 'voluntarist assumption' (Birch 1990: 67) that God can do anything, and whatever God does is by definition good.

The view of the physical universe as a product of pure chance cannot be sustained either. Ecologists discern in Earth and beyond an almost limitless set of interlocking systems—or 'closing circles' as Birch calls them—that form an internal or in-built design that still remains a mystery (Birch 1993: 18). These systems suggest a governing force at work, according to which (1) matter has an inherent tendency to be life-like, and so life emerges from matter; and (2) life has its own inherent sense of purpose: to continue to live, to prosper, to reproduce itself and to interact with other life forms—sometimes competitively, sometimes cooperatively or symbiotically (Birch 1990: 67).

In articulating this concept of purpose, scholars like Birch are also exploring the principle of voice according to which Earth and its components are identified as subjects in the ecological paradigm. According to Birch:

> The individual entities that constitute matter are subjects, be they protons or people. They are sentient to the possibilities of their future, within the limitations imposed by their past. What they respond to…are the persuasive possibilities relevant to their future. Creation is not by [dictatorial command] but by persuasion. Order by persuasion is the factor limiting chance… The combination of sentience in individual entities, together with the lure beyond themselves for their possible futures, is the source of their creativity (1990: 42).

That is to say, there is a principle of sentience and self-organization in nature. Birch has already identified this with an ecological (as opposed to a mechanistic) model of nature: 'in the ecological model of nature all molecules and cells are recognised as subjects' (1990: 27). These subjects 'take account of their environment' (1990: 79) internally, and are active (1990: 85), not passive, as they appear to be to our senses and as they are regarded in a mechanistic model of nature.

Further, Birch links this understanding of the natural world with the Socratic distinction between mechanical and final causes, or mechanical causation and causation through purpose. 'The one involves external relations, the other involves internal relations' (1990: 48). Internal relations imply an inner directionality, a *telos* or purpose—within the parts—an *inner* will and thus some sort of emergence or agency.

The mystery of the this inner *telos* continues to be explored in works such as *The Sacred Depths of Nature*, a work that challenges the biblical scholar and theologian to examine again whether the biblical texts reflect an inner sense of purpose for nature (Goodenough 1998). Is a genuine *Erdgeschichte* discernible in these texts, one that reflects the persuasive forces of life at work in the world—a divine design that balances the *Heilsgeschichte* that focuses so forcefully on the well-being and future of humankind?

Following the general lead of Moltmann that God is 'in creation' (1985), is it consistent with the biological principle of purpose—evident in the life-drive of nature — to point to the incarnation texts as indicators that God does not stand outside the natural world, but is an integral part of the life-drive itself. Does God 'becoming flesh' mean that God becomes the essence of the biotic? Or is there an underlying belief, as Habel suggests in the challenge he raises in relation to John 1 in this volume, that the transcendent God is viewed as outside creation and that when the Word 'tents' in flesh this is only a transitory abode of a God who descends 'from above' only to return there again.

Can a bios that has been 'infected', entered, by the divine ever be the same again? Does God's incarnation become an integral part of how all life is and represent God's indwelling in all things in a mystical way that is beyond pantheism or panentheism? Does the text of Romans 8 envisage creation's 'mourning and yearning' as a state of being prior to the 'now' state of incarnation, achieved with God's entry, as the God–human Jesus Christ, into the time and place, the being and life of all creation?

> [F]or the creation was subjected to futility, not of its own will but by the will of the one who subjected it, in hope that the creation itself will be set free from its bondage to decay and will obtain the freedom of the glory of the children of God. We know that the whole creation has been groaning in labor pains until *now* (Rom. 8.20-22; NRSV).

Perhaps Christian theologians have 'heavenized' the 'now' of this text, because the perspective of 'forever-changed creation' is too outrageous in their heavenist eyes.

Does Paul assert in this text — as in other sections of his writings preserved in the Christian Scriptures — a view of a God who 'breaks into and across' the limitations and irreconcilable difference of the divine–human separation? Does this text promote a view that God's incarnation is an audacious and challenging event that forever changes the way things are? Does this text provide an insight into the way things are from God's perspective — and does this text demonstrate that God's point of view challenges the view of humans at the centre, and the heavenism of contemporary Western theology? In God's eyes, everything is intrinsically valued as 'very good', and will experience a 'setting free' and participate fully in the 'freedom of glory'. And the implication in the text is that the 'now' of the incarnation has already changed creation's groaning into celebration.

Voice and Value

The search for the voice of Earth — suppressed, silenced, mediated or expressed — within the text of the Scriptures continues. As a team we explored the concept of Earth's voice as something more than metaphor in volume 4 of the Earth Bible Series (2001: 23-28). In that volume the voice of Earth was variously heard. Shirley Wurst, for example, retrieves the voice of Earth in Jeremiah 4 (2001: 172-84) and William Urbrock reconstructs Psalms 90–92 to allow the voice of Earth to be heard (2001: 65-83).

Samuel Rayan (1994), one of the great biblical scholars of India, explores the question of Earth's voice from another perspective. In a challenging study he speaks of Earth as also being 'the Lord's self-manifestation'. 'The Earth and everything in it', he maintains, are 'loving and saving words addressed to us and addressing each other' (1994: 132). Earth is full of spatial signs and symbols that speak to us. He continues:

> The cherished language of symbols is silence. The earth speaks in the eloquent silence of hills and trees. 'Silence, my soul,' said Tagore, 'these trees are prayers.' A language the earth loves to speak is the silence of night and the silence of the womb, the silence of seeds as they sprout and the silence of buds smiling into blossoms... But the earth communicates also in the roar of the sea, the warble of birds and brooks, the murmur of the breeze. The heavens in their blue silences and their thunderclouds declare the glory of God. No speech, no words, no voice heard, but the call goes on throughout the universe (Ps. 19.3-4). And 'deep calls to deep at the thunder of your cataracts' (Ps. 42.7) (Rayan 1994: 133).

The rich poetic language of Rayan should not blind us to the underlying truth—grounded in biblical traditions—that Earth is a voiced subject in the cosmos. We dare not ignore, however, that many biblical traditions suppress the voice of Earth and prevent its song or suffering from being expressed. Bill Loader in his article in this volume, seeks to discern that voice mediated through the wilderness, the rent skies and the animals who attend Jesus in the desert.

Perhaps the ecojustice principle most frequently examined by writers in this series is the principle of value or intrinsic worth. In this volume, Alan Cadwallader explores whether or not the symbolism of the plough in Lk. 9.62 suggests that the kingdom of God endorses the subjugation of women and Earth. Keith Carley's study of Ezekiel's formula of desolation demonstrates the frequency with which Earth is devalued in that text. 'For the most part, Earth is the passive object of horrifying mal-treatment' (2001: 143-57).

The intrinsic worth of Earth and the Earth community is frequently linked with the affirmation of these components of the cosmos as good creations of God. Reading Mt. 6.25-34 in the light of Second Isaiah, Adrian Leske, for example, argues in this volume that the Sermon on the

Mount values the natural and human worlds as both part of God's good creation. Reading John 9 from her Yoruba background, Oyeronke Olajubu, recognizes that water has value as a healing agent independent of any healing act performed by Jesus.

The question which we may pose at this juncture is whether the principle of intrinsic value, as expressed by ecologists, has the same import as it has been interpreted to have by our writing team. Lilies may have a glory greater than Solomon, waters may have healing power, the wilderness may break into blossom and celebrate the value of these elements of Earth. Ultimately, however, we are faced with the worth of every molecule, mouse or mountain, regardless of its beauty or blessing for humans. Or, in the language of the Wisdom tradition, every creature or force of nature has its own 'way' that gives it identity, value and purpose regardless of whether Job or any other human ever discovers its presence, or discerns its way.

Intrinsic value is frequently distinguished from utilitarian value, which asserts that something has value if it is a resource for humans. Working through the various texts chosen by writers in this series, it has also become apparent that we need to distinguish between 'intrinsic value' and 'added value'. Something has intrinsic value because it exists within the natural order. Many parts of nature are selected for special attention in the biblical tradition and have a value added to, or bestowed, upon them. The seventh day of the week is part of the cycle of time and as such has intrinsic value: as the Sabbath it has a bestowed or added value and is declared 'holy' or separate. Even the declaration that parts of the Earth community — such as humans — are 'special creations' of God suggests that they carry added value. The issue before us is whether texts that speak of added value tend to negate the principle of intrinsic value, and also suggest a hierarchy of values in some biblical traditions.

The question of value also raises the ethical issue of whether, when we engage in the act of writing about being Earth-sensitive, we are able also to practice an Earth sensitivity. The task not only involves the kind of paper we use in publishing, but also the act of transforming a component of Earth into text — whether that be as a clay tablet, papyrus or modern paper. As a consequence, we need to read Earth with as much respect for Earth's agency and active participation in life on Earth as Indigenous Australians have as they read the landscape.

Valuing Earth demands that we acknowledge Earth not only as our life source but as our text source, too. When we read Earth, we are reading another living being; and, as contemporary reading theory asserts, in every reading there is a projection of ourselves, and also a

projection of the being of an Other — Earth. And perhaps, as we read
Earth, we are also read: in our reading of the 'Other', we are reading
ourselves. Our task is to read all the texts' perspectives: the texts of us,
the texts of Earth community, and the texts of Earth. And, in the process,
not confuse the texts and their meanings.

Sustaining and Resisting

Sustainability is now one of the technical terms current in policies relating to the environment. The aim is to find ways to sustain the resources
of Earth while maintaining the current standard of living for humans.
The concept underlying this ecological/economic policy is similar to the
traditional model of stewardship. It is in the self-interest of humans to
control the household (*oikos*) of Earth by managing the ecosystems of
Earth in ways that are sensitive to the dynamics of those systems.

The principle of mutual custodianship espoused by the Earth Bible
Project has a somewhat different focus: first, we ascertain how Earth has
sustained and nurtured human beings and all life; and second, we
explore how we, as part of Earth community, learn to nurture Earth as
Earth has nurtured us. In various articles in this series we have emphasized that the model of stewardship frequently espoused by ecotheologians remains hierarchical and anthropocentric. The claim that the
mandate of Gen. 1.26-28 has been misunderstood and can be interpreted
in terms of a benign stewardship model is untenable (Habel 2000c: 31).
This mandate, however, continues to influence most biblical writers who
assume that humans are, in some sense, 'ruling' for God on Earth.

Few writers have explored how Earth has sustained humanity and all
life on Earth. There is a tendency to discern God as the sustainer of life
without also recognizing Earth as the immediate agent of sustenance,
support and creative energy. As the 'servant song' asserts, Earth is being
'Christ to us'. The task for those reading from the perspective of Earth is
to recognize whether Earth as the life-giving subject is valued or negated
in the text. Job 38–39 is a biblical text that highlights how the domains of
Earth function without — indeed, unconscious of — human control. When
God takes Job on a journey through the cosmos, Job discovers a wisdom
embedded in the world that governs and sustains all life (Habel 2001).
Earth is not a subject — or object — to be ruled but a life partner to be
understood, respected and appreciated.

The value and voice of Earth, it seems, are frequently suppressed in
the text. Earth as a subject is regularly ignored by many ancient writers
and modern interpreters. Are there, in line with the principle of resistance, texts where Earth resists suppression, devaluation and relegation

to the margins of significance? Barbara Rossing, in her article in this volume, recognizes the role of Earth in resisting the forces of a human empire and a biblical tradition that would reduce Earth to a silent captive. A radical reorientation to the text of Revelation 12 occurs when the initial Greek word *ouai* is rendered 'alas' rather than 'woe': the voice of Earth's lament emerges stridently from the text as a result.

Another text where the lament and resistance of Earth may be heard is the book of Joel; unfortunately, it has not been explored in this series. In Earth's lament in Joel, the ground mourns, the animals groan and the wild beasts cry out in anguish. As Cunanan (1994) recognizes, the prophet identifies with the groaning creation. It takes but a small step to move from recognizing the empathy of the prophet to discerning the resistance of nature.

The task before us, envisaged in the Earth Bible Project's quest for a viable hermeneutics from the perspective of Earth, is to reread many texts where the groaning Earth is recognized, such as Romans 8 and Joel, — where Earth, as our life partner, resists our human acts of suppression and oppression.

Another step in recognizing the role of Earth in our human history is to investigate whether the suffering of Earth is in any sense viewed as vicarious or redemptive. Are there texts where Earth suffers for, with, or in place of, humans? Reading against the grain, Shirley Wurst suggests that the curse in Genesis 3 is taken on, assumed, by Mother Earth on behalf of her children. She writes, 'The *adamah,* like other mothers in Genesis, will do just about anything for her child' (Wurst 2000a: 99). Is Earth and the Earth community frequently the scapegoated 'mother' in the biblical tradition, the one who suffers instead of 'her children'?

In a later reading, Wurst demonstrates that Earth in the text of Jeremiah 4 is an abused victim of a patriarchal and jealous God who requires revenge — suffering and death — to appease his shame as the wronged partner, the deserted *baal,* the husband/overlord of the three women in the text. Though the voices of the victims — the partners: Earth, the older woman, and her younger 'replacement' sister-wives, Israel and Judah — are scarcely heard in the text, the cries of abused women throughout history echo in their words:

> My anguish! My anguish! I writhe in pain!
> Oh, the walls of my heart!
> My heart is beating wildly; I cannot keep silent... (Jer. 4.19a).

To what extent is Earth as a subject willing to assume this vicarious role? And to what extent does Earth resist this abusive expectation that a 'good' mother suffers on behalf of her children, or that a woman should suffer when her partner is, from a patriarchal perspective, shamed by her behaviour? These are challenges for future readings, and future discussions and debates.

A Continuing Need

The need to pursue the approach of the Earth Bible Project has not diminished. The ecological crisis facing the planet persists. The *Earth Charter*, whose latest version was produced after the first volume in this series was published, makes it clear that the social and environmental well-being of peoples on Earth includes a spiritual as well as an eco-justice dimension. This well-being demands that we take into account how our religious heritage, including our biblical heritage, has contri-buted to the degradation of the planet and how it can play a key role in sustaining Earth. The inclusion of an Earth Bible seminar in the 2001 Asia Pacific *Earth Charter* Conference illustrates a heightened awareness of the role religion and spirituality can play in making the *Earth Charter* an effective vehicle for the United Nations (for more detail, see the *Earth Charter* web page: www.earthcharter.org).

Despite the growing volume of literature on ecotheology and related fields, the need for critical ecojustice readings of the biblical tradition continues. Contemporary ecotheology literature explores a wide range of creative interactions: ecological principles, theological traditions, con-temporary issues and biblical texts. Rarely, however, is the problem-atic nature of the biblical text as a source of ecofriendly concepts taken into consideration. Even the highly sensitive and creative essays published under the title *Earth Revealing/Earth Healing* (Edwards 2001) do not tackle the question of whether the biblical tradition can be colonized for eco-theology without prior and critical examination of its diverse ecological orientations.

While this task may not have been overtly stated in the brief of these writers and other ecotheologians, it is hard to see how in the twenty-first century, facing the global ecological issues we are, and with the chal-lenges to the 'master narratives' mounted by minority perspectives claiming a view from the centre, we can proceed with an approach named ecotheology without first facing the challenges of discerning the ecofriendliness of the text. In the second half of the twentieth century, the Judaeo-Christian tradition was charged with responsibility for humanity's rampant destruction of the Earth. The problem of biblical texts that do not seem to support the perspectives of modern eco-theology still demands attention, if this charge is ever to be addressed. To change the way we move into the future, we need to acknowledge our past—including those beliefs that have led us to place ourselves at the centre incapable of recognizing let alone respecting the implicit mutuality of our responsibility as Earth citizens.

The challenge of ecojustice readings for Christian theology, presented at an Ecotheology Conference in Christchurch (Habel 2000a), focused on both the untapped potential of some biblical traditions and the Earth-negative orientation of others. This concern is summarized as follows:

> Ecojustice calls for Earth to be valued as a subject. The biblical tradition reflects two conflicting portraits of how Earth is treated, one negative and the other positive. According to the negative tradition God is depicted as devaluing Earth by cursing without provocation or manipulating Earth forces for reasons unrelated to Earth's actions. Humans are portrayed as subduing Earth and members of Earth's community without concern for Earth itself. The positive tradition, which has largely been hidden or ignored, presents Earth as a living domain of majesty, presence and mysterious design that both humans and God celebrate (Habel 2000a: 141).

Margot Käsemann, in a series of Bible studies prepared for a Gurukul Summer Institute on Ecological Theology (Bangalore), begins her focus on the tradition, significantly, with the story of the Flood, rather than Genesis 1 (1994: 28-31). As she notes, the Flood story takes into account the reality of a broken creation and violence in the world. Like many other fine studies, this work does not take the step of identifying with Earth and recognizing the injustice rendered upon Earth by the God depicted in the text. Why should all non-human life—the entire Earth community—suffer oblivion because of human violence? God covers the Earth with destructive primordial waters before revealing it again. And only a chosen remnant—those saved along with the human family perceived as worthy because of their connection with Noah—survives.

In like manner, in the earlier narrative of the Fall, God uses Earth to punish humans, by pronouncing the curse of Earth because of human rebellion.

One can hardly speak of the Flood story as Earth-friendly, in spite of the final rainbow of divine promise. Unless, of course, one understands God as being within the land, within Earth, and hence being a participant in the suffering of Earth in the Flood, a position adopted by Wali Fejo in his Indigenous reading (2000), and an insight explored by Shirley Wurst in a study entitled 'God's Face in the Flood Story' (2000b: 218-22).

Conclusion

The biblical scholars included in the Earth Bible Team, faced with this continuing need and the contributions of scholars from around the world who have undertaken to read the text from an Earth perspective, recognize that there are still many challenges facing those working within, and with the texts of, the biblical tradition. Numerous texts need to be thoroughly analysed in terms of the ecojustice principles — both as described in this project and developed in response to or independently of it — to determine their relative contribution to ecotheology, ecoethics and the practical task of reconnecting us with our environment. We hope the ecojustice principles we outlined in the initial volume in this series will continue to be refined and employed in a dialogue between ecologists, biblical scholars and students of religion. We, as a team, are indebted to all who have contributed to this series, to those who have challenged us along the way, to Indigenous voices that have made us rethink our own Western assumptions and last, but not least, to Earth. Earth has sustained us since our beginnings as humans and now assists us — in mind, body and spirit — as we seek to hear the voices of Earth in the biblical text and the world around us.

Matthew 6.25-34: Human Anxiety and the Natural World

Adrian M. Leske

Some years ago in a chapter titled 'Cosmogony and Ethics in the Sermon on the Mount', Hans Dieter Betz stated that what he found surprising was the positive manner in which the natural order was treated in the Sermon, and particularly in Mt. 6.25-34, since little interest in this subject had been shown in the rest of the Christian Scriptures (1985: 121; repeated in 1995: 465). Of course, the Christian Scriptures is essentially theo-anthropocentric: it deals primarily with relationships between God and people and how that affects relationships with one another. Consequently, any alliance with the Earth community is evidenced often only by implication that the restored harmony between God and people will lead to a renewed recognition of the goodness of all of God's created world in accordance with Gen. 1.31. Nevertheless, it is particularly in the sayings of Jesus that we do often find allusions to the natural order, allusions which draw on the heritage of the Hebrew Bible. Matthew 6.25-34 has generally been understood to be a collection of wisdom sayings. For this reason Betz holds that the Sermon on the Mount derived from Jewish-Christian groups residing in Jerusalem around the middle of the first century CE, who saw God as the father of the cosmos. Thus, these sayings in Mt. 6.25-34 demonstrate that ethical behaviour consists 'in learning the way and manner in which God loves and preserves his creation' (Betz 1985: 123). However, it is my contention here that when we look at Mt. 6.25-34 in the light of the prophetic writings, we find a greater depth of meaning, and a deeper understanding of humanity's relation to the Earth community. As such it gives greater credence to this passage having originated with Jesus himself who consistently emphasizes the prophetic tradition.

Further, it will be argued that on the basis of the influence of Second Isaiah and other prophetic writings on our text, as on the rest of the Sermon on the Mount, the principle of interconnectedness is assumed in which all living things are mutually dependent on each other for well-being and fulfilment of God's eternal plan. Becoming a member of the kingdom of God means becoming a member of God's family, as Jesus' insistence that his disciples think of God as 'Father' (Mt. 5.16, and 44 times) and themselves as God's children (Mt. 5.9, 45) implies. This kinship with God thus implies not only kinship with other human beings, but also with all the Earth community which God feeds and clothes. This relationship of all things is an integral part of the prophetic message, and an underlying assumption in Mt. 6.25-34.

Allusions to the Natural Order in Matthew's Gospel

In order to put Mt. 6.25-34 into the context of the whole Gospel of Matthew, we need to see what is said in it concerning the natural order, particularly in the sayings of Jesus.

First of all, following in the traditions of the prophetic writings, people are often likened to trees. Jesus calls his disciples in the sermon to beware of false prophets who will be known by their fruits. Kingdom members will be like sound trees which by their very nature bear good fruit, for grapes cannot be gathered from thorns or figs from thistles. Thorns and thistles, an allusion to the Fall, had become a common metaphor for the curse that would come upon the land of those who rejected their covenant with God (Mt. 7.16-20; 12.33; cf. Gen. 3.18; Hos. 10.8; Isa. 5.6; 7.23-25; 10.17; 32.13). It is in this context that Jesus later cursed the fig tree that bore no fruit as a metaphor of the fruitlessness of the Jerusalem priesthood (Mt. 21.18-22). John the Baptist had warned that every tree that does not bear fruit would be cut down and thrown into the fire (Mt. 3.10; cf. Isa. 10.33-34; Mal. 4.1) as a metaphor for judgment on those who did not live fruitful lives in accordance with God's will and purpose. The implication here is that humanity comes under the same judgment as the rest of the Earth community when it fails to fulfil its God-given purpose. There is a common justice for all.

While the wicked were often depicted as shrubs in the desert (Jer. 17.6) or as chaff that the wind drives away (Ps. 1.4), the righteous in contrast were likened to a tree planted by the waters which 'in the year of drought is not anxious and does not cease to bear fruit' (Jer. 17.8, cf. Ps. 1.3). Moreover, considering the many quotations and allusions to the book of Isaiah in Matthew's Gospel (Leske 1998b), when Jesus said, 'Every plant that my heavenly Father has not planted will be uprooted' (Mt. 15.13), he was alluding to Isa. 60.21. There the prophet has God saying of the faithful: 'Your people shall all be righteous; they shall possess the land forever. They are the shoot (*neser*) that I planted, the work of my hands, so that I might be glorified.' These faithful are then described as growing up into 'oaks of righteousness, the planting of the Lord, to display his glory' (Isa. 61.3). Yet there is still opportunity to return for those gone astray. For Jesus points out that God still reaches out in blessing to all, 'for he makes his sun to shine of the evil and on the good, and sends rain on the righteous and on the unrighteous' (Mt. 5.45; cf. Isa. 45.8; 55.10, 11).

Besides the tree metaphor, there are the parables of the kingdom of God in Matthew 13 set into the context of nature: the sower and the seed, with its allusions to Isa. 55.10-11; the weeds among the wheat; the mustard seed; the catch of fish.

The faithful are also likened to members of the animal world. Continuing the common prophetic metaphor of likening people to sheep (Jer. 23.1-4; Ezek. 34; Isa. 40.10-11; Zech. 10.2-3), Jesus spoke of the crowds as 'like sheep without a shepherd' (Mt. 9.36). He saw his mission as being sent 'only to the lost sheep of the house of Israel' (Mt. 10.6; 15.24). He sent out his disciples to participate in the mission as 'sheep in the midst of wolves' (Mt. 10.16, cf. 7.15). But they were to be subtle as serpents and innocent as doves. Other members of the animal world were referred to in order to get across a vital message to the disciples. Jesus advised a potential disciple that 'foxes have holes and birds of the air have nests, but the Son of man has nowhere to lay his head' (Mt. 8.20) in order to teach that discipleship called for a greater trust in God to supply what is needed and to recognize that God is in control of his universe. Even common sparrows, which are sold two for a penny, do not fall to the ground apart from God (Mt. 10.29, cf. Isa. 34.15-16). There is a principle of interconnectedness in these references. Human beings are to learn from other members of the Earth community how God takes care of his creation.

There are also references that imply a desired unity between heaven and Earth. In Mt. 11.25, Jesus addresses God as 'Father, Lord of heaven and Earth', a rather unique title in the Christian Scriptures. It is a title that acknowledges the sovereignty of God over all creation, with clear allusions to Isa. 40.12-31; 42.5; 43.10-13. God has created heaven and Earth for a purpose, they are called to stand forth united (Isa. 48.13). So Jesus taught his disciples to pray, 'Your will be done on Earth as it is in heaven' (Mt. 6.10). It is the faithful who are given the task to bring about this unity. They shall inherit Earth (Mt. 5.5) and have authority on Earth to forgive sins (Mt. 9.6-8) so that whatever they bind or loose on Earth will be bound or loosed in heaven (Mt. 16.19; 18.18-20). It is in this context that the risen Jesus gives to his disciples the assurance that 'all authority in heaven and on Earth has been given' to him (Mt. 28.18) as he sent them out to make disciples of all nations.

Many of the parables of Jesus emphasize this idea that those living in harmony with God are to act as faithful servants to bring all members of the Earth community into harmony with God. Such are the parables of the vineyard (Mt. 21.33-46, drawing on Isa. 5.1-7), the marriage feast (Mt. 22.1-14), the faithful and wise servant (Mt. 24.45-51), wise and foolish maidens (Mt. 25.1-13), the talents (Mt. 25.14-30), the great judgment (Mt. 25.31-46). For this reason, kingdom members are called the salt of Earth, the light of the world (Mt. 5.13-16; cf. Isa. 42.6-7; 49.6-8). Of course, it is primarily the transformation of the human element that is sought here. But there is an underlying assumption, as we shall see, that through this transformation, all elements of Earth community will be brought into greater harmony with heaven and with God's will. For this reason neither heaven nor Earth are to be belittled or abused, for one is God's throne and the other is God's footstool (Mt. 5.34-35; 23.22; borrowed from Isa. 66.1). This does not imply here that Earth is in subjection or inferior, but that both heaven and Earth are God's possession and under God's authority and dominion. While Matthew generally prefers to use the term 'kingdom of heaven' rather than 'kingdom of God', he uses 'heaven' here simply as a pious Jewish circumlocution for 'God'. No tension or opposition between heaven and Earth is implied here, for both are part of the realm of God.

General Approaches to Matthew 6.25-34

Most of the commentators put this passage into the category of Jewish wisdom sayings (so Guelich 1982: 335; Strecker 1988: 136) that deal with the same concerns common in Hellenistic philosophy (Betz 1995: 471, 473). In doing so, they have missed the point I believe. Sayings like Job 12.7-10 ('Ask the animals, and they will teach you') or Prov. 6.6-11 ('Go to the ant, you lazybones') are often noted as similar. However, what is said in the latter example is almost entirely opposite to what we find in our text. In fact, there have been critics of our text who see the sayings as somewhat superficial, economically naive, and supporting laziness (see Luz 1989: 402, 403). Some, however, recognize that Mt. 6.33, with its concept of seeking after the kingdom of God and his righteousness, does not fit into the Wisdom category (so Betz 1985: 119) and creates a disruption in the flow of the text. This has led Ulrich Luz to conclude that Wisdom material has here been put into the service of a specific statement about the kingdom of God, originally aimed at those disciples who for the sake of the kingdom had become itinerant radicals, and were no longer practising their trade (Luz 1989: 408).

While some scholars make passing reference to these sayings as reflecting belief in a cosmic piety wherein the Lord of nature holds sway over all creation (Davies and Allison 1988: 649), most are concerned to identify the typical wisdom formula of arguing from the lesser to the greater. More than any other, Betz has emphasized the order of nature in this pericope, suggesting that the progress from food to clothing has been determined by the hierarchy of beings in nature. Thus, the highest are human beings, followed by animals (the highest of which are birds of the air), followed by plants (highest of which are the flowers). Alluding to Cynic philosophy Betz argued that in the ancient world animals were often seen as models for human behaviour because they were looked upon as an integral part of nature. Humans, however, had become alienated from nature as a result of civilization. Therefore, he concluded, 'animal behavior, because it conforms to nature and thus to cosmic and meta-physical reason can serve to establish what is ethically reasonable human conduct' (Betz 1995: 473). But such an argument does not fit well with reference to the plant world. In regard to plants, Betz preferred to focus on the fact that while animals are clothed in fur and feathers, and plants in flowers, human beings enter this world naked. In Gen. 3.21 God himself had to make garments of skins to clothe Adam and Eve. Thus, Betz argued, God is seen as the inventor of culture. On this basis, Betz concluded that God fulfils human needs through culture, providing 'those needs remain "neutral" and therefore ethically justifiable' (Betz 1995: 480).

All this seems to be missing the real point of these sayings about anxiety as they lead up to the central message of seeking 'first the kingdom of God and his righteousness' (Mt. 6.33). Clearly, the point being made is that God feeds the birds of the air *even though they neither sow nor reap nor gather into barns* (Mt. 6.26), and the grass of the field is beautifully adorned *even though the flowers neither toil nor spin* (Mt. 6.28). Thus the central point being made is that one enters into and accepts God's kingdom and his righteousness as God's gracious gift, and then all these things will follow from this relationship (Guelich 1982: 344-47; Hagner 1993: 166). When one is in proper relationship with God, there is no reason for anxiety since God supplies whatever is needed to live as a member of God's kingdom. However, Betz sees God's kingdom as a future reward to the faithful, and interprets 'his righteousness' (*ten dikaiosynen autou*) as the sum total of what God requires as a prerequisite for entering the kingdom (1995: 483-84), and thus essentially negates the purpose of the similes.

But Betz is not alone in this. Some of those who assume that *dikasiosyne* here is to be interpreted as the righteousness that God requires, and as the law of the kingdom (so Davies and Allison 1988: 661), but yet recognize a conflict, prefer to see 'righteousness' as a Matthaean insertion. After all, it is not found in the Lukan parallel (Strecker 1988: 139-40; Luz

1989: 407). However, this does not solve the problem, since the assumed conflict still remains. One has to ask whether there is not a better approach to this saying on anxiety that will render a clearer understanding of its relation to the kingdom of God and the natural world.

The Prophetic Approach to Matthew 6.25-34

The Gospel of Matthew was written by a Jewish Christian primarily for Jewish Christians in order to reassure and remind them of the meaning and significance of Jesus' teaching of the kingdom of God and his actions relating to it. The Gospel contains many Semitisms: words and phrases in Hebrew idiom, and unexplained Jewish customs that indicate Jewish readers are in the author's mind as he writes. Moreover, the author assumes that his readers know a lot about the faith outlined in the Hebrew Scriptures, and that they are familiar with the Hebrew Scriptures' text, particularly the prophetic writings. The evangelist makes frequent use of quotations and allusions from these, more so than any other writer included in the Christian Scriptures. These quotations are not merely superimposed on the narrative, but are an integral part of the story, giving added meaning and significance to the words.

Fulfilment is the all-pervading basic concept in this Gospel. All Israel's history, hope and purpose are seen as coming to fulfilment through Jesus and his message of the kingdom of God. The most profound influence on Jesus' message and mission in Matthew's Gospel comes from the prophetic literature, specifically from Second Isaiah and in varying degrees from those prophets who followed in that prophetic tradition: Third Isaiah, Malachi, Zechariah 9–14, Jonah, Daniel, Wisdom of Solomon, and the Parables of Enoch (*1 En.* 37-71; see Leske 1998a). That is already evident in Matthew's summary of Jesus' activity in Mt. 4.23 (repeated in Mt. 9.35) that Jesus went about 'teaching…and proclaiming the good news of God's kingdom and healing every sickness and every disease among the people'. The phrase 'proclaiming the good news of the kingdom' clearly has its origin in the announcement in the book of Isaiah of the good news of the coming deliverance from exile and the restoration of the kingdom when God himself would reign as King (see Isa. 40.9; 52.7). Second Isaiah, like many of his time (e.g. Ezek. 45.8-9) saw the failure of the monarchy as being primarily responsible for the exile. Hence, in the restoration, it would be a return to the ideal of Exod. 19.5-6 where God is King and the people a royal priesthood under God (cf. Isa. 41.21; 43.15; 44.6). Also, the phrase 'healing every sickness and every disease among the people' is a strong allusion to the suffering and restoration of servant Israel depicted in Isa. 53.3-4, 10-11, and the references to Israel being healed of its infirmities in Isa. 35.5-7; 41.17-20; 42.7, 18-22; 61.1-3.

The good news of God's kingdom is the news that brings restoration and healing (Isa. 57.18-19). This is what is being joyfully proclaimed in the opening verses of the Sermon on the Mount, in the so-called Beatitudes (Mt. 5.3-12). These are not new laws or new entrance requirements; they are proclamations of the renewal of the covenant blessings (Leske 1991). Matthew thus demonstrates that Jesus has come to fulfil the message of Isaiah and the prophets by proclaiming the good news of the kingdom of God, by teaching the true meaning of being a member of that kingdom as God's servant Israel. Jesus fulfils the promises of Second Isaiah by gathering together the 'lost sheep of the house of Israel' to be a living 'people–covenant' (cf. Jer. 31.31-34; Isa. 51.7) and a 'light to the nations' (Isa. 42.6; 49.6-8; cf. Mt. 28.19-20), and thus carry out their role as true Israel. It is the announcement of healing and restoration and the call to live as God's kingdom people, 'the planting of the Lord, to display his glory' (Isa. 61.3).

It is in this light that we must look at this pericope on anxiety. Since Jesus is addressing people here who have earlier been described as members of the kingdom, as the 'salt of Earth' and 'the light of the world' (Mt. 5.13-16), he is reminding them to live now as the restored covenant people. It is important to note in this context that the three things they are not to worry about anymore in Mt. 6.25 are what they will eat, what they will drink, what they will wear. These relate to the summary of the covenant curses in Deut. 28.48, which warns the people of God that if they did not serve God with joyfulness and gladness of heart, they would serve their enemies 'in hunger and thirst, in nakedness and in want of all things'. But those who have received the covenant blessings need not be anxious about these things.

While Isaiah of Jerusalem could speak of hunger and thirst as a curse that came to those who had set themselves apart from God (Isa. 5.13; 29.8), and Jeremiah and Ezekiel could give their constant warnings of impending judgment in terms of hunger, sword and pestilence (e.g. Jer. 14.12-18; Ezek. 5.12-17), Second Isaiah spoke of the deliverance from exile as the people no longer having to experience hunger and thirst because they would be led by springs of water (Isa. 41.17; 49.10; cf. Ps. 1.3; Jer. 17.8). The invitation to the celebration of God's reign and the transfer of the everlasting covenant made with David to the people (Isa. 55.1-5) is to eat and drink to the full 'without money and without price'. Later, after the return, the warning to the opponents of the faithful is put in this way:

> Therefore thus says the Lord God:
> My servants shall eat, but you shall be hungry;
> my servants shall drink, but you shall be thirsty;
> my servants shall rejoice, but you shall be put to shame (Isa. 65.13).

That is why the people in Matthew 6 are exhorted to 'seek first the kingdom of God and his righteousness' (Mt. 6.33) because all these other things come with God's kingdom.

In Second Isaiah God's righteousness is a common theme and is always used in terms of God's covenant faithfulness in restoring his people and establishing his reign in their hearts. In his writings (Isa. 35, 40-55) both the masculine (*sedeq*) and feminine (*sedaqah*) forms for 'righteousness' are used of God, but only the feminine form is used for human righteousness. Moshe Weinfeld's suggestion that the masculine refers to the abstract principle and the feminine to the concrete act (1995: 34) does not fit well with Second Isaiah. Rather, their use throughout reveals that the masculine is used to indicate initiative and the feminine indicates a response. Thus, God takes the initiative for deliverance and acts in righteousness (*besedeq*) when he arouses Cyrus to deliver oppressed Israel (Isa. 45.13), just as he calls his servant Israel in righteousness (*besedeq*) whom he takes by the hand and keeps for his special purpose (Isa. 42.6). Without Yahweh's initiative the people would have remained in exile. For they worshiped Yahweh 'not in faithfulness nor in righteousness' (*bisedaqah*; Isa. 48.1). So it was necessary for them to experience Yahweh's righteousness in order to be able to respond in righteousness to God. Consequently, the prophetic cry is:

> Shower, O heavens, from above,
> And let the skies rain down righteousness (*sedeq*),
> Let Earth open, that salvation may spring up,
> And let it cause righteousness (*sedaqah*) to spring up also;
> I the Lord have created it (Isa. 45.8).

Those who are longing for Yahweh's righteousness (*sedeq*, Isa. 51.1) are assured that it is coming speedily (Isa. 51.5), and then they will experience his gracious response (*sedaqah*) forever (Isa. 51.6-8). Therefore, those who have this experience of God's righteousness (*sedeq*), and have God's teaching in their hearts (Isa. 51.7), are ready to carry out their God-given purpose with God at their side (Isa. 50.8). It is this understanding of righteousness that is so crucial for the interpretation of Mt. 6.33. In the light of this, it is clear that 'his righteousness' in that verse refers to God's gracious act of covenant faithfulness in restoring his people, a 'righteousness' that then enables those who seek it to respond in faithfulness as members of the kingdom.

Following Isa. 55.1-5, which depicts the celebration of God's kingship and the transference of the covenant made with David to the people, the vindication of God's servants was later depicted as a great banquet (Isa. 25.6-8). This led to the concept of a messianic banquet as manifestation of God's kingdom. This is reflected in the feeding stories (Mt. 14.13-21; 15.29-38) and in the parables of the marriage feast (Mt. 22.1-14; 25.1-13). The phrase used in those feeding stories—'they all ate and were satisfied'—was meant to recall the feeding of the people of Israel in the wilderness (Exod. 16.4-12), a phrase often used to indicate covenant blessings that God graciously bestows (e.g. Deut. 6.11; 8.10; 11.15; cf. Mt 5.6!). Thus, in the Gospel of Matthew as well as in the prophetic literature, eating and drinking are very much a part of celebrating the kingdom of God. So kingdom members obviously have no need to worry about those things anymore. Just as God takes care of and feeds the birds of the air which rely on his goodness (Mt. 6.26), so God will care for those people who turn to him in trust.

The same must be said also about those who are concerned about covering their nakedness. From the story in Genesis 3, nakedness had come to depict shame and humiliation. It was when the primeval couple had gone against God's will that they realized they were naked and tried to cover themselves, an action which led to their removal from the Garden of Eden. Consequently, nakedness was seen as a curse that would come on those who had forsaken God (Amos 2.16; Ezek. 16.7-39; 23.29). In order to get his message across that putting hope in Egypt rather than in God would be disastrous, Isaiah of Jerusalem walked around naked for three years as a sign of the judgment that would come upon Egypt and Ethiopia (Isa. 20.1-6). So when Second Isaiah proclaimed the impending restoration of Zion/Jerusalem (as representing the people) in Isa. 52.1-2, he did so by calling them to wake up, cast off the bonds of captivity, and 'put on your beautiful garments'. Later, after the return, the faithful one rejoices in the Lord: 'for he has clothed me with the garments of salvation, he has covered me with the robe of righteousness, as a bridegroom decks himself with a garland, and as a bride adorns herself with her jewels' (Isa. 61.10). This image is alluded to in Jesus' parable of the marriage banquet, where the man without a wedding garment is cast out (Mt. 22.11-14). So a kingdom member has no need to be anxious about clothing! For God clothes with beauty even the grass of the field, which lasts only a short season (Mt. 6.30).

Matthew 6.33 is really a declaration of the fulfilment of the prophetic longings for future restoration and a complete reversal of Deut. 28.48. No longer is there to be hunger, thirst or nakedness. The phrase, 'all these things shall be added to you' (Mt. 6.33), incorporates all the blessings of relationship and harmony in God's realm. The verb used here, *prostithemi* ('to add'), often has the meaning of 'to join, to incorporate' (cf. Acts 2.41, 47; 5.14; 11.24; 13.36). The phrase is the reversal of 'in want of all things' in Deut. 28.48. It expresses the blessings of harmonious relationship with all of nature, expressed in Deut. 28.2-6. The time of restoration has come. The kingdom of God is here. They now live under the covenant blessings, no longer under the curse. All they have to do is ask and it will be given them, to seek and they will find (Mt. 7.7-11; cf. Isa. 55.6; 65.1).

Now how does all this fit in with the natural order? It is true that the pleasant picture of the birds of the air in Mt. 6.26 may be somewhat idyllic, but that is intentional. It is part of the writer's expression of the restoration of God's kingdom. They are God's creatures, he knows them and cares for them (Ps. 50.11; Mt. 10.29), and they have their place and carry out God's purpose in his glorious creation (Ps. 104.12). Yet human greed and self-centredness are seen by the prophets as not only breaking covenant with God but also with God's creation. Thus Hosea laments because the people were not living according to the covenant stipulations, and so 'the land mourns, and all who live in it languish; together with the wild animals and the birds of the air, even the fish of the sea are perishing' (Hos. 4.3). Other prophets speak of the birds of the air and the animals fleeing the land or being swept away, leaving the land a devastation because of human unfaithfulness (Jer. 4.25; 9.9; Zeph.1.3). Restoration of relationship with God would also mean a return to the proper relationship between humanity and the animal world as partners in Earth community, as it was meant to be before the Fall (Hos. 2.18; cf. Isa. 11.1-10). God can change and restore Earth, devastated and polluted as part of the curse on humankind for having broken the everlasting covenant (Isa. 24), when God's Spirit is poured out from on high (Isa. 32.12-16; 27.2-5; 35.1-10). Second Isaiah constantly uses the imagery of the transformation of the desert into a flourishing garden to illustrate the restoration of Israel. But it is more than a metaphor. As William Brown, commenting on Second Isaiah, has so aptly put it:

> Nature is in need of redemption as much as Israel requires a new genesis. As Yahweh's judgment on Israel is inseparably tied to the land's desolation, so Israel's redemption is closely associated with the land's fructification. Such is the new thing Yahweh promises to Israel within the conflictive world of nations and nature (1999: 264):

Second Isaiah puts the principle of interconnectness so beautifully: all creation rejoices at the restoration of God's people.

> For you shall go out in joy, and be led back in peace;
> the mountains and hills before you shall burst into song,
> and all the trees of the field shall clap their hands.
> Instead of the thorn shall come up the cypress;
> instead of the brier shall come up the myrtle;
> and it shall be to the Lord for a memorial,
> for an everlasting sign that shall not be cut off. (Isa. 55.12-13):

Contrary to Betz's view that birds were the highest level of the animal world, and flowers the highest of plant life (see above), birds of the air were obviously chosen because they were two a penny, and flowers of the field because of their brief span of life (Mt. 6.26, 30). This was done not simply to make a contrast of value, but to emphasize that if God takes such care of even the most insignificant aspects of his creation, surely he will show love and concern for his redeemed ones. This is particularly evident in the use of the flowers of the field. In earlier writings humans had been likened to flowers of the field in order to emphasize the brevity of human life (Job 14.1-5; Ps. 90.5), often to contrast that with the love of God which lasts forever (Pss. 102.12, 26-29; 103.15-18; Isa. 40.6-8; 51.12). Isaiah 40.6-8 – 'Surely the people is grass; the grass withers, the flower fades, but the word of our God will stand forever' – leading up to the announcement of the good news of the reign of God (Isa. 40.9-11), most likely influenced the forming of this section of Matthew's Gospel. Because God gives so much care to dressing so beautifully the grass which has such a brief life, there is no room for anxiety about clothing in the kingdom of God. The *oligopistoi* – that is, disciples whose faith, though positive, is still hesitant – need to open up their vision to encompass the whole impact of God's kingdom in their lives. They need to heed the voice of the Earth community speaking silently of the goodness of God and of their own intrinsic value. Then they will truly grow up into 'oaks of righteousness, the planting of the Lord' (Isa 61.3) and 'all the trees of the field shall clap their hands' (Isa. 55.12)!

Implications of Matthew 6.25-34 for Ecojustice

The good news of the kingdom of God, which is the central theme of Mt. 6.25-34 – and, indeed, of the teaching of Jesus throughout the Gospel – is that God's reign is here now as well as in the future. That kingdom comes as a gracious gift when people seek it. It is there for the asking. That had already been proclaimed at the beginning of the Sermon on the Mount in the announcement of the series of blessings (Mt. 5.3-12). This proclamation of the kingdom of God as theirs is the new heaven and new Earth being created that was spoken of in Isa. 65.17; 66.22. Mt. 6.25-34, together with the whole Sermon on the Mount, is a call to be part of this new creation. Matthew deliberately placed the accounts of the healing miracles in the next two chapters after this sermon to impress upon the reader that the promised restoration, the new creation, was already taking place (Mt. 8–9). Significantly, he placed the healing of the leper first to indicate that this was the restoration of Israel, since the suffering servant of Isaiah 53 was sometimes depicted as a leper (*t. Sanhedrin* 98b). Even more significant is the fact that nature was brought into the healing process with the account of the calming of the storm (Mt. 8.23-27). Storm and tempest were symbols of God's wrath towards the wicked (cf. Isa. 29.5-6; 40.24; 41.16; Jer. 23.19; 25.32), and calming of the natural elements was a sign of God's blessing (cf. Ps. 107.25, 29; Jon. 1.4, 12). All this is tied together with the Sermon on the Mount by means of the inclusio in Mt. 4.23 and Mt. 9.35.

The ushering in of the kingdom of God thus brings about transformation. The whole Earth community is tied together. Like Second Isaiah, Jesus weaves together the natural and the human world; all are part of Earth, all are part of God's creation. Just as in the past, the failures of Israel led to the devastation of the land, so the restoration of the people is to mean the renewal of Earth. The prayer of the restored was to be that God's will would be done on Earth as it is in heaven. God's caring for Earth community members, be they birds of the air or flowers of the field, is strong indication that God also takes care of all those who are members of God's kingdom. The implication of the interrelationship between human beings and the rest of Earth community is thus made clear. Human beings are, after all, of Earth and cannot survive apart from Earth. The healing of Earth comes with the healing of humanity. When that happens the one serves the other in a divine harmony.

All beings have value, even the most insignificant like the birds of the air or the grasses of the field. Jesus calls on his followers to learn from nature around them, to listen to the voice of God's created world. This must inevitably awaken in them a greater sensitivity to the harm being done to Earth, and to their becoming involved in the healing of the Earth community. While Mt. 6.25-34 deals primarily with the divine–human relationship, it thus also implies a kinship with other members of Earth community. All share in common judgments and blessings. The one God is God of all, who cares for *all* creation, and regards it *all* as very good. It also implies that every aspect of the Earth community—be it human, animal, or plant life—has its purpose in God's design, and thus is of intrinsic worth. Considering the prophetic background to these verses, the further implication is that members of the kingdom of God are called to share in the renewal process of all of creation and thus to do the will of their Father in heaven (Mt. 7.21). Ecojustice is an integral part of the will of the Creator.

It is this principle of interconnectedness which is an underlying theme in Jesus' saying on anxiety in Mt. 6.25-34.

Good News—for the Earth? Reflections on Mark 1.1-15

William Loader

Introduction

What happens when we approach Mark from an Earth perspective? The approach taken in this paper seeks to avoid colonizing texts with cherished views, especially my own, so far as that is humanly possible given our natural capacity to see reality as we want to see it. My own commitment to an Earthed spirituality, one which values the whole creation and not just human beings, stands without my feeling I have to substantiate it with ancient texts. As an interpretive historian and theologian dealing with biblical texts, I consider it essential to try to hear what a text is saying in its own terms, both when it coheres with and perhaps inspires my values and when it heads in the opposite direction. In dealing with Earth, a hermeneutic of suspicion and openness entails critical listening to the texts and a good deal of the time interpreting their silences and conjecturing where they might lead in what they have not articulated.

Sometimes the broader cultural context allows assumptions, such as that the created world is of worth, even though it may appear on stage only as a prop for human drama. It is not evil in itself, as we might suppose in Gnosticism. Similarly Earth does not consist of desiccated segments of reality strewn across the stage without connection or coherence. In part the connectedness and coherence flow from the assumption of a creation and, with that, the notion of some divinely rooted purpose and function. Usually that function is anthropocentric. Earth in its vastness lies largely out of sight and offstage. The values of custodianship have no scene for themselves. But already we move too quickly. The text deserves to be heard, inviting us to listen to its world, where we hear voices and guess our way through the interconnectedness that gave John and Jesus a place in the wilderness. Our focus is the beginning of Mark's Gospel.

Mark 1.1-15 forms the prologue or overture to the Gospel. In it we hear the melodies of later chapters and the scene is set for what follows.

The transition to what follows is somewhat fluid. Some would see the prologue concluding at Mk 1.13 with a change of time and place commencing in Mk 1.14 as the writer reports John's arrest and Jesus' entry into Galilee preaching the good news. In an oral culture where gospels were written to be read aloud, such transitions were common. Mark 1.14-15 belongs both to what follows and to what precedes. Importantly it recapitulates the themes of the first verse. Jesus is preaching 'the good news of God' (Mk 1.14). Mark 1.1 spoke of 'the good news of Jesus Christ, the Son of God'. In this way good news both embraces the prologue and serves as a title for the account that follows.

Jesus both brings the good news and is the good news. In the course of time 'good news' (*euangelion*) became a standard term for Christian proclamation ('gospel') and from there, ultimately, a description for a written account of Jesus' life, such as we find in titles given the Gospels from the second century. But here the good news is to be found in the events that follow, events Mark has 'begun' to tell in Mk 1.1. This is 'the beginning'.[1] Hearers of Mark's opening words might recognize the echoes of Isa. 52.7 and Isa. 61.1, which speak of a messenger of good news and of one anointed to tell good news to God's people. These had become texts of hope as Jews faced successive regimes of oppressive conquerors in the centuries that followed.[2] Others might have heard echoes of imperial proclamations that declared that Rome's imperial power was good news for the world, bringing peace and stability.[3] Some might have greeted any such claim with disbelief and despair.

The good news overture, itself, includes many voices: 'the voice of one crying out in the wilderness' (Mk 1.3); the voices of those confessing their sins in baptism (Mk 1.5); a voice 'from the heavens' (Mk 1.11); and the voice of Jesus himself (Mk 1.15). What about the voice of Earth? Can we articulate its silence? What about this good news? Is it also good news for Earth?[4]

---

1.   Ancient writers took great care about the opening statements of their works. The word 'beginning' was what one might expect at one level in such sentences, but within the Jewish–Christian tradition it comes frequently as an echo of Gen. 1.1 in a way that claims that something just as fundamental is about to be told. Mk 1.1 reflects this. Other famous examples are Jn 1.1 and 1 Jn 1.1.

2.   For instance, in the document, 11QMelch, found among the scrolls at Qumran. See also Lk. 4.16-20; 7.22.

3.   The word *euangelion* is found in an inscription at Priene hailing the achievements of Caesar Augustus. See Marcus (1999: 146); see also the excursus in Guelich (1989: 13-14). As van Iersel (1998: 91) notes, even the term 'Son of God', would for some immediately evoke the claims of the emperors.

4.   The later addition to Mark, found in some manuscripts, speaks of preaching

The Wilderness – Voices in/of the Wilderness

Road-making

After the joyfully triumphant bars with which the overture greets us in Mk 1.1 we hear a discordant note, at least from an Earth perspective. Three texts from the Hebrew Scriptures combine to declare that John the Baptist will build a road, a straight road (Exod. 23.20; Mal. 3.1; Isa. 40.3).[5] More dramatically in Luke we hear the fuller text of Isaiah 40, 'Every valley is to be filled in and every mountain and hill levelled' (Lk. 3.4-6), immortalized in Handel's famous aria from 'Messiah'. It is a disastrous image. Mother Earth de-breasted to make a new highway! While it is only an image, our choices of images reflect value systems. The hymn 'Onward Christian Soldiers', for instance, uses an image now widely acknowledged as discordant because of the values it reflects.

Mark's text does not include the levelling, but only the road. The road is not in the wilderness; only the voice is in the wilderness. This reflects the fact that Mark is using the Greek translation of Isa. 40.3, which speaks of the voice as crying out in the wilderness. In the original Hebrew the phrase 'in the wilderness' belongs with the instruction to prepare the Lord's way: 'Prepare in the wilderness the Lord's way.' The community at Qumran had already used that text to describe itself as a community preparing such a way – in the wilderness (1QS 8.15)! In Mark the road is not mapped to run through the wilderness. Thus the image in Mark is not as violent. It focuses less on road-making and more on marking out the path, ensuring it is a way that can be travelled. Mark will later picture Jesus as 'on the road', a road that will lead to the cross.

The image is incidental to the theme, but choice of images may sometimes reveal important presuppositions. These may also have relevance for the relative place of Earth in all of this. What is the image of the way doing in Mark? In the immediate context its focus is on readiness and access. Get ready for the one who is coming: Jesus, the Christ. In Isaiah it was more in the nature of promise and encouragement: the Lord is going to lead his people out of exile and back to Jerusalem. Isaiah 40.1 declares:

the gospel to 'the whole creation'. Contemporary usage in Mark's time indicates that this does not demonstrate a special sensitivity to the world beyond humanity. It was a common way of describing humanity, in a similar way to contemporary usage of 'the earth', 'the world' today.

5.   It is best to see Mk 1.2-3 as continuing the statement begun in Mk 1.1. Thus, 'The beginning of the good news of Jesus Christ [the Son of God was] as is written in the prophet Isaiah...' Most recently, Marcus (1999: 141-42) also discusses 'Son of God' as likely scribal addition to the text; similarly Guelich (1989: 7) cf. Hooker (1991: 33).

'Comfort, O comfort my people!' In the rest of Mark the image of the way describes Jesus' ministry, his journey, especially to Jerusalem and the temple (Mk 8.27; 9.30, 33; 10.1, 32, 46; 11.1, 11), beginning in the far north, in the city that honoured the empire – Caesarea Philippi: a symbol of the Gentile world; and reaching its climax when Jesus enters the temple in Jerusalem.[6]

One possible focus could have been the journey as an experience of passing through. The goal is all that matters, sometimes spiritualized as the heavenly Jerusalem. All else is incidental, perhaps even a hindrance and a distraction. Such snubbing of the world became characteristic of those groups that made Mark their favourite Gospel in the following centuries, the Gnostics, who read Mark as implying that the heavenly dropped into Jesus at his baptism, endured being on Earth to inform its inhabitants of how to escape, and flitted back to heaven just before or just after the crucifixion, leaving an Earthly corpse on the cross. While Mark does employ the image to describe Jesus' journey to Jerusalem (and also inspired Luke to elaborate the image to great lengths), Mark's Jesus was not on an escape path, nor was he just passing through. Rather he spent most of his time stopping and attending to people who were in need. The span of Caesarea Philippi to Jerusalem may have more to do with celebrating the inclusion of Gentiles in Jesus' journey than with geography.

For Mark, then, 'the way' means more a 'way of being in the world' than a 'way out' of it. In fact it was a particular way of being, one that entered into solidarity with people along the way and deliberately entered and embodied their suffering. It was a way of inclusiveness. The cross was not the low point of its meaning, something to be left behind, but the high point, something to be held up as revealing the way God is in the world. This Earthed-ness in relation to Earth's people quite naturally invites us to contemplate an Earthed-ness in relation to Earth, too, though Mark does not articulate that. Just as Mark's Jesus depicts God on the ground of real human experience, Mark's theology would not be a source of distraction from Earth but generate a sense of solidarity in which the oneness with humanity might have expressed itself also as a oneness with the life that we live on Earth. Perhaps the wilderness is a place of merged identity, an entering into not only a deep encounter with the divine but with primal Earth.

Wilderness and Hope

In composing his overture Mark is not inventing new tunes, but re-working melodies familiar both from known stories of the life of Jesus

6.   On the symbolic role of 'place' in Mark's narrative see Malbon (1991).

and from the great compositions that formed Israel's heritage in the Hebrew Scriptures. We have already noted the quotation of Isa. 40.3 in 1.3 and its words about wilderness. Wilderness—in Australian English, 'the outback'—is a central theme running through the prologue (Mk 1.3, 4, 12, 13). As an image it called up many associations for the Gospel's contemporary audience.

The quotation in Mk 1.2-3, which Mark introduces as coming from Isaiah, is a combination of three different texts from the Hebrew Scriptures. The Isaiah text, cited in Mk 1.3, alludes to the wilderness lands through which Isaiah asserted God would lead the exiles triumphantly home (Isa. 40.3). This explains why Mark treats the combined quotation as coming from Isaiah. In fact Mk 1.2 is not a quotation from Isaiah at all but a combination of two quotations from Exod. 23.20 and Mal. 3.1. The Exodus passage also links us to the wilderness. Wilderness was the way for Israel in their escape from Pharaoh's Egypt. Exodus 23.20 contains the promise: 'I will send an angel in front of you, to guard you on the way and to bring you to the place that I have prepared.' That angel—in the Greek translation of the text, 'my angel'—would go ahead of Israel on its journey through the wilderness. Whoever linked these quotations together (someone before Mark) took the text to be referring not to an angel, but to a messenger—an ambiguity possible with the word in both the Greek and Hebrew. The text was then read as a promise by God to Jesus about John the Baptist (similarly Mt. 11.10).

The promise in Mal. 3.1, which also speaks of sending a messenger in advance, has also influenced the text. That promise—'I am sending my messenger to prepare the way before me'—was commonly linked with Mk 4.5-6, which spoke of the return of Elijah to restore right relationships in Israel. John is identified with Elijah in Mk 9.9 and like Elijah, according to 2 Kgs 1.8, wears the hairy garments of a prophet (cf. Zech. 13.4). Thus the opening statements in Mk 1.2-3 already create a whirl of associations linked with Israel's hope and the wilderness.

Wilderness was, therefore, a favourite place for great expectations and preparations for new acts of liberation that echoed those of old. Josephus reports individuals and movements that made the wilderness their base.[7] Wilderness was a place of hope in transition. Some people expected a repeat of the great miracles of the wilderness period of Israel's history: miraculous feedings, river crossings, military formations, revelations about Torah. This informs the way wilderness functions in Mark's narrative (and also later—for instance, in the feeding of the five thousand where people sat down in army formation). So John starts the work of

---

7.   See Josephus, *War* 2.258-64; *Ant.* 20.97-99, 169-72. See also Acts 5.35-36; 21.38.

preparation in the wilderness and, later, Jesus undergoes his testing in the wilderness before setting out with the good news for the towns and villages of Galilee. The wilderness is the vestibule of hope. But is it more than that?

Wilderness and Lifestyle

What about the wilderness itself? In the text it is silent. Yet the wilderness does have character and to some extent it is very ambiguous. One apparent ambiguity is just a fact of geography: the River Jordan passes through the foot of the wilderness of Judaea. It was wilderness nevertheless and still is. Another ambiguity is John's nourishment. We, today, might squirm at the thought of eating locusts, but they were good 'bush tucker', as was wild honey.[8] According to Mk 1.13 angels nourished Jesus in the wilderness. That sounds more palatable, but probably amounted to the same kind of diet. Unlike the depiction in Matthew and Luke, Jesus was not fasting in Mark. 'The angels' also enhance the allusion to precedents in the Hebrew Scriptures, like Elijah (1 Kgs 19.1-8).

There is something romantic about simply living off the land like this. It recalls the movements in the 1970s, when many chose to go bush and pursue alternative lifestyles. The phenomenon has deeper roots, however, reaching back to age-old tensions between living by cultivating the land and building settlements on the one hand; and on the other, living by herding, or simply by hunting and gathering the food that nature provided, before moving on. The tension reproduces itself in various forms: settled peoples and nomadics; city dwellers and country people; urban and rural (cf. Jer. 2.2; 31.2; Hos. 2.14; 9.10; Amos 5.25). Beside the romantic appeal of the rustic is the very serious question of whether the globalized values of the international city dwellers are not only marginalizing the rural peoples but threatening the well-being of the planet and all its inhabitants. When someone deliberately returned to the wilderness to live off the land, that act was a challenge to the lifestyle chosen by others. John's behaviour was a challenge, a call to repentance. This had a lot to do with confrontating lifestyle choices. Through Israel's history and its stories, from Cain and Abel to the Rechabites, from John to Jesus, the alternative lifestyle called people back to a sense of God in

---

8.   The diet may also indicate that John was non-meat eating (as Mt. 11.18/Lk. 7.33 report), although usually this kind of stance is more characteristic of Jews living in a strongly Gentile environment where meat is deemed polluted (as in Daniel). Hooker (1991: 37) writes: 'Locusts and honey would not be John's entire diet but might well be his greatest delicacies.' Lev. 11.22-23 show that these were acceptable meat substitutes; cf. Painter (1997: 28), who sees a problem of purity here.

the natural world and to a way of trust that inevitably sought to live with the land and not against it.

Trust in the Land

Jesus did not remain in the wilderness like John. Was his experience with John just a stage he had to go through, a bit of radical growing up to be abandoned for mediocrity at the age of 30 as happens so frequently in our society? On the contrary, Jesus, according to Mark, carried these wilderness values into his ministry and this doubtless reflects the earliest tradition about Jesus. Jesus was calling for the same repentance as John. The direction did not change. Jesus carried the confrontation into the settled areas of Galilee and its surrounds by living the lifestyle he followed; he invited his followers to share this lifestyle. They were to live off a bare minimum, travelling for town to town, depending on the network of hospitality and caring that the good news advocated and produced (Mk 6.7-11). By calling many to abandon wealth, land and family, Jesus was subverting traditional values and calling for a radical reassessment of priorities. At one level his challenge could bring dislocation. At another it invited a new and different relationship to land and to people.

In this context he called people to look at the lilies of the field, the ravens, the grass (Mt. 6.25-34; Lk. 12.22-32). It was a call to trust, a challenge to the anxiety that hoards and frets and as a consequence exploits and often destroys. It assumed the possibility of coexistence with Earth. The lifestyle advocated by Jesus was a protest against prevailing values. We know of similar teaching among popular Stoic and Cynic preachers. Like them, Jesus conducted himself in a way that confronted the norms that made possessions and power central to the good life. Instead, the alternative preached by Jesus asserted that the good life involved living in harmony with God.[9] That profile in the case of Jesus was informed by prophetic visions that went far beyond the individual fulfilment espoused by the philosophers; Jesus' dream involved transformed communities and an inclusive compassion. While not articulated as part of his vision of the future reign of God, it is a logical extension of his teaching elsewhere to assume that Jesus' vision of God's reign would include also a right relationship with creation, a synergy such as we find in Mark's prologue. The lifestyle confrontation that the good news brings is, indeed, good news for Earth and for all creation.

---

9.   For discussion of the Cynic parallels to Jesus' teaching, see Downing (1987); Crossan (1998: 333-35) where he reassesses his earlier work; see also the strongly negative assessment of Boyd (1995).

The Rent Heaven — Voices from/of the Heavens

John was a voice in the wilderness (Mk 1.4-6). Jesus would also spend time in the wilderness (Mk 1.12-13). Before replaying that tune in relation to Jesus Mark draws the listener's attention to an event that reveals the significance of all that follows in his Gospel. It is an event of cosmic proportions: the baptism of Jesus. The scene begins quietly as Jesus allows John to submerge him in the none-too-clean waters of the River Jordan. Jesus is embracing or being embraced by the same waters that bring life and bear life as everyone else who came to the river.[10] The stream articulates divine grace. It may also prefigure divine judgment. Jesus descends like his compatriots into the deep, with no qualms about solidarity with all sorts who have come to be baptized in hope. As Jesus emerges, Mark decribes a dramatic cosmic event.

The heavens are 'torn apart'. God rips a hole in the curtain; at least, that, according to Mark, is what Jesus saw. In Matthew and Luke, the more genteel image of opening is used: the curtain is drawn, the dove alights and the voice is heard. Mark's dramatic image probably derives from Isa. 64.1, where the prophet pleads: 'O that you would tear open the heavens and come down!' Those who heard Mark's Gospel read many times over might have thought of the ripping of the curtain when Jesus died on the cross. There the focus is judgment and an ironic response to the mockery of Jesus as one who would 'destroy the temple' (Mk 14.58; 15.29), but there, as here, we also find a voice declaring him, 'Son of God' (Mk 15.39).

The image has inspired many other reflections, including that — as it is expressed in the book of Hebrews — it might be symbolizing the new and living way for all, mediated by Christ alone, or a new immediacy of the divine presence. While the theme of access was not, in my view, in the forefront of Mark's narrative,[11] it was certainly possible that Mark's hearers may have sensed both there and here that we have a celebration of removed barriers, and a new open access to the divine. It is almost as though now, by divine fiat, heaven springs a leak and Earth is to be filled with the glory of God. Something of that is certainly present in delicate refinement in Mark.

The focus in Mark is on the urgency of divine love. The image, despite its violence, is not one of destruction and judgment. The assumption is

---

10. On Mark's description of John as 'the baptizer' in contrast to Matthew and Luke's 'the baptist' see Guelich (1989: 16-17), who also discusses the variant texts. Cf. also Mk 6.14, 24.

11. See my discussion in Loader (1997: 120-21); see also van Iersel (1998: 100).

that the heavens flow together again unscathed. There is no sensitivity, even in the imagery, to consequences of such acts for Earth or the heavens in a literal sense. The inanimate creation is silent. The urgency makes open the way for the Spirit, pictured here not as a rushing wind, or mighty storm, or burning flame, but as a gentle dove.

In this moment heaven and Earth touch, much as some religious traditions understand temples and sacred sites as places of convergence. The focus is primarily on God and humanity, but the event engages heaven and Earth in a way that probably goes beyond mere symbolism. For Mark, as we shall see, there is the hope that now God's goodness will fill Earth and that evil will be banished forever. This is ultimately hope for all creation. John the Baptist had announced the coming of the Spirit in Jesus' ministry when he declared that Jesus would baptize with the Spirit (Mk 1.8). His is the image of the engulfing flood. The Spirit belongs to 'the stronger one', who will later 'bind the strong man' of the demonic world and subvert his rule (Mk 3.27). The language of power resounds throughout the overture. When, however, Jesus receives the Spirit to equip him for this task, and is anointed as Messiah for this role, the image is the dove. At most we might imagine a small voice cooing.[12]

'Like a Dove...'
Creation also speaks in the image of the dove. Luke dramatizes the narrative, emphasizing that the Spirit came not only like a dove, but in the physical form (*somatiko*) of a dove. For Mark the dove is just an image — and one that evokes many echoes. Some hear the story of the wind or Spirit hovering over the waters of creation (Gen. 1.2; similarly 4Q521); others find here the language of foreign deities baptized to serve better purposes; still others recall the great Flood and the good news of a new beginning for Noah — but also for all of life.[13] While for Mark the Spirit becomes the source of power for Jesus' victorious battle against the forces of evil, the broader allusions invite us to receive the Spirit as one who also groans for the liberation of all creation, as Paul put it once. As John predicted, Jesus is to baptize with the Spirit. That baptizing is about to begin as a new flood of God's goodness finds expression in Jesus' ministry.[14]

---

12. Rabbinic literature later spoke of the *bath qol*, the quiet voice of God, as like a dove's cooing, but the words that come from on high in this scene are more like trumpeted acclaim.

13. See Gundry (1993: 51) for discussion of the range of options.

14. On Jesus' ministry as baptizing with the Spirit see Guelich (1989: 25; Gundry (1993: 38, 46).

This Jesus who descended in solidarity into the waters now rises to reassuring words that affirm his identity. With echoes of Isa. 42.1 he is affirmed as God's servant; with echoes of Ps. 2.7 he is affirmed as Israel's royal Messiah, the Son of God; with echoes of Abraham's love for Isaac (Gen. 22.2, 12, 16), he is affirmed as God's beloved Son. This central affirmation underlies all that is to follow. He is the man of the Spirit. He embodies the divine agenda. Mark will follow his path. Is Earth simply the sand beneath his feet or does this embodiment also entail good news for all creation?

Animals and Angels – Voices in/of the Struggle

Jesus' path leads him directly back into the wilderness. We are back to powerful language. The Spirit is compelling. At one level it is John the Baptist's story repeating itself with all the same associations of simplicity and hope. But Mark describes Jesus' venture differently, raising further ambiguity about the wilderness. Jesus 'was with the wild animals' (Mk 1.13). The wilderness was wild! Was Jesus thrown by the Spirit into the wilderness den of wild animals, like Daniel? Is that what Mk 1.13 means? Was that part of the testing of Jesus?[15]

Or is the image evoking the opposite? Is Jesus pictured as being in a kind of new paradise, as a new Adam, tempted but remaining true; living at one with the animals, who therefore pose no threat?[16] That would enhance the sense of the future ideal as one of coexistence with Earth and its creatures, as in Isa. 11.2; 65.25; 2 Bar. 73.6). The image of the dove might even be contributing the thought of a new paradise after the Flood. Some have noted that Jesus would later enter Jerusalem riding an untamed (literally, 'unridden') colt and have wondered whether Mark intends here to portray Jesus as having a calming influence, perhaps

---

15.   Lane (1974: 61) argues in relation to the wild beasts that 'their affinity in this context is not with paradise, but with the realm of Satan'.

16.   Marcus (1999: 157) emphasizes the paradisical features as influencing already the portrait of John the Baptist (his garments and food). He draws attention to the hope expressed in Isa. 11.2 and writes: 'Mark apparently believes that this restoration had now happened in Jesus, the new Adam' (Marcus 1999: 168; see also 169-71). He does, however, emphasize that it is a place of struggle – with Satan – and that it is of fundamental importance for Mark that Jesus emerges victorious; cf. Gundry (1993: 58-59) who rejects not only a paradisical interpretation, but also the notion of a struggle with the animals. Rather, he argues that the scene serves to bear witness to Jesus being Son of God, whom none can harm; similarly van Iersel (1998: 102) see also Bauckham (1994).

even the magic of a super tamer.[17] Did he tame the wild animals as well? Part of our problem is that the Greek does not speak of the animals as 'wild'. It uses a word designated specifically for non-domestic animals, but in English we lack one. When we speak of 'wild' animals, we create the impression that the focus is on wildness, whereas the Greek wording need not imply this at all. Nevertheless the idea that Jesus had a taming influence is possible—although, from an animal's perspective, it might not be in their interests to be tamed in this way. It could reflect just another instance of human beings wanting to force all other realities into a shape that serves their interests.

An underlying issue is: did Mark mean the scene to resemble paradise, a foretaste of restored order? In this case, animals are present peaceably as once they were in Eden according to popular thought. The struggle was then only with Satan—as it was in the garden of Eden. Or do the animals also feature, not as combatants, but as dangerous, as 'wild'? Then Jesus tames them, or at least is able to protect himself, as well as resisting Satan. The *Testaments of the Twelve Patriarchs*, which contains many parallels to the Gospels, promise such power to the people of Israel in direct association with the devil and with angels as here: 'The devil will flee from you; wild animals will be afraid of you, and the angels will stand by you' (*T. Naph.* 8.4; similarly *T. Iss.* 7.7; *T. Benj.* 5.2).[18] The difficulty with the seeing Mk 1.12-13 as a foretaste of paradise is that paradise motifs do not feature elsewhere in Mark.

Whether wild animals are incidental idyllic scenery or, as is more likely, feature as part of the wild and dangerous, the primary focus is on the successful outcome of the conflict between Jesus and Satan. The context both in Mark 1 and the rest of the Gospel certainly does not suggest a holiday; rather the Gospel depicts a struggle. This is also what we might expect in the light of similar accounts of great people written at the time. A common feature of these is the hero facing tests and trials before going off to perform exploits.[19] Mark (as well as Matthew and Luke) is most likely to be writing under the influence of these contemporary texts. Therefore the focus is not magical bliss, but struggle. The mention of animals may have been to enhance the sense of danger— but the struggle was not with the animals; it is with the arch spiritual enemy, Satan. The Q version of the story, preserved in Matthew and Luke, makes strong links with the wilderness struggles of Israel. How-

17.   See the discussion in Gundry (1993: 628).

18.   The image of wild animals as inimical to human life is particularly strong in Ezekiel. See most recently the discussion in Olley (2001: 55-56).

19.   On the background to the temptation narratives see Kloppenborg (1987: 258-62).

ever, aside from the symbolic numeral 40 – which need not point in that direction – nothing in Mark's account particularly suggests that those struggles form the primary background to his text.[20]

For Mark the wilderness is the place of Jesus' struggle. Jesus emerges victorious. Angels sustain Jesus. Mark is introducing us to one of the major themes of his Gospel, fundamental to his version of the good news and central for our consideration of whether this good news is also good news for Earth and the created world.

Earth and Struggle

Central to the struggle is the demonic power of Satan. We may feel estranged by such thought and see his power reducing Earth's significance to incidental background scenery. Struggle is, however, important and dominates what follows. The assumption in Mark's Gospel is that Earth is the habitation for angels and demons. In the wilderness you can meet both. Mark offers no explanation for how Earth came to be this way, unlike some of his contemporaries. Mark assumes that Earth is not demonic. Some did think that way with disastrous consequences; in this view, Earth is depicted as being in an even worse state than when it is seen as a sphere to be passed through. Earth becomes the enemy to be conquered and subjugated. It becomes a hopeless junkyard and an embodiment of evil.

Not so in Mark's eyes. He would have shared the view that Earth was God's creation. But in a number of ways the struggle between Jesus and Satan inevitably expands to include Earth and its creatures. For Mark, hope would have included also a new or renewed heaven and Earth.

Normally wilderness was a place to avoid in Jesus' time, much as settler Australians have hugged the coast and avoided the inland. Mark shows Jesus led by the Spirit into the outback, the place of dried bones and deep mystery. Here Earth articulates the fragility of life. Human beings shrivel in size, lost in the greater-than-human elements of wind and heat and wasteland. Here is the boundary of human confidence and competence – but also the locus of revelation where the cultivated gods of human settlement are silent. In both modern and ancient times people have experienced the wilderness as the raw terrain of the soul, not simply as a metaphor for personal inwardness, but as an Earthed colloquium about existence. Here the world of nature has the upper hand. Earth dances to its own rhythms and does not answer our questions. For

---

20.   As Hooker (1991: 49) notes, 40 could also allude to the days Moses spent on Sinai (Exod. 34.28) or the time Elijah travelled to Horeb (1 Kgs 19.8). Note also the 40 days of the Flood story (Gen. 7.4, 12).

Jesus to face the wilderness is another way of saying Jesus faced reality. That means he faced exposure and struggled to overcome the challenges he experienced. For Mark and people in Mark's world, wilderness was numinous space where good and evil met head-on; it was a place of demons and angels, of destruction and new life. Here Jesus would be confronting head-on the central issues that he would meet for the rest of his life.

When Jesus completes his retreat, his journey is not away from the struggle; with eyes open Jesus journeys into its heart, suppressed and disguised beneath the constructions and myths of human community. Raw conflict and raw Earthedness continues to set the tone of the struggle. Under the meaning dressed up by religious systems, Jesus is able to see both Earth's issues and God's issues. He is able to be good news to those severed from their connection to the land by exploitative landlords and the leeching occupation of the Romans and their local henchmen.

Was wilderness merely the convenient setting for uninterrupted thought, punctuated by moments of natural beauty to inspire; a nice and appropriate context for contemplation? Or did the wilderness speak, disturb, evoke, whine, shout and wail, giving voice to the pain of the struggle? More likely the latter, just as once more, in Gethsemane before his death, Jesus was bowed in brokenness and overwhelmed by grief and the struggle with evil as he contemplated the cosmic drama about to unfold in evil's revenge.

Mark locates this struggle not simply in the hearts and minds of people or the heart and mind of Jesus, but on the cosmic stage. In harmony with other Christians of his age, Mark portrays the struggle he is about to relate and which his overture intones as a major world event where superhuman forces are at play. Larger issues are at stake and they have an impact on all people. It is a small step to allow that expanding logic to encompass the whole of creation. Mark does not articulate this breadth of concern, as does Paul, but the conceptual links that connect Mark to communities under Pauline influence make it likely he would have shared their hope.[21]

'Collateral Damage'

We must avoid idealizing Mark, however. Part of the victory of the Son of God over the demons in the Gospel of Mark also includes acts that impinge negatively on Earth and have produced patterns of thought and behaviour that are destructive. There appears to be a callous disregard,

---

21. See Marcus (1999: 73-75); similarly Painter (1997: 5-6).

for instance, for the pigs who catapult themselves into the lake when the Gerasene demons enter them (Mk 5.1-20). They are 'collateral damage' – to use a favoured term of the military establishment – in the war against evil. Nor is there sympathy for the economic loss experienced by the local farmers as a consequence of this 'act of God'. Unlike Mark, the earlier storytellers would have seen the destruction as doubly appropriate: these were unclean animals in an unclean land. The plight of the pigs is a non-issue for them and for Mark. Innocent of intended harm, such disregard easily plays itself out, however, in patterns of exploitation and destructiveness where the Christian gospel and those who espouse it bring great mourning to Earth.

Miracle and Natural Processes
In a similar way Jesus' actions in calming the storm (Mk 4.35-41), walking on the waters (Mk 6.45-52), and in the food-multiplying miracles (Mk 6.35-44; 8.1-10), all subordinate the natural processes of Earth to manipulation that benefits human beings. No harm is done, but the approach is symptomatic of a world view that can disregard natural processes. In the case of the water miracles, we can probably assume that Mark and his predecessors would have seen the natural and demonic intertwined. The stilling of the storm is an exorcism ('He rebuked the wind and the sea and told them, "Quiet! Calm down!"'; Mk 4.39). Earth is not inanimate. There are angels of winds and rain and fire. There are also demons who inhabit and manipulate these, but the focus is the battle not their embodiment.

Such scenes are also alive with deliberate echoes of the past. Sea miracles recall the Exodus – both as departure and as crossing the River Jordan. Food miracles recall both the Exodus and the wonders performed by Elijah and Elisha. The point of such stories is that the hearer should recognize the divine powers at work, and that these powers are none other than those of YHWH, as manifest in Moses and the prophets and sometimes hailed as direct epithets of God. They are not, however, inaugurating a new order or new possibilities of relating to the natural world. How we might long for such skills to control weather patterns and multiply scarce resources! People vary in their views about possible historical realities behind such stories, but their impact changes little about the view of Earth or values relating to Earth. Too often, moreover, they encourage a stance that sees Earth as an obstacle, to be subordinated to human (and divine) purposes without regard for the consequences. But it need not be so.

Healing for Creation

On the other hand, some aspects of the good news in Mark do entail positive changes that involve healing for creation. This is apparent in the exorcisms. Throughout his ministry Jesus baptizes the world with Spirit; human beings are released from demonic distortions; people are healed; the paralyzed are set free. Behind these acts is the notion that good news means 'bringing [back] into good order', one of the meanings of 'righteousness'/'justice'. While in Mark and the Gospels righteousness is focused on human beings, the principle of restoring order and wholeness has rich possibilities when applied, with awareness, to the fullest extent of the disorder. It is, indeed, good news for all creation when righteousness is made a fundamental axiom for values and behaviour.

A Call to Change; a Vision of Renewal

This brings me back to the fundamental values of the passage, the main melody of the overture. Mark's overture is about change—a change of attitude, which is the basic meaning of the word often translated as 'repentance'. This is the message both John the Baptist and Jesus share. With it goes the grace of forgiveness. It is about facing up to reality. John encourages his hearers to celebrate change and forgiveness with a sacramental encounter with Earth through Earth's waters. Here there are multiple allusions: to the days of creation, to Noah and the flood, to the Exodus; but there is also a fundamental acknowledgment that human words fail and that truth will sometimes best emerge when in our bodiliness we find a way of allowing Earth to speak to us and for us. All this is there in John the Baptist as it is in Jesus.

The new in Jesus builds on John the Baptist's future vision, but emphasizes a new age when God will rule Earth. It is a future hope, informed by prophetic visions of inclusiveness, of feasting and community. It is also both an agenda that drives Jesus' ministry and a reality that is beginning to emerge as Jesus' ministry lives it out in the here and now. This is the good news of Jesus Christ and about him. It is not about a pathway to heaven, as if hope lies in abandoning Earth. That kind of theology diminishes creation and will lead to espousal of popular Platonic notions that the body and material reality are a tomb or cage from which the soul must break free like a bird or, worse, to speculation that materiality is a demonic plot hatched by a demigod who from the beginning thwarted Adam and Eve's best aspirations out of insecurity and trapped their offspring in the molasses of the flesh. It is more about a way of life than a way through it.

Jesus' vision of God's reign remains at some points undefined in Mark's Gospel, but appears to take its origins in hopes for restoration of

Israel, and, often connected with that, involves both the inclusion of all peoples and the renewal of all creation through the gift of the Spirit. While not identified as such in the prologue nor in Mark's Gospel, this hope includes more than human beings and, when fully embraced, celebrates the restoration and renewal of the whole creation.

Solidarity in the Renewal of all Creation
While Paul, reflecting this context, wrote of the groaning of the Spirit and its yearning for such total renewal, Mark's composition knows these chords, but we hear them only in the one groaning for escape in Gethsemane, the one crying the cry of forsakenness from the cross. Despite the battle motif, Mark's symphony, especially the final movements, is not triumphalistic.

Instead we see Jesus treading the way John the Baptist prepared, a way of change and transformation, a way that would see him wounded and dying at its end. Jesus' way of death and resurrection did not 'leave it all behind', but Jesus' way is a model to inspire others to take the same journey. To tread that path invites us not to rush through the countryside to be in time for a heavenly parking space, but to live in solidarity with the Spirit, to share out the baptism of the Spirit with all creation.

Mark has no illusions: this is the way of vulnerability and compassion, not of happy peace of mind and ethereal victory. That exposure, celebrated in the waters of baptism also connects us to the vulnerability of Earth and ultimately, the vulnerability of God.

When Is the End Not the End?
The Fate of Earth in Biblical Eschatology (Mark 13)

Keith D. Dyer

The blame for exploitation and abuse of the environment by Christians is often laid on the 'Genesis mandate' (Gen. 1.28), particularly when it has been interpreted as giving humans 'dominion' over all creation. At least as culpable however (and arguably even more influential as the reason behind for President Bush's refusal to sign the Kyoto Agreement, for example),[1] are certain biblicist convictions about how creation *must* degenerate and collapse, which are usually derived from texts at the other end of the canon to Genesis. It is my aim here to retrieve some of these 'texts of cosmic terror' from the grip of both fanatical and scholarly apocalypticism, to re-evaluate them in light of Earth Bible principles, and to wrestle with those texts that seem to persist as words against Earth. The focus will be on the Synoptic Gospel eschatological texts and Mark 13 in particular, but since they are dependent on the prophetic literature and in turn influential for those texts in the Christian Scriptures written afterwards, the question of the fate of Earth in biblical eschatology is the ultimate topic addressed.[2] It is my contention that we should not burden these texts with the full scope of our relatively recent apocalyptic imaginations, nor excuse our own responsibility for human and environmental calamities by appealing to divine necessity (*dei genesthai*, 'this *must* take place'; Mk 13.7).

In this context, the Earth Bible principle of interconnectedness — 'Earth

---

1. The dominance of conservative, even fundamentalist, Christianity in the south of the USA — Florida and Texas (the heartland of President Bush's support base) — sets certain parameters for the language within which political issues must be expressed, or at least be seen not to contravene. Long-term ecojustice issues are simply not part of that religious or political vocabulary, and can even be perceived by fundamentalists as a threat to the sovereignty of God and human freedom.

2. This paper was first presented at the ANZATS/ANZTS Conference on Eco-theology in Christchurch, July 2000, (my thanks to those who provided feedback), and has been redrafted in this form during the week of the terrorist attacks on the World Trade Centre, September 2001.

is a community of interconnected living things that are mutually dependent on each other for life and survival' (principle two) — informs the readings that follow here, though I shall extend the interconnectedness to include the 'heavenly bodies' as viewed from Earth. It follows that the Earth Bible affirmations of the intrinsic worth of the universe *and* Earth (principle one) and the principle of purpose of the universe, Earth and all its components (principle four) are also foundational for the interpretations offered here (Earth Bible Team 2000b: 42-53). The re-examining of the texts selected below from this more integrated perspective (which is how they once used to be read), should suggest alternative interpretations to the obsession with the eschatology of inevitable disaster that dominates so much of popular theology.

The Fate of Earth in Popular Eschatology

The eschatological convictions that can limit Christian engagement with Earth issues may be outlined by suggesting (somewhat tongue in cheek) a fundamentalist Christian version of the Earth Bible's six ecojustice principles. Let's call them the six Biblicist Eschatological principles:

1. *The principle of imminent cataclysm* — Earth is headed for disaster (sooner rather than later).
2. *The principle of disconnectedness* — we humans don't have to share or feel responsible for Earth's fate (salvation is for humans, not Earth).
3. *The principle of inevitability* — there's nothing we (or Earth) can do about it.
4. *The principle of transcendence* — what really matters is the next world (or 'heavenism' as Habel describes it).
5. *The principle of sovereignty* — God is in ultimate (even direct) control of all this.
6. *The principle of self-interest* — God will rapture 'believers' out of this mess in the nick of time.

It comes as no surprise that within this kind of operational framework, every ecological disaster and every sign of degenerating human behaviour is seen as proof that 'the end times' are indeed upon us. This in turn tends to reinforce faith as a kind of grim paralysis, stoically enduring the decline of our planet in the hope of something better in the next life. Any motivation to take action in support of a suffering humanity — let alone a suffering Earth — is limited to the immediate concerns of caring for one's own and seeking revenge on anyone who can be implicated in causing the catastrophes. Long-term policies to address the underlying causes of environmental and social degradation are simply irrelevant to those who are convinced that things have to get worse before they can get better, and that they will only get better through the direct intervention of God to bring this sorry planet to an end. In Norman Habel's words, those who hold such a perspective 'reduce Earth to a ball of corrupted matter about to be thrown onto the waste dump of eternity' (Habel 2000a: 125).

Yet what of those biblical texts used as the basis for such a jaundiced view of the future of creation? Have the developing understandings of our solar system and the relatively recent possibility that humans can destroy planet Earth affected the way we read these texts of cosmic terror? Do the descriptions of the sun being darkened, the moon not giving light and the stars falling from heaven (Mk 13.24-25, using Isaiah and Joel) *necessarily* indicate a pessimistic view of the future of the cosmos? We should realize that it is not just the fundamentalist right who read these texts in this way. Even scholars such as Mary Ann Tolbert interpret the Gospel of Mark, for example, in these terms, claiming the author sees 'this present evil, oppressive, and suffering-filled existence' as 'a passing interlude before the coming of the Son of Man on the clouds and eternal life for the faithful'. She argues further that 'the world in which Jesus and his followers live is a bleak, ugly and painful place filled with wars, persecutions, trials, betrayals, death, and a yet to be experienced last blood bath of cosmic dimensions' (Tolbert 1989: 264-65). At least Tolbert is honest about the predicament that such an interpretation presents to her:

> The difficulty Mark furnishes for modern appropriation is not its negative assessment of the human situation but its solution to the problem. Mark argues that only direct divine intervention can preserve the elect from the mess this generation is making of the cosmos. While some even now may wish to continue affirming Mark's view, such acquiescence has unfortunately permitted this generation to keep increasing the mess for almost two thousand years (Tolbert 1989: 310).

Adela Yarbro Collins also speaks of the acute problems that arise for Markan interpreters 'who are conscious about the fact that they do not share the world-view presupposed by Mark' (1988: 148-49). This is a valid problem to raise, and we should not seek to resolve it simply by assuming that a common world view exists between these ancient texts and ourselves, an assumption often characteristic of a fundamentalist reading. Nor should we replace arbitrarily the six biblicist eschatological principles with six Earth-friendly ecojustice principles, just to see if we achieve a more relevant exegetical outcome. Of course we cannot help but approach the text with certain assumptions, and it is helpful to be as open as possible about them, but they are already products of our engagement with our context, our community of meaning and many past readings of the text. As such, I do not simply impose a new set of hermeneutical principles on the texts below (and insofar as I do, I outline them beforehand), so much as meet those principles already embedded in the texts (in both positive and negative manifestations) and in the questions that our present context urges upon us. The cognitive dissonance generated by the application of biblicist eschatological principles to our current social and environmental crises, demands this re-examination of our exegetical assumptions.

Tolbert and Collins suggest that we should confront the world view presupposed by the Gospel of Mark and expose its inadequacies for meeting today's problems. That may well be necessary, at least in part, for the texts and their traditional interpretations are not innocent. A credible argument can be mounted, however, that the origin of the bleak apocalyptic outlook they have described is not to be found in the earliest Gospel and its setting—be it in Galilee, Syria or Rome in the late sixties or early seventies of the Common Era. Rather, we should search closer to home for the source of the heightened dualisms of apocalypticism: in nineteenth-and twentieth-century America, and wherever else we find that particular combination of modern Western science and fundamentalist biblicism.[3] The language of 'the end' used in the popular media today seems to be dominated by this combination of the more colourful biblical concepts and the language of contemporary science. Together they produce a taxonomy of ultimate terror, what Eugene Boring has termed 'molecular eschatology'. As a result, apocalypse and armageddon have become two of the most public biblical terms used in our 'secular' vocabulary. They have been reinterpreted in the light of the splitting of the atom to take on meanings far beyond the ancient imagination and observations of the cosmos. We are told how many

3.   I'm not suggesting for a moment that Tolbert and Collins are fundamentalist or biblicist, but rather that they operate within a culture dominated by an apocalyptic paradigm that originates in the conjunction of Western science and fundamentalist biblicism, and which desperately needs reconstructing. They have no choice but to subject their own culture and its dominant hermeneutic to scholarly critique, but where this acquiesces in the imposition of modernist polarities on ancient texts we have an obligation to point to other ways of reading these texts. Of course, Collins herself was instrumental in overcoming the spiritual–political polarity in the reading of Revelation, just as Tolbert has recently made enormous contributions to 'readings from this place' which challenge many Western polarities: spiritual–material, heavenly–earthly, and so on. These dualisms are described more fully by the Earth Bible Team (2000b: 40-41) in volume 1 of the Earth Bible Series.

hundred times more potent the weapons of today are than those used on Japan, raising the spectre of imminent nuclear meltdown. Even if we survive such cosmic suicide, our understanding of the universe suggests that eventually Earth will one day spin off into outer darkness (no doubt with weeping and gnashing of teeth) or else be swallowed up by the sun and the unquenchable fire.

This peculiar combination of modern Western science and uncritical biblical thought can lead to an eschatological myth so powerful that it impels faith communities towards sectarian fantasies—or at the very least disables any possibility that they might respond more creatively to the present environmental crises. It may sound harsh, but the major cause for alarm is not really the occasional groups of 'apocalunatics' who self-destruct across the pages of our newspapers from time to time, but the large numbers of Bible-believing Christians who seem to be trapped into inactivity by such a world view (or rather, world-denying view)— faithfully tending our rose gardens while the tropical rainforests are destroyed to appease our own profligate consumption.

The power of such a myth rests on a set of tired old oppositions that still have not been fully deconstructed or reconstructed, polarizing our understanding of spirit and matter, ethics and eschatology, ideal and real, politics and religion, this world and the other, the present and the future, the sacred and the secular. Many of these distinctions are made by appealing to 'apocalyptic', as if this were some consistent body of thought and literature that either makes sense of all these ideas (if you're that way inclined), or else that can be marginalized as excusable in times of severe persecution or labelled as sectarian fantasies. They are dangerous polarities because inevitably they devalue the 'material' in favour of the 'spiritual', Earth in favour of heaven, and the present and distant future in favour of the imminent future (Earth Bible Team 2000b: 40-41). Even when they have been denied or marginalized, these polarities often continue to define and warp the discussion.

Yet even if we can retrieve some texts from the distortion of this apocalyptic paradigm (as I attempt below), we should not think that this will solve all the tensions between Earth and eschatology. There remains a huge problem for ecotheology in those texts that resist retrieval and advocate our 'earnestly desiring [hastening] the parousia of the day of God through which the heavens will be torched and dissolved, and the elements melt with fire' (2 Pet. 3.12). The problem is not the imagining of an end to the created order as such—that has been inevitable not only since Nagasaki and Hiroshima, but really since Copernicus, Galileo and Kepler, and the dethroning of Earth as the centre of the universe, the apple of God's eye. Rather, the problem lies in 'earnestly desiring' such an end, and in seeing it as part of the Creator's immediate plan for the creation, as a 'good thing' that cannot happen soon enough. Such a conviction can only result in passive disinterest in the fate of the environment at best, and may even underlie active exploitation and despoiling of the created order.

What do we do, then, with those biblical texts and images that seem to support such an understanding, and especially when such images seem to resonate with the deepest fears of our contemporary world — 'lurking at the edge of the abyss'? Which texts can be retrieved and which still resist?

Challenging the Distorting Polarities of the 'Apocalyptic Paradigm'

We need to remember that the genre 'apocalypse' is a modern category that has been imposed retrospectively on ancient texts, most of which regard themselves as prophecies — as urgent words of God to their own generation. The label 'apocalypse' was used to draw attention to a perceived heightening of transcendent language and symbolism in some 'prophetic' texts, though the distinction has never been an easy or obvious one (Collins and Collins 1979: 21-121). As such, the use of the word 'apocalypse' can fulfil a useful descriptive function, but it should not be used to impose a set of polarities, arising out of high modernism, on to ancient texts. While these supposed dualities may indicate tensions in prophetic and apocalyptic literature, they have often been polarized into binary opposites by subsequent developments in our understanding of space, time and the cosmos. These oppositions are then read back into prophetic texts with devastating consequences. I shall use the relationship between heaven and Earth (space), and between present and future (time), to illustrate this process, before briefly examining any implications for interpreting some select eschatological texts.

The claim by Yuri Gagarin — that he didn't see God on his trip to the heavens in the first crewed space flight in 1961 — both illustrated the polarization between heaven and Earth that had already taken place in popular thought, and contributed further to the distance between them. The increasing modern scientific awareness of the vast regions in space coupled with a biblicist insistence that heaven is somehow 'up there', have led to a spatial duality quite foreign to the thought world of prophetic and apocalyptic literature. Rather, biblical and other early texts portray heaven and Earth as interactive parallel universes, where heavenly messengers and humans in dreams and visions may cross the boundaries and 'time zones' on an everyday basis. The ambiguity in both Hebrew and Greek of the messenger/angel ('heavenly' or 'earthly'?) illustrates this well, and interestingly, the 'angel unawares' motif has again become a popular theme in this 'new age', especially in film and television. But biblical interpretations often lag behind when hermeneutical paradigms begin to shift. We stubbornly refuse to admit to an angel at the beginning of Mark (Mk 1.2), insist one is present at the end (Mk 16.5), and assume the 'angels in heaven' (Mk 13.32) must also be the 'other-worldly beings' involved in some kind of transcendent parousia at Mk 13.27. But God's messengers cannot be pigeon-holed so neatly. In the cosmic understanding of the first-century Mediterranean world, they are intermediaries between a heaven and Earth that coexist on the inside of a sphere, suspended above the abyss, mirroring each other as God(s) and humans interact:

> In *4 Ezra*…the heavenly world exists alongside the earthly one (*4 Ezra* 7.49-51). Similarly, divine time – or timelessness – exists alongside human time, and may be accessed by the privileged few who are granted divinely sent visions and dreams, in which the normal constraints of time (and space) are erased (Dailey 1999: 240).

Dailey goes on to argue that any supposed temporal dualism between present and future is also challenged by the assumed world view of prophetic and apocalyptic literature:

> The idea is not simply that one period of time will end, and that a new period of timelessness will begin, but rather that both exist simultaneously. Regarding the endtime, *2 Baruch* states '…they shall see the world which is now invisible to them and they will see a time which is now hidden to them. And time will no longer make them older' (*2 Bar.* 51.9) (Dailey 1999: 239).

Such an understanding of the interconnectedness of Earth and heaven challenges popular religious assumptions about the ontological space between them – that heaven is the opposite to, and distant from, Earth and replaces Earth after its demise. Rather, heaven (and the heavens) interact with, mirror and initiate activities on Earth.[4] These ideas also challenge our assumptions about heaven as the (only) abode of God. If heaven is immanent and interconnected with Earth as part of the divine ecosystem, then there is no longer any usefulness in the concept of a

---

4.   There is no room here to cite examples from Josephus and the Graeco-Roman historians of the way they use cosmic language as part of their description of significant historical events. Comets, falling stars, darkened sun and moon, and rivers reversing are all understood as *part of* (and not just signs or symbols of) tumultuous historical events, such as the destruction of Jerusalem and the assassination of a Caesar. See examples and the literature cited in Dyer (1998: 230-31; 1999: 106 n. 6) and Adams (2000).

divine residence beyond the farthest reaches of the universe. If heavenly bodies are seen as mutually interdependent with human existence and sharing in consequential relationships, then there is no longer any need to read ourselves as victims of these texts of a cosmic terror ordained by God. We may indeed interpret our role and God's role in some events in that way retrospectively, as the biblical narrative does on many occasions, but the future consequences of our present actions are always open, prophecy is always conditional, and repentance (in the true sense of 'change of direction') is always a possibility.

Retrieving Mark 13.24-30 from the Distorting Polarities of the 'Apocalyptic Paradigm'

Reading the texts in Mark 13 about the darkened sun and moon and the falling stars from a more 'historical' (Earth-based) and less 'apocalyptic' (transcendent) perspective does not deny the cosmological dimensions of the text. It does not seek to impose a 'metaphorical' reading on texts that are very clearly meant 'literally', though these two terms themselves betray an underlying modernist duality that can no longer be sustained. They also betray certain urban Western assumptions about what can and cannot happen in our natural environment. From the perspective of Earth, and away from bright city lights, stars can be seen 'falling' every clear evening. From the perspective of ancient oral cultures, these heavenly movements are significant for interpreting events on Earth (Mt. 2.2). The smoke of great battles darkens the sun and turns the moon blood red, and any other approximately concurrent natural wonders are pressed into service as ways of describing, interpreting, remembering and dating significant human events. What is remarkable about the history of interpretation of these texts in ancient literature is that we have in recent times forgotten how to read them in this way.[5] Since the

---

5.   Joseph Verheyden (1997) has restated the common modern interpretation of Mk 13.24-25 as recycled theophany/day of the Lord language used to describe a transcendent parousia of the Son of Man at the end of time. His detailed analysis of the theophanic motifs from the prophetic literature is very helpful—and correct in identifying the Markan focus on the gathering of the elect rather than on judgment themes—but any challenge to the assumption that these motifs must be interpreted as a transcendent parousia in Mark is dismissed without engaging the issues: 'I think one also misses the point when arguing that [Mk] 13.24-25 merely announces an important turning point in history' (Verheyden 1997: 526 n. 3). Recent commentators who have taken a more 'historical' interpretation of these verses include: Thomas R. Hatina (1996), N.T. Wright (1996: 339-68), Keith D. Dyer (1998: 230-31) (all of whom refer to the earlier work of R.T. France). Support for similar interpretations of these

Copernican revolution, because we can now imagine these texts in a new 'literal' way, we have burdened them with the full force of modern apocalyptic terror, and insisted that Mk 13.24-27 must therefore be a parousia text, a text of 'the end'. A brief perusal of pre-Copernican exegesis will readily establish what used to be the range of interpretations of this and parallel passages.

Jean Calvin, in his harmony of these synoptic texts, interprets them as referring to the 'continual rising and falling that we observe in the world': 'As for the stars, He does not mean that they shall fall in actual fact, but according to men's way of thinking'; 'In other words, as long as the Church's pilgrimage in this world lasts, the skies will be dark and cloudy' (Calvin 1972: 98, 94). Augustine and Ambrose connect them with leaders and persecutions in their own time:

> then the stars shall fall from heaven and the powers of heaven shall be moved, when many who seemed to shine brilliantly with grace will yield to persecutions and will fall, and even the strongest of the faithful will be shaken (Augustine, in Oden and Hall 1998: 187).

Similarly: 'Also the stars, that is, leaders surrounded by fellow Christians, shall fall, as the bitterness of persecution mounts up' (Ambrose, in Oden and Hall 1998: 187). It is natural that these interpreters should see the stars as mirroring leadership within their own contexts, but the particular setting of Mark 13 suggests a further adjustment.

The cosmic events of Mk 13.24-25 can be understood in similar terms to those above as reflecting the falling leaders and powers immediately preceding Mark's day. In this setting, they would be understood as the realignment of temporal powers in the East after the fall of Jerusalem and the establishment of the House of Flavian in Rome. These are the powers (the 'they' of Mk 13.26) who will witness the vindication and exaltation of the 'human one' before God in heaven, just as the High Priest will (Mk 14.62). There is no messianic return, earthly parousia or second coming implied here, but rather, as in Daniel 7, the exaltation of 'one like a human' before the 'Ancient of Days' in heaven. This vindication will also be manifested on Earth in the form of the gathering, by the messengers/angels, of the elect from Judaea and from the four corners of Earth and heaven in the formation of the new community of faith ('his' elect; Mk 13.27). The eschatology and missiology of the Judaean remnant is thus redefined in one inclusive moment as they are welcomed into the Markan communities in the north.

texts also comes from the socio-literary readings of Ched Myers (1988: 343) and Herman C. Waetjen (1989: 200), both of whom cite Walter Wink (1984: 162).

Mark 13.29 is usually translated as 'He is near, at the gates' to accord with the view that Mk 13.26-27 speaks of some kind of parousia. But the comparison with the fig tree and summer (in Mk 13 and in Mk 11) requires that the impersonal 'it is near' (Mk 13.29) refers instead to the time of harvest that summer brings. Certainly this is how Luke, one of Mark's earliest interpreters, reads it, when the early summer harvest festival of Pentecost becomes the occasion for the gathering of the multi-ethnic community, and the coming of the kingdom with power (Mk 9.1; Lk. 21.31). This usage of the personification of a season waiting at the gates is well attested in Aristotle ('Winter-at-the-gates') and not as clumsy as we might think.[6]

The affirmation that all these things will happen within a generation of Jesus speaking these words (Mk 13.30) is the assurance to Mark's community that they are *already occurring as they hear the Gospel.* This emphatic time reference in Mk 13.30 has caused much debate, although it is undoubtedly the most unambiguous reference of all. Despite many ingenious attempts to find alternative meanings, it is clear from its usage elsewhere in the Gospel of Mark and in Hebrew literature that its primary meaning is a literal 40-year generation. It is equally apparent that its location in this discourse implies that 'all these things' must include everything up to Mk 13.30 as events in the recent memory and current experience of the Markan community, and the refugees it now welcomes.

Texts that Resist Retrieval from the Ruin of Earth

'Heaven and Earth Will Pass Away' (Mark 13.31, cf. Matthew 24.35)
I have argued elsewhere that this affirmation by Jesus should be understood as more than just a figure of speech used to illustrate the permanence of his words (1999: 117). Certainly there are versions of this saying that *have* been remembered in the tradition in a figurative way: 'But it is easier for heaven and Earth to pass away, than for one stroke of a letter in the law to be dropped' (Lk. 16.17, cf. Mt. 5.18: '*until* heaven and Earth pass away'). Interestingly, the majority of scholars arguing for a transcendent eschatology in Mk 13.24-27 seem to prefer a figurative reading of Mk 13.31, even though this leaves them with the awkward collapsing together of v. 30 (all these things happening within a

---

6. J. Jeremias (1965), 174 note 8. The personification of seasons and virtues/vices ('love' and 'lust') waiting 'at the door(s)/gate(s) is common in classical and koine Greek, and provides a more appropriate framework for Mark 13.19 than James 5.9 or Acts 5.9.

generation), v. 32 (no one, not even the Son, knowing the day or hour) and v. 33 (you/we not knowing the time). If, however, v. 31 is permitted to signal a transition between 'all these things' (Mk 13.30) that occur 'in those days' (Mk 13.24), and the singular event of 'that day and that hour' (Mk 13.32), then it follows that the passing away of heaven and Earth is not just a figure of speech. Rather, it can be seen as the beginning of Jesus' response to the second half of the disciples' question in Mk 13.4.

The first half of the question ('When will this be?'), refers to the throwing down of the Temple building, which is addressed by Mark's compilation of the words of Jesus and early Christian prophets regarding the fate of Jerusalem in v. 6-23. But these events have no direct connection with any ultimate 'end', nor do they even function as a sign (Mk 13.4, cf. 8.12), since the Temple, for Mark, has stood condemned since Jesus first entered it (Mk 11.12-25). The cosmic realignments and the regathering of the elect (the time of summer harvest occurring as Mark writes) are then described in Mk 13.24-30, followed finally by a brief allusion ('Heaven and Earth *will* pass away'; Mk 13.31) to that second half of the question (Mk 13.4b), the 'fulfilment of *all* things' and its supposed sign. Jesus denies any knowledge of such an event and its timing (Mk 13.32), and ignores the request for a sign (again, Mk 8.12). Yet arguably, the text does affirm the prerogative of the Creator to de-create the cosmos. Even if this is so, the parable that follows immediately — the parable of the returning householder/Lord (Mk 13.34-36), and the need to move to a heightened level of watchfulness (Mk 13.33, 35, 37), are interpreted existentially in the Passion narrative that follows, as the four watches of the night are acted out (Geddert 1989: 94-105; Dyer 1999: 117-18). In Mark's narrative, it is not so much 'the end' that is inevitable and imminent (contra Tolbert), as those ends we encounter on the road of discipleship and testing. It is not the parousia that dominates Markan eschatology (in fact it is *never* mentioned) as much as the *appearances* of the returning Lord: three times leading up to midnight (Mk 14.32-42: he finds them sleeping at cock crow [Mark 14.72: Peter remembers]), at early dawn (Mark 15.1: Jesus alone), and then the appearance promised again in the new beginning in Galilee (Mk 14.28; 16.7). The logic of Mark's narrative insists that any cosmic eschatology motivates, not paralysis, but existential alertness and faithful action.

2 Peter, Stoicism and Cosmic Conflagration: End, Cycle or Spiral?
If Mk 13.31 contains the affirmation of the end of Earth as we know it, other traditions in the Christian Scriptures develop the idea much further. The passing away of heaven and Earth is linked explicitly with a

new heaven and Earth in Rev. 21.1.[7] Even here, though, the language is not necessarily to be taken as referring to the annihilation of Earth and its replacement by a totally new creation (Reid 2000; Howard-Brook and Gwyther 1999). This is because it is not clear whether any concept of an absolute end to the cosmos has been clearly expressed in the literature of the ancient world. The closest analogy to the implosion of the solar system or the modern nuclear holocaust was the Stoic idea of cosmic conflagration (*ekpurosis*), which seems to have been understood as a cyclical (*paliggenesia*) or perhaps a spiralling event, with each cosmic cycle beginning and ending with fire. Edward Adams is inclined towards a destructionist position himself in interpreting both the biblical and the Stoic texts, but he admits that affirmations in Stoic writings of the destructibility of the cosmos 'are somewhat offset by statements affirming or implying its immortality' (Adams 2000: 54). Thus if cosmos is used of any one particular world-cycle 'it can be described as destructible', but since it is used by the Stoics to encompass 'the endless sequence of world-cycles and conflagrations' it can be 'affirmed as everlasting' (Adams 2000: 55).

The biblical language that comes closest to expressing these Stoic influences is undoubtedly that of 2 Peter (quoted earlier). The melting of the elements (*stoicheia*) with fire (2 Pet. 3.12) and the burning up of Earth and the heavens (2 Pet. 3.10, 12) seems to use language and concepts shaped specifically to appeal to those within the Greek cultural world (Neyrey 1993: 241). Whereas this might make for a graphic contextualization of eschatological exhortations for the hearers of 2 Peter, it presents insurmountable problems for a retrieval of the text from the perspective of Earth. This is so even if these texts are understood in terms of the renewal rather than the annihilation of Earth, since they also exhort the hearer to actively desiring, if not hastening (2 Pet. 3.12), that day. Texts that at the most maintain the prerogative of the Creator to de-/re-create the creation (Mk 13.31; Rev. 21.1) here have become texts that encourage our eager expectation of, and even participation in, that process. This suggests a questionable heightening of meaning that occurred when the Gospel tradition was more thoroughly Hellenized and expressed in Stoic

---

7.   Space permits only a brief reference to the Isaianic background to these texts (e.g. Isa. 65.17; 66.22), and two readings that are supportive of the positions taken here. Westermann uses eschatological language, but argues that the texts imply that 'the world, designated as "heaven and earth", is to be miraculously renewed' (Westermann 1969: 408). Watts historicizes the texts thoroughly, and claims that they do not present 'an eschatological picture of the distant future' but presume 'a position in which the former age is already gone and a new age with Cyrus and his successors has begun' (Watts 1987: 354, 353).

terminology. Such a shift is analogous to that occurring when these same Gospel traditions were modernized and interpreted in post-Copernican terminology, as we have argued above. The process of re-contextualizing the text as a living Word requires a sensitivity to wider shifts in meanings and cosmologies, and attention to the history of interpretation of texts which spans pre-modern, modern and postmodern eras.

Conclusion (An End, Not 'The End')

What, then, of the fate of Earth in Mark 13? There has been no space here to develop the dimensions positive to Earth in the wider Markan story: that Jesus 'was *with* the wild beasts' (Mk 1.13); that Jesus reclaims the 'sea' of Galilee as a bridge for disciples to cross between cultures, rather than a fearful chasm (Gill 1991: 35-41); that Galilee as *place* is integral to the mission of, and encounter with, the resurrected Jesus (Mk 16.7). Some texts in Mark 13 have been retrieved from the brink of the apocalyptic abyss (Mk 13.24-27) and interpreted in the light of an interconnected cosmos (heaven *and* Earth), where human activity and cosmic consequences *cannot* be separated, and Earth has intrinsic worth and purpose together with humanity.

One text still remains that affirms the exclusive knowledge of 'the Father' regarding the ultimate fate of heaven and Earth (Mk 13.31-32). The text seems to assume, rather than assert, the transcendence of the Creator. Even so, whether this text necessarily speaks of cosmic annihilation is doubtful. Its function within the narrative of Mark is to trigger a call to be on the alert for 'ends' as we encounter them in all aspects of human existence. That is, a call to act responsibly as humans in the face of trials, rather than to hide human and environ-mental disasters under a cloak of divine inevitability.

The same things cannot be said of the tradition preserved in 2 Pet. 3.7-13. Even though the context may again be hortatory, and the destructive process understood as part of a cyclical renewal, the 'hastening' or 'earnest desiring' of the torching and dissolving of the heavens and the fiery melting of the elements presents irretrievable problems for an ethical response to ecological problems. Again, the hope is for a (re)new(ed) heavens *and* Earth (2 Pet. 3.13), but the active encouragement to hasten the demise of the old Earth is an invitation that too many Christians have accepted too easily already.

Swords into Ploughshares: The End of War? (Q/Luke 9.62)[*]

Alan H. Cadwallader

Swords into Ploughshares: The Crisis of an Image

The prophetic clarion call of 'swords into ploughshares' (Isa. 2.4; Mic. 4.3) has echoed through the ages as eschatological hope for an end to the ravages of war and a return to idyllic pastoral life. Old American folk songs dream of the day when war will be no more, signalled by the refashioning of swords into ploughshares. Contemporary examples are trumpeted as fulfilling the hope — the United Nations Mission in Sierra Leone, for example, hails the recycling of armaments into productive farming implements.[1] The life of humanity is secured in harmony and as a signature of that tranquillity, steel is forged to cut Earth open.

This 'myth of innocence' (Mack 1988) — if not of origins, then at least of aspiration — does not dwell in untrammelled light.[2] The violence of the plough lurks in the shadows. Without any technological modification, the plough becomes a weapon for the mass destruction of Philistines; swinging Shamgar is memorialized as judge of Israel (Judg. 3.31).[3] The pastoral utopia suddenly stalls when ploughshares are turned back into swords and agricultural images are conscripted into militaristic service (Joel 3.9-13). The reputed implement of productivity becomes the instrument of destruction as cities and territories are ploughed into oblivion (Jer. 26.18).[4] The plough, it seems, can be a battalion of violence and dispossession.

---

[*]   I wish to record my thanks to a former student, Stuart Hill, whose doctoral work on Q provided the initial prompt to this essay. See Hill 1998.

1.   See 'Swords into ploughshares' (www.europaworld.org/Issue 35; accessed 18/5/2001). Multitudinous Christian organizations, whether they have a peace agenda or not, latch on to the scriptural text as their flagship.

2.   'Traditional romaniticism' and 'a thinly disguised biblicism' are but two of the assessments of the editors of a Festschrift to Burton Mack (Castelli and Taussig 1996: 9).

3.   A dispute exists about Shamgar's ethnicity: Canaanite or Israelite (Gottwald 1979: 418, n. 342).

4.   Cf. *Sibylline Oracles* 5.505. The same metaphor occurs in non-Jewish writings: see Horace, *Odes* 1.16.19-22; Seneca, *On Tranquillity* 1.26.4. The 'metaphor' was a tactic employed by invaders and colonizers.

The Plough, the Police and the Loss of Peace

The linkage of plough and destruction is far from unique in the history of Earth. The collusion of land holdings and state power is known in many cultures (Beinart, Delius and Trapido 1986; Farquharson 1976). The slowly dawning realization, however, is that the plough has brought neither peace for humanity nor peace for Earth. Evan Eisenberg writes:

> As humankind — or farming, or civilisation, or what have you — disperses from its point of origin and fills each new place, there is a sense of loss. The game thins out, the soil washes away, neighbours quarrel over wells and boundary stones. Armed men appear everywhere demanding rent and taxes (1998: xxii).

Such violence has an intricate web of associations, all woven around the plough.

On one level, there is Ernest Gellner's disturbing trinitarian collation of plough, sword and book, or production, coercion and cognition (1988: 19-20). The land is turned to the needs of a growing population; it supports and is accompanied by the need for a (low-paid, disenfranchised and hence dependent) labour force and defence personnel to protect 'interests'. The ruling wisdom, over time sectioned to a seemingly independent clerisy, 'covertly served the social ends' which bound together, authorized and directed thought about any member of that trinity. Thus, thinking about the land connects with elements of trade and production on the one hand, and ideology and policing on the other (Gellner 1988: 16, 122, 205). The first-century Jewish philosopher Philo of Alexandria expressly compared logic with the fence that encloses a field.[5]

In other words, the text, the mediaum, is not innocent. Moreover, it 'tricks' us (Gellner 1988: 257) into an acceptance of the arrangement, in part because the governing text becomes a participant in the idyllic picture of agricultural pursuits that it has itself idealized (Castelli and Taussig 1996: 16). The text becomes as 'natural' as Earth, even though it contrives to record Earth's epigraphy in a form that authorizes its own (manufactured) existence.

Here another level of violence surfaces. The evidence is accumulating that the plough, and the technological executions and developments that it symbolizes, has wreaked havoc upon Earth. 'Drought', claims Michael Glantz (1994; 1995), 'follows the plow'. Countries with substantial semi-arid land masses readily attest to this, but global warming is subjecting

5.   See Philo, *Husbandry* 14, cf. 33; used of the role of the mind to establish control over the unruly animals of our senses.

Earth as a whole to a level of devastation that resembles a battlefield. 'Laid bare by plowing', the root systems of intricate communities of plants have been ripped to shreds, and the soil—now exposed to the ravages of wind, sun and rain or irrigation—has been either carried off or denuded of its nutrients (Eisenberg 1998: 30). The plough, for all the scientifically constructed texts that assert the Earth-friendliness of the tool (cf. Isa. 7.25), has turned a declining return for human consumption and debilitating harm to Earth.[6]

There is one element missing from such analyses, even though there is a recognition of the division of labour and levels of control and dependency that such technology initiated and sustained (Glantz 1994: 173-74). It was recognized long ago by John Gribble, an Anglican priest-missionary in nineteenth-century Western Australia. He exposed the connection between abrogation of the land from Indigenous Australians for huge farming stations and the attendant abrogation of Australian Aboriginal women as 'gins', 'fuck-meat' of white pastoral gentlemen. His protests unleashed the alliance of establishment forces against him: pastoralists, media, government...and the Church. He and his cause were crushed (Wood 1994: 134). Ploughing may turn out to be an arm of patriarchal identity. Accordingly, the Earth Bible principle of intrinsic worth needs to be alert to 'associated political, sexist, ethnocentric and class issues' (Eaton 2000: 64) as it confronts the plough.

Ploughing as a Gospel Activity of the Kingdom of God

These are the overarching historical contexts for our reading. Agricultural images of course dominate the Gospels. And yet, the plough (*arotron*) is not a frequent player in the pages of the Christian Scriptures—three references in all and, significantly perhaps, tied to urban authors Luke and Paul (Lk. 9.62; 17.7; 1 Cor. 9.10).[7] Nevertheless, the citation of dominical words in Lk. 9.62 has secured a status for this saying and its metaphor far above others in later Christian writers:

> No one who puts a hand to the plough
> and looks back is fit for the kingdom of God.

---

6. Australia's level of salinization of land is but one of multitudinous examples around the globe. See R.L. Heathcote's contribution to Glantz 1994, and other essays in that volume.

7. 'Yoke' (*zuge*), however, probably is connected with ploughing (Mt. 11.29, 30; Acts 15.10; Gal. 5.1; 1 Tim. 6.1) and, with its metonymous signification of slavery (cf. Juvenal, *Satires* 6.206-207), may derive from times when slaves were themselves the traction animals shackled to a plough.

Jerome, as but one example, often alludes to this verse. He turns it into an ascetic counsel intertextually combined with bearing one's cross, not taking thought for the morrow, climbing Jacob's ladder,[8] not returning home from the field or descending from the roof to gather another garment.[9] The handle of the plough is equated with the fringe of the Saviour's robe, and locks of his hair.[10] Right choices and perseverance are the content of this instruction. The only legacy of recognition of Earth lies in his reminder of the bad choice of Lot who chose land that was watered 'by Jordan's muddy stream made salt by the Dead Sea'. The only acceptable land was 'the holy land from heaven'.[11] He may advocate tilling Eden but this is executed in a hermit existence on a desolate rocky island, an adversary against which one must stand with Christ.[12] Eden, the holy land, heaven — this is now the focus of ploughing, an activity of and for the kingdom of God. With this other-worldly orientation, the material realm, the Earth of Australian Aboriginal peoples, sheep and swaggies,[13] is consigned to that which is opposed to the kingdom. But the plough with all its subtle aggressive symbolism is retained as the kingdom's marketing logo.

Ploughing (and) Women: The Division of Labour, Body, Earth and Wisdom

The fundamental connotation — of making productive, of manipulating to another end, of gaining control — this locks onto the plough. The plough is an implement of civilization, of technological advancement that enables the culture of man (*sic*) to subdue the potentially chaotic, uncontrolled material realm. Spontaneous generation is construed as harbouring a mysterious force over which cultivation must assert control.

And, in the ancient world, it *is* man's culture and cultivation, at least as reified by a society controlled structurally and ideologically by men. While peasant women and primitive societies might work the hoe (Schottroff 1991: 99-100; Scheidel 1990)[14] the plough is a mark of man's

8.   *Letter* 3, 'To Rufinus', citing Mk 8.34; Mt. 6.34; Gen. 28.12.
9.   *Letter* 22, 'To Eustochium', citing Mt. 24.17, 18. See also *Letter* 118, 'To Julian'.
10.   *Letter* 71, 'To Lucinius', citing Mt. 9.20; Song 5.2.
11.   *Letter* 71, 'To Lucinius'.
12.   *Letter* 3, 'To Rufinus'.
13.   'Swaggie' is an Australian term for tramp or hobo but has a distinct 'bush' (i.e. country) connection.
14.   The conventional symbol of women's work was the distaff. The hold of this gendered labour division is manifest in the title of Mrs H. Dudney's 1904 work: *Spindle and Plough* (London: Heinemann).

authority, one of many gender-role distinctives that were deployed in the ancient world.[15] Autumn Stanley (1982: 297-302) suggests that the plough marked male colonization of women and their environment-sensitive horticultural pursuits in the ancient world, just as surely as male agriculture colonized the land. The plough, writes Robert Sallares, required low labour inputs; this goes 'a long way towards explaining the spatial and sexual division of labour'. Man was outside (ploughing) and woman (apart perhaps from harvest) was inside in the labour intensive work of food preparation (Sallares 1991: 83).[16] A sign of poverty therefore was the hoe. A sign of considerable wealth was having slaves and multiple yokes of oxen to perform the ploughing (cf. Lk. 14.19; 17.7). As Carol Palmer (1998: 143) writes of traditional agricultural methods, the plough 'is a powerful image…which can symbolize status, masculinity, and production'.

Indeed, as the urbane Jesus Ben Sira would counsel, 'How can one become wise who grasps the plough?' Wisdom comes with the opportunity for leisure (Sir. 37.24-25). This is not to sacrifice ploughing however. Field ploughing is left to one's slaves/labourers.[17] And the fit image for the male pursuit of (Lady?) Wisdom is ploughing (Sir. 6.19). As we shall see, this imagery is far from innocuous or idyllic.

Turning swords into ploughs (which are then grasped without looking back, to signify attentiveness to the kingdom of God) is human work[18] and for human (salvific) benefit. This could be constructed over against

15. The anthropologist, Paul Leser, notes the widespread use of the plough as a signification of the division of labour and argues for a gender-specific translation of the Greek *oudeis* and *euthetos* accordingly (1974: 251-52). For a modern-day survival of this gender demarcation, see Palmer (1998: 152, 154).

16. And the equally labour intensive 'female' role of wool carding and spinning. This coheres with Jewish practice, even allowing for a probable lack of rigid observance among Galilean peasants (Horsley 1995: 200, 204 citing *m. Ket.* 5.5, 9). Horsley does not notice the gender and status symbolics of the plough in his analysis. Cf., however, Stegemann (1995: 371-72, 376-77).

17. Slave farm labourers could themselves act as the beasts of burden hauling the plough or may themselves have the charge of the animals yoked to the plough (Bishop 1936: 269, 271, giving Egyptian examples of each). There may be an allusion to human traction in *T. Job* 32.3 where the gift of animals is seen as relief for the needy ploughmen (cf. *T. Job* 10.5). In Israel it appears that oxen were the preferred beast of burden (Philo, *Virtues* 146, contrary to Greek and Roman choice: Homer, *Iliad* 10.351-53; Pliny, *Natural History* 8.68). One yoke per plough was the usual (Firmage 1992: 1130).

18. Hesiod (*Work and Days* 443) speaks of putting hand to plough as beginning work. This may well have been known by Tertullian who substitutes 'work' for 'kingdom of God' (*Idolatry* 12.2).

the world by embrace of an ethereal realm or by scoring the plough's furrows through the texture of Earth in order to bring it into line(s). No one has paused to ask whether this ploughing really is beneficial for either Earth or women, or whether the war continues, simply using different rapiers to achieve its ends.

Ploughing is the primary androcentric metaphor for sexual intercourse in the ancient world,[19] even as the plough is a metaphor for the male member (Adams 1982: 24, 83). Page duBois writes:

> This metaphor, associating the woman's body and the earth, which establishes a metaphorical connection between the field and her sexual organs, is a traditional analogy…it expresses a relationship that is not merely stereotypical but is so deeply felt by the culture that it appears everywhere: in literary texts, in ritual practices, monuments, and in mythological narratives (1988: 39).

The associations are numerous. First, the prime point of fertility is the male — he is the true parent according to Aeschylus's character Orestia, since 'he is the one who mounts'. The woman is no more than a nurse.[20] The connection is blatant in the naming of semen, 'seed'. Thus, the Epicurean philosopher, Lucretius, comments on a prostitute's contraceptive practice of *coitus interruptus*:

> [she] withdrew from the man's passion with her buttocks and receives the moist fluid with all her breast relaxed. For thus she drives the furrow of the plough from the true direction of the path and turns aside the blow of seeds from the vital parts.[21]

Secondly, penetrating Earth and depositing seed is the source of productivity. This is ploughing, men's work; and the 'promiscuous' Earth, who will nourish any seed sown in her body, responds to that plough. There is a need is to protect the boundaries of that land so that other inseminators might be denied access.[22] Thus ploughing and policing are intimately connected (cf. Mt. 13.24-30).

Greeks gave this human activity religious significance.[23] Even Ben Sira's analogy of seeking wisdom as by ploughing, comes perilously

---

19. The metaphor is still alive in some Mediterranean cultures (Herzfeld 1985: 152-62; Palmer 1998: 141, 144).

20. Aeschylus, *Eumenides* 660.

21. Lucretius, *On the Nature of Things* 4.1269-77.

22. The sexual–agricultural combination is intricately interwoven by Herodotus in his retelling of Oedipus' union with 'double-sown' Jocasta, his mother; see *Histories* 1207-12, 1255-57.

23. Homer, *Odyssey* 5.125-28; Hesiod, *Theogony* 969-71.

close.[24] In any case, the notion of ploughing as intercourse remains unchallenged. Samson's bitter reference to ploughing 'with' his heifer is charged with adulterous and promiscuous overtones (Judg. 14.18).[25] There may even be a coarse denigration: Septuagintal *en* and Hebraic *b'* can be translated locatively (i.e. as 'in') rather than instrumentally ('with').[26] This ethological reductionism of the woman is designed to enforce her bestial collation (Soggin 1981: 242), every bit as subject to dominance of the man/men as Earth.[27] Philo castigates those who mate with barren women, by comparing them with those who plough hard and stony ground, which 'quench[es] the seed as it drops'.[28]

The context of this Samson story exposes the inherent power differentials between Earth/body and the plough/penis. Thus we find that ploughing might ignore productivity simply to assert the supremacy of the plough and the one 'who puts his hand to it'. The Roman satirist, Juvenal, bitingly portrays the malakite, Naevolus, as whining 'The slave who ploughs his master's field has less trouble than the one who ploughs him'.[29]

Far removed from this portrait of abuse — but no less assertive of power used against others — is the image found in a Septuagint addition to Isa. 45.9. The familiar belligerent defiance of the clay against the potter (recalled by Paul in Rom. 9.20) is prefaced by a synonymous metaphor ploughing beyond the boundaries of time, despising the limits of creation that provide seasons for when ploughing can occur (Isa. 28.24). Ploughing is empowering.

Carving Up the Body: From Ploughing Earth To Writing Text

Page duBois (1988) demonstrates how the ploughing metaphor is extended. The writing receptacle often associated with (elite) women in the ancient world is the wax tablet.

---

24. Compare however, Namaan the Syrian's desire to connect with his new religious boundaries through the soil of Israel — 2 Kgs 5.17.

25. In the light of the rare word for 'sun' in this verse, Burney, along with others, amends the text to *hachadrah*: 'before he entered the bridal chamber' (1920: 365). This heightens the sexual tension of the riddle. This conjecture has not met with universal acceptance.

26. On the range of possible meanings for *b'*, see Dahood (1980: 13-18).

27. Philo sees the oxen yoked to the plough as one of many proofs from animals of human destiny to rule (*Creation of the World* 84b-86; *Decalogue* 77).

28. Philo, *Special Laws* 3.34-36.

29. Juvenal, *Satire* 9.45-46.

Sappho, printed with permission, Naples Museum

The instrument of writing was the stylus. The parallelism was constructed: as the stylus is to the plough penis, so the receptive wax is to Earth/body. Hence the act of writing was interpreted as an act of productive, boundary-making male expression. Writing may be more mediated than agriculture, but it too is directly related to commerce and culture (duBois 1988: 130-66). Even when the woman writes, her wax tablet is frequently contrasted with the scroll-holding man — a symbol of permanence, antiquity and authority. Her literacy by contrast is receptive, malleable and imitative. In the paintings this meaning was conveyed by the woman holding the phallic stylus to her mouth. The stylus ploughs the furrows of letters in the wax.[30] The female body is written and given its form by the male, just as the plough styles and inscribes Earth (cf. Eaton 2000).

The second-century CE dream diagnostician, Artemidorus, offers a clear statement: 'in dreams, a writing tablet signifies a woman, since it receives the imprint of all kinds of letters'.[31] The rise of a textual medium supplemented gender symbolics in the ancient world. The woman's body was handed the terms by which the writing medium was known —

30.   Philo, *Husbandry* 16. The problem often found with wax, however, was that a 'wandering' occurred — that is, the stylus found it difficult to hold a correct line, just like the inattentive ploughman. This, however, reflected a problem — not of the stylus, or even the technician, but of the wax itself, which, like the woman's body was prone to wandering promiscuity. The Roman rhetor Quintilian's solution was to cut the boundaries of the letters onto the base of the board, so that the stylus might follow the predetermined limits; see *Education of an Orator* 1.1.27.

31.   Artemidorus, *Oneirocritica* 2.45.

the *pinax* and *deltos* on which writing occurred were also applied to the
woman's body, the latter term with specific genital location. The body is
not merely a site for agricultural imagery; it 'is a space for scriptural
labor' (duBois 1988: 165). The same is true of Earth. Both become objec-
tified and marked by the stylistic plough. And as the plough harbours a
potential (and predilection?) for violence, so too the stylus is sharp for
the attack.[32]

The Argument: Luke Ploughs Up Q and Earth

This triangulation of body (especially with its configuration into gender
distinctives), Earth and textuality plot the reference to the plough in Lk.
9.62. Far from subverting the signification of the plough, it divinizes
ancient symbolic conventions of male power. What I suggest however, is
that this is Luke's conservative, urban-influenced, textually protective
adjustment to a much more radical saying (at least in Q, and probably
oral, in origin). Luke's clerisy has not only domesticated the saying. He
has retracted the release of Earth from the plough, reinscribed all its
associations (especially the division of labour and related subjugation of
women), and shackled the subversive impulse of the first two sayings
(Luke 9.57-60).

The Third Saying: How Anti-Social?

The most important debate however turns us back to the plough. The
use of Elisha motifs is identified as influencing the second saying (Lk.
9.59-60) and deemed part of the Q tridents. Fledderman (1992: 551-52)
repeats that Luke simply extended the invitation of that allusion into Lk.
9.61-62. Regardless of the assessment of the origin of Lk. 9.61-62, it is
generally proclaimed that the Jesus saying is a radicalizing of the Elisha
call (Marshall 1978: 412). Elisha, after all, had been permitted by Elijah to
bid farewell to his relatives. Jesus refused such a request.

This warrants closer examination about whose is the more radical
action. Elisha certainly is encouraged to return from whence he came
(*anastrephe*; 1 Kgs 19.20) but this is not the accent of the narrative: after
Elijah's direction, there is no farewell scene recorded. Rather, the

---

32. The power of writing to destroy an enemy is amply demonstrated in the
satirists. The Roman Martial betrays his own consciousness of the power of the pen in
Epigram 10.5. But it goes back as far as Homer's reference to 'murderous symbols
inscribed in a folding tablet' (*Iliad* 6.167-70). This takes on a literal expression in an
account of a pedagogue (Christian at that) being punctured to death by stylus-
wielding students; see Prudentius, *Peristephanon* 9.

concentration is upon Elisha's sacrifice of the farming implements and the cattle. Elisha has 'burned his bridges'[33] — there is no employment to which he can now return. Even today, 'following the plough' is a metaphor for staying at home (Palmer 1998: 129). Given our previous recognition of the connection between ploughing and the home, of the division of labour between public and private, Elisha has destabilized the conventional securities. Elisha's devotion is now to Elijah ('his father'; 1 Kgs 19.21).[34]

The dominance over interpretation of the espousal of the unique radicalness of Jesus and the early Jesus movement compared to its Jewish matrix is exposed.[35] The release of the land from being furrowed, the removal of class distinctions so that the people may be fed (1 Kgs 19.21), the subversion of family ties — all these belong to the Elisha call narrative. Two of these elements are retained in Luke's section on the cost of discipleship (Lk. 9.57-60), *but the plough is not sacrificed.*[36] Craig Evans' (1993: 79-80) effort to interpret this analogously as the rejection of the self-righteous Pharisees, the rich man and the rich young ruler (Lk. 16.15; 17.19-31; 18.9-14, 18-30) fails precisely because the mark of wealth — the plough — is *retained* for the kingdom.

The civilizing culture of Luke's 'kingdom of God', with its concomitant gender and status division of labour, is scored in the wake of the plough (cf. 1 Cor. 9.9-12). Earth is constrained to produce. Mutuality between Earth and humankind, seen in the images of peasant farming in parables such as the sower (especially in Mark's version), is adjudged inadequate. The urbanization — and the growing hegemony of textualization — of Christianity demanded the technological advance and symbolism of the plough. This is clearly indicated by Luke's opprobrious reference to the plough in Lk. 17.7 with its endorsement of master–slave relations, the hierarchy of eating order (Lk. 17.8) and the implication that the control over house and field are interrelated.

33. And in spectacular fashion. The usual number of yoked oxen for a traction-plough in ancient Israel was one pair (Firmage 1992: 1130). The reference to five 'yoke' of oxen in Lk. 14.19 similarly indicates great wealth (cf. Palmer 1998: 139).

34. Note that the 'loss' of Elijah is greeted in familial terms by Elisha: 'father, father' (2 Kgs 2.12).

35. This is yet another instance of the triumphalist blast of Christian commentary that has been most clearly critiqued by growing feminist awareness of the depth of anti-Semitism in academic analysis (Levine 1994: 8-13).

36. Even Steinhauser, who argues strongly for the Q origin of Lk. 9.61-62, acknowledges the difference of perspective in the third saying where someone has begun a task and is called to perseverance (1989: 152, 153, 154).

The Third Saying: How Anti-Earth, How Anti-Woman?

More deeply hidden is the relationship of these structures to attitudes to Earth, attitudes which range from inconsequential to utilitarian; they are certainly conventional. There is no question in this text that Earth is to be ploughed, cut open in order to make it more productive, more controlled, more bounded. In fact, that assumption becomes divinized: (right) ploughing becomes a qualification for the kingdom of God.

Accordingly, the occasional suggestion of a Q source for Lk. 9.61 seems to surrender to that of the Lukan author. Of course, this assumes that Q promoted a more egalitarian community, inclusive of women (Batten 1994; Schottroff 1991), and that Luke 'upholds the traditional submissive role of Greco-Roman women' (Corley 1993: 183; Schaberg 1992: 275-93; Schüssler Fiorenza 1992: 52-76). These assumptions are not unques-tioned. Amy-Jill Levine, for example, is dubious about how much inclusivity the Q community can bear (1994: 21-33). A third assumption has, however, not been challenged: regardless of whether Q or Luke lies at the origin of Lk. 9.61-62, the verse structure is fixed.

For the moment, however, the recognition of the connection between gynaecological and ecological attitudes in the ancient world means that where there appears an indication—symbolic or otherwise—of a hier-archical diminution of women, there too one will likely find a domi-nation of Earth. The plough provides just that symbolic arrangement. The choice of a particular metaphor is indicative of a world view. The adoption of the plough as a positive figure for the kingdom of God in Lk. 9.61 carries with it an array of associations.

The kingdom of God becomes a realm that incorporates many of the assumptions and expectations found in the very kingdom of this world against which it is supposedly pitted. In particular, the kingdom of God is found to endorse the subjugation of women and Earth—they are both to be ploughed as a work of the kingdom. Without the man's determined and focused hand to the plough, that man will lose the kingdom, potentially compromising it in the process. And, if the role of the male (leaders) of the community is to educate and control (d'Angelo 1990: 461), then women and Earth will be adversely affected as well if this is abdicated. Women will wander and Earth will encourage weeds—both indicators of dangerous promiscuity.

There is a subtle reinforcement of the dangers of this accepted feminine propensity in an allusion built into the text. 'Turning back' (*strafeis*) would conform the text more closely to the Elisha call story (*anastrepse*; 1 Kgs 19.21);[37] in fact a cognate (*epistrepsatô*) is found in Lk. 17.31, a verse warning against the dangers of turning back from the field. But Luke intends a more demeaning allusion for a failure of discipleship.

'Looking back' (*blepon eis ta opiso*) has rightly been seen as an allusion to the destruction of Sodom.[38] Jerome certainly recognized it[39] and it is noted by Fledderman (1992: 552). The Septuagintal expression is couched in a general warning offered to Lot by the angels as he and his family are rescued from the incineration of the city (Gen. 19.17). He is earnestly instructed not to look back (*me periblepses eis ta opiso*). Lot specifically is instructed (note the singular verb and the absence of any wider ambit). His wife presumably is expected to have received the same direction from her husband (cf. 1 Cor. 14.35). She takes no heed of what the narrative assumes she has heard, and finds herself encrusted in unheralded consequences (Gen. 19.26).

If this is the case, then the woman/wife is granted no independent significance such as to warrant this life-determining knowledge; she is totally dependent on the male for her survival, and she is ultimately culpable for becoming embroiled in the annihilation of a city. Mrs Lot meanders from the designated path and becomes a stereotypical womanly paradigm (Lk. 17.32). If handling a plough is man's work, then looking back is woman's propensity. Hence the failure of the man who puts his hand to the plough is defined as an effeminate collapse – the standard vilification of a man's failure of prescribed direction in the ancient world.[40]

At this point, one might surrender hopes of finding within the text a valuation of Earth in its own right, an encouragement of mutuality of relationship between humanity and Earth or even a breath of an alternative voice – the silencing of Earth as surely as women's voices are seen to be muted in Luke–Acts. Indeed, at the level of the dominance of written Gospel traditions, this would appear to be so. Luke's stylus has won, inscribing the woman's body as the paradigm of a failure of reliability, and Earth as devoid of value or productivity without human/male intervention.

---

37. *Strafeis* is in fact the reading in a number of minuscules, ancient lectionaries and texts of the fathers.

38. There is, however, another intertextual connection which has been ignored: 1 Sam. 24.9.

39. Jerome, *Letters* 71. See also Tertullian, *Against Marcion* 4.23; Cyprian, *Epistle* 7.

40. Dio Chrysostom, *Oration* 3.50; *P. Hibeh* 54, cf. David's distaff curse on Joab's line (2 Sam. 3.29).

Recovering an Earth-Friendly Saying

The hegemony of Luke's inscription is challenged in two directions, anthropologically and text-critically. The anthropologist Paul Leser (1974) had a life-time's interest in ancient farming practices, particularly the origin, development, diversification and dissemination of mechanical adjuncts to agricultural settlement.[41] He notes different ploughs and varieties in blade designs that demand different techniques in their use. A plough with wheels, coulter, one-sided share and mould-board has no place in the picture of the implement in use in the Israel of Jesus' day (Leser 1974: 242).

The tool was rather an 'ard', sometimes called a 'scratch-plough' (Firmage 1992: 1130; Palmer 1998: 139-44). It has a symmetrical shape. Though the Greek term remained the same (*aratron*), the technology and mechanics were quite distinct. From the references in the *Testament of Job*, the ard could still be used, albeit with difficulty, even if no animals were available to assist.[42] Leser is adamant that, unlike the European plough, the ard does *not* require constant attention. Indeed, one can easily look back without running into trouble — the ard is light enough to stabilize easily and the method of ploughing allows for ready correction on the return path. In any case, the ard was used to plough the soil two or three times, and went across or even diagonal to the initial 'scratching'. In such circumstances, looking back became irrelevant (Leser 1974: 243-46).

It now becomes important to recall that the only Christian Scriptures writers who mention the plough are Hellenized urban-cultivated citizens: Luke and Paul. Their visualization of ploughs is governed by the technically more advanced implements working the farms surrounding and tied to the cities they frequented. These ploughs had mould-boards, side-share, often a wheeled fore-carriage and coulter (Bishop 1936: 273). They demanded different ploughing techniques, including constant, undivided concentration on the forward movement. Local knowledge of Palestinian conditions and ard manufacture[43] has disappeared and been replaced by the ploughs used in the familiar territory

---

41. One of his earliest works was *Entstehung und Verbreitung des Pfluges*, published in 1931.

42. See n. 19 above. It probably meant that one labourer performed the function of the hauling animal.

43. The Roman plough was probably next to useless in Palestine, if nineteenth-century English attempts to introduce the mould-board plough are any indication. Yet again the technological improvement brought a decline in yields (and increased damage to the share from rocks) (Leser 1974: 244 n. 2).

around Graeco-Roman cities. This is the plough that appears in an embellishment in the *Acts of Thomas* (147): 'my hands have I put to the yoked plough and have not turned back, *lest my furrows go crooked*'.

Consequently, Luke is either ignorant of actual farming practice in Palestine or determined to employ the image to reinforce gender stereotypes (or both).[44] If the former, then ploughing as a sign of the kingdom sets itself over against local farming knowledge. The result is a blatant disregard for the season or the land that dictates to the plougher the limits of ploughing. Rather, ploughing is arraigned for its own (metaphorical) sake, much like Naevolus's attitude to his abused slaves (above). The plougher sets himself against the Creator, by arraigning himself callously against creation. Yet Luke scripts it as modelling the kingdom of God.

This 'ignorance' of actual ploughing practice accentuates the gender/power differentials more strongly. In the use of the imagery, Luke has dispensed with productivity or fertility but has concentrated upon the assertion and demonstration of control. Ploughing for/as the kingdom proffers no reason for ploughing. Perhaps the reason was to be provided by the reader (as in the *Acts of Thomas*), conventional values being elicited and thereby reinforced. Or perhaps ploughing becomes its own end and own gratification. If so, even the defence that ploughing might deal with weeds that have overtaken the land (Isa. 7.25) evaporates. It has become infected by a blood-lust that delights in the thrust of the lance.

The second challenge is perhaps more significant. Surfacing in the wake of textual transmission is a small but determined bubble of oral tradition that upsets the plough. To be sure it is textualized, but this may only reorient textuality as a servant rather than master of orality. The survival of the variant undermines the attempt of the dominant text to silence other approaches (Cadwallader 1994a: 332-40). Yet, few commentators refer to it.[45] Metzger dismisses it as scribal inadvertence

44.   For a similar religiously inspired ignorance, see Philo's assessment of the ox as a stronger and more durable plough animal than the donkey (*Virtues* 146-47, *Special Laws* 4.206). Pliny in his *Natural History* (8.68) makes the contrary assessment. The foundation of Philo's judgment is his division between clean (ox) and unclean (donkey), cf. Deut. 14.1-8. The desire for (ethnic) religious distinctives is determinative.

45.   Fitzmyer (1981: 837) recognizes a 'slightly different nuance'. He apparently assumes that the reference to ploughing is positive, now made the more difficult by having one's gaze directed away from the handle (and hence generating difficulties in grasping). He refers to L. Cerfaux (1955: 326-28; *non vide*). In fact, the nuance is far more significant than he recognizes, once the plough is removed from its privileged position.

because, to him, it 'scarcely makes sense' (1971: 149). Plummer (1922: 509) points to a 'similar' inversion in Lk. 22.42 though I suspect the similarity is formal only. But the different manuscripts attesting the variant probably reduce the 'inadvertence', the more especially because the reading, though in a sense harder, *does* make sense. The reading, translated, is:

> no one who looks back and puts a/his hand to the plough
> is worthy of the *basileia*[46] of God.[47]

The double participle construction joined by a conjunction is now *contrasted* with the *basileia* of God. The act of looking back *and* laying a hand on the plough is a rejection of the radical demands of Jesus' call. On this reading, ploughing is no fit image for discipleship. It represents a 'staying at home', symbolic and symptomatic of the patterns of behaviour at loggerheads with the new world view of the *basileia* movement. Moreover, the combining of the allusion to Lot's wife 'looking back' and the return to ploughing fractures any essentialist functionalism of male and female. The plougher, the man, is as capable of looking back as Lot's wife. Neither male nor female is inherently pre-determined to stereotyping behaviours — hence woman and man are released from any predisposition to either promiscuity or rapaciousness.

Luke 'Looks Back' to the Plough

The positing of another, earlier tradition that repudiated the plough is more in keeping with the radical disturbance of social conventions of the previous two sayings (see *Appendix*). Luke, it appears, has looked back — like Lot's wife — to retrieve the plough; the saying becomes modified to the needs of a church that is now struggling for acceptance. The images of its existence, however, are now drawn not in complete contradistinction from its surrounding culture but in measured accommodation to it.

---

46. *Basileia* is preferred to the translation 'kingdom' both to accent the contrast between the Lukan symbolic world and to restrict (if not avoid) the militaristic and dominating semantics of the English word.

47. The variant is attested most significantly in D with P[45] *vid*, the latter being the probable surmise on the basis of what is left from a lacuna. Quite a number of Old Latin manuscripts support the reading. Significantly, the reading is also found in Eastern and Western authors (e.g. Clement of Alexandria; Cyprian; Hilary; Zeno). The verse itself is subject to a massive array of options, which may attest in part to a conflict of traditions. On the range of readings, see the *International Greek New Testament Project: Luke* (Oxford: Clarendon Press; 1984): II, 217-18.

The metaphor cannot be dismissed as a 'mere' metaphor for the range of nuances and values upon which its success as a metaphor depends is what gives it power. However ploughing the kingdom be described—as training in asceticism, as perseverance or as keeping (morally?) straight paths or furrows—the notion is that the Earth of the kingdom must be ploughed for the kingdom to be realized. The metaphor thus reinforces the notion of a rapacious attitude to Earth as a heavenly virtue.

The days of total reliance and dependence upon the providence of God and the fecundity of God's creation are, it seems, consigned to the primitive past. The sword is back (Lk. 22.35-37). Just as Luke has reconfigured the stories of women to restore male control over them, so also Earth, with whom they are commonly allied and compared, is to be subject to the same control again. It is to be furrowed, according to the presumption/ideology that a yield for the worker is assured.

Alternatively, given that Fitzmyer credits the plough-slave illustration of Lk. 17.7 to the special L source (1985: 1145), Luke may have made his choice between the *Tendenz* of his sources. The adjustment to the socio-economic practices of the surrounding culture rescues the plough from the fire of Elisha's sacrifice, so that it now becomes a key implement of the kingdom. The third saying of the trilogy, in Luke's form, stands in tension with the two prior anti-social sayings. It reinstates conventions—the attitudes and practices that reserve ploughing to men and use the plough as a mark of superiority over both women and Earth.

Radical Discipleship: Valuing Earth Means Devaluing the Plough

The third-century bishop, Cyprian of Carthage, is one writer who appears to have been raised on the alternative reading. Significantly, he ties this to another text commonly identified as Q, namely, Q 12.24 ('consider the ravens').[48] For him, the rejection of the plough is the signification for total dependence on the Creator. While Cyprian spiritualizes through massive intertextual connections, his writing does demonstrate that the re-linquishing of traditional ties was not only recognized but encompassed material provision as much as it did to shelter and familial obligations.

Here we notice a subtle difference between Paul's dismissal of creation in 1 Cor. 9.9-10 (*not* concerned about oxen) in favour of human beings (or, more narrowly, apostolic Christians) and Q's argument from the lesser ('the ravens') to the greater ('you') in Q 12.24. Though the argument operates from an inherent hierarchy of structure, Q leaves no doubt that Earth's creatures are valued in and of themselves. Such prizing of the

---

48. Cyprian, *Testimonies to Quirinus* 3.11.

material reality is not measured in terms of its potential for fecundity but its actuality. The plough is not needed. This is a lesson for human beings both in recognition of their material importance and in their collation with creation. Creation does not have value because human beings turn their technology upon it; neither do human beings gain their value because of their technological prowess exercised upon Earth.

Moreover, the eradication of the plough removes the fundamental signification of the division of labour in the ancient world and the super-structure of gender dualism and sexual domination. Thus Q 12.27 con-trasts the innate beauty of the lilies with images drawn from women's work: 'carding', 'spinning' and 'becoming worn out'.[49] If the plough is no longer able to demarcate men and women, then Earth is also granted new opportunities, including the long-awaited Sabbath rest (Lev. 25.4). Philo's embellishment of the '*hebdomadal* year' notes that, in addition to a ban on sowing and pruning, no ploughing 'or any other operation of husbandry' was to take place.[50]

Conclusion: The Possibility of a New Beginning for Earth

The presence of the alternative reading destabilizes the singularity of endorsement of the plough as an image of the *basileia* of God. It has been argued here that the alternative reading is prior to Luke's Gospel. While pillaged by Luke's redactional activity—with its momentous symbolic implications for Earth and women—this radical saying survived. Whether its survival was assisted by a tenacious oral tradition or simply as a respected written artefact, the offering of an option breaks the strength of the plough, sword and book triad. The saying's probable priority to Luke and the value it restores to Earth in its own right by leaving behind the plough for the *basileia* of God, denaturalizes the ideology of the Scriptural-socio-politico-economic alliance, leaving it exposed as one but not *the* solitary attitude. Simply by avowing the existence of a choice, Earth might become free from the domination that texts frequently authorize.

Of course, this neither resolves nor sanitizes an Earth reading of Q as a whole. Moreover, it must confront the charge of romanticism that in-evitably is mounted against a questioning of technological (i.e. 'scientific') method. The assumption, however, that 'scientific' approaches are free

49. Following Robinson's reconstruction of the earlier (oral then prior written) form of the saying (1999: 61-77).

50. Philo, *De decalogo* 162-63 cf. Josephus, *Antiquities of the Jews* 11.343, where a minimalist position (no sowing) is mentioned.

from eisegesis is precisely what this paper has challenged. The marginalization of the plough rather invites Earth, not the plough, to be the spring of admiration, contemplation and learning…and non-violent fecundity:[51] 'Behold the lilies of the field.' And that must be the praxis qualification placed even on my textual act.

Appendix on Q 9.61-62

The dominant debate regarding the verse is whether Lk. 9.61-62 derives from the text of Q (even though there be no Matthean parallel) or is a piece of Lukan redaction. John Kloppenborg has been the main proponent of its presence in Q (1987: 190-91 n. 80),[52] but has had to sacrifice the degree of probability for its inclusion in the recent *Critical Edition of Q* (Robinson, Hoffman and Kloppenborg 2000: 156-57).[53]

Interestingly, the redactional arguments for the inclusion in Q are sometimes used for the counter-argument. Harry Fledderman (1992) identifies three sources for the construction of Lk. 9.61-62, namely the previous couplet of Q sayings (Q 9.57-60), Luke's characteristic vocabulary, and that of the Septuagint, notably Gen. 19.26 and 1 Kgs 19.19-21. The problem, however, is the danger of circularity and the limits of editorial or redactional practice. Identifying characteristic Q vocabulary may do nothing more than confirm the redactional activity of the Q scribe(s). Luke's characteristic vocabulary is as evident in the redactional reworking of the two prior sayings as this (Fledderman 1992: 550), and hence could be argued as an editorial mechanism to tie the three *chreiai* together, engineered either by Luke or the Q editor.[54] The clearest example of circularity is the analysis of *euthetos* ('fit'): 'The adjective *euthetos* appears twice in Luke and nowhere else in the gospels. It is probable that the other use (Lk. 14.35) comes from Q, and that Luke introduced the Q expression here' (Fledderman 1992: 551). There are a number of arguments that support a serious consideration for the alternate reading as belonging to Q. Though the reading brings the third *chreia* closer to the radicalism of the call of Elisha, the Elisha narrative is more radical in its description than this element of the Lukan call to discipleship. Elisha burned his plough and accessories. This inverted (or rather, reverted) reading matches that level of severance. In fact, the plough is not to be revisited at all.

51. Technology, therefore, becomes anchored to and assessed by Earth (Fritsch 1994).

52. The arguments are repeated with one significant addition—a cohesion to the 'country-life language of Q' (Kloppenborg 1988: 64), where he lists the main proponents (to that time) of the various positions (cf. Tuckett 1990).

53. Borrowing the United Bible Societies model of a four-level grading of probability for its critical readings i.e. the omission of Lk. 9.61-62 is {B}, some doubt remains.

54. Some in fact argue that *heteros de…eipen* and *kurie* in Mt. 8.21 are drawn from the wording found in Lk. 9.61 and thus indicates that even though Matthew does not have a third saying, he does retain a remnant from his Q source (Steinhauser 1989: 152).

The radical edge to the reading brings it closer to the intensity of the first two sayings which eschew any imagery of a settled lifestyle. No home, no filial obedience, no plough—here is a coherent crescendo of commitment to the providence /cost of the *basileia*. There is dispute as to whether this couplet/triad of radicalism is attributable to 'elective vagrancy' (Kloppenborg 1987: 192) or a response to rejection of the *basileia* message (Tuckett 1996: 182). But the alternative reading is fundamentally coherent with the extreme disconnection of Q 9.57-60.

Codex D, the most important extant witness to this reading, has been noted elsewhere for its ability to collect independent traditions that circulate outside or alongside the Gospels and Acts. The most famous *agraphon* is Lk. 6.4-6 where an additional beatitude is found, one which is deemed, at least by some, as authentic (Delobel 1989: 105-16).[55]

It has long been recognized that the history of transmission may contain important evidence for the establishment of Q, if only because of the recognized propensity of Gospel manuscripts to assimilate to each other. James Robinson (1999; 2000) has argued persuasively that occasionally copyists are influenced by their knowledge of other traditions. One particular example he cites is Q 12.27 where a form of the saying about the lilies (of the field) earlier than that known to Matthew and Luke has yet survived in other writings and even in transmission of the Gospel text (in Codex ‭א‬; Robinson, Hoffman and Kloppenberg 2000: lxv-lxvi, xcix-ci).

There is no question that the Lukan reading in our Christian Bible has dominated scholarly interpretation and allusion from Irenaeus and Tertullian onwards.[56] The suggestion that there may have been an alternative form of the saying, which is likely to be present in the Q tradents, indicates that Luke has probably exercised his redactional prerogative on the pre-existing tradition.[57]

55. Delobel notes that of 23 non-received sayings of Jesus, 14 of them occur in Codex D, 3 of them in D alone.

56. Irenaeus, *Against Heresies* 1.8.3; Tertullian, *Idolatry* 12.2.

57. There is also the possibility that the textual transmission of Luke was itself early divided. It is less likely, or at least has less evidence to assess, that Q in its own transmission possessed variant readings here. However exploration of this hypothesis must be delayed.

An Ecojustice Challenge: Is Earth Valued in John 1?

Norman C. Habel

Introduction

John 1 has long been read as one of the *sedes doctrinae* for teachings of the Christian Church on the incarnation, the second person of the Trinity and *creatio ex nihilo*. Given its exalted status within the Christian faith, the very suggestion that this text could be read critically from a particular hermeneutical perspective may seem sacrilegious. If, however, we rigorously analyse this text in the light of the ecojustice principles associated with the Earth Bible Project, we may discern dimensions of the text that are problematic in terms of how it views Earth and the physical universe.

In attempting this analysis, I acknowledge that my understanding of the text is influenced by my past Western Christian orientation. I have been conditioned by my intellectual heritage to assume a popular dualism that separates reality into the domains of heaven and Earth, spiritual and material, mind and matter, humans and nature, flesh and spirit. The significance of this Western dualism is outlined in more detail by the Earth Bible Team in the first volume of the Earth Bible Series (2000b: 40-42).

In the past, I have read the text with this assumption as part of my heritage, an assumption that may be challenged not only by a particular ecojustice reading of the text, but also by alternative readings that reflect a deeper understanding of the ancient ideology of the Johannine narrative. And I welcome that challenge. In this reading, however, I begin with the suspicion that the prologue of John, written in an ancient Greek social context, is likely to reflect an ancient dualism similar to the popular dualisms that have developed in Western society.

My approach to this task will be to examine how key sections of the first chapter of John's Gospel seem to reread the text of Genesis 1 and related passages of the Hebrew Scriptures. Taking my cue especially from the principle of intrinsic worth (Earth Bible Team 2000b), I pose the question of whether John 1 rereads Genesis 1 in a dualistic way that tends to devalue Earth and the physical universe. My aim in this paper is to throw out a challenge: Is creation valued in John 1?

In the Beginning

Both Genesis 1 and John 1 begin with the primordial world of the beginning. Whether we render the first verse of Genesis 1 as a temporal clause: 'When God began to create sky and Earth' or as a superscription: 'In the beginning God created sky and Earth', the locus of the plot is the primordial world. The reader is transported back before the mysterious beginning of the known world.

As I have demonstrated previously in my article on Genesis 1 in the second volume of the Earth Bible Series (Habel 2000b), the world that God creates is the physical universe consisting of 'sky and Earth'. *Shamayim* is explicitly identified as the sky (Gen. 1.8), and *erets* is the name given to land or Earth (Gen. 1.10). There is no reference here to a spiritual or celestial domain where God and heavenly beings dwell, though such a domain is found elsewhere in the Hebrew Scriptures. Genesis 1 is about the formation of the physical cosmos.

The primordial components of the unformed physical world are given in Gen. 1.2: Earth, waters (the deep) and darkness. In the midst of this physical scene the *ruach elohim* ('wind/spirit of God')—hovers freely. In this verse, and in the narrative that follows, there is no action or characterization of any of these primordial components—that suggests they are negative or alien forces that must be conquered. They represent the status and stuff of the primordial that are transformed into the cosmos.

Some have sought to discern in the waters of the deep a reference to the *Chaoskampf* tradition of the ancient Near East and to the figure of Tiamat in the Babylonian creation myth of *Enuma Elish*. As Peter Trudinger states in his article in volume four of the Earth Bible Series (2001: 30), 'the *Chaoskampf* was seen throughout the biblical writings, whenever references to a water-being and the architecture of the cosmos occurred in proximity to each other'. He adds, moreover, that the '*Chaoskampf* pattern precludes any intrinsic value being ascribed to a significant component of Earth community' (2001: 30).

It is now clear that, in passages like Gen. 1.2, the waters of the deep need not be interpreted as negative or destructive chaos forces, but as the stuff of the primordial that is reordered as part of the current cosmos (Habel 2000b: 39). The same is true of the darkness in the primordial; the text nowhere suggests that darkness is an alien force that needs to be conquered. The text of Gen. 1.2 depicts a dormant primordial world of components yet to be ordered into the cosmos familiar to the writer.

When these physical components are ordered into the known world, they are all pronounced 'very good'. It is significant that God only makes this pronouncement after looking and discovering that they are good. They are discovered and declared by God to be 'good in themselves'. Nothing in the physical universe, either in its primordial or ordered state, is negative, alien or evil. All of the Earth community pleases God who declares it good.

The question before us is whether the same can be said for the cosmos and the Earth community in John 1. Does the God of John 1 see Earth as good?

Two Discrete Subjects

The central subjects in the texts of Genesis 1 and John 1 are quite discrete. Both texts identify the central subject at the beginning. After the superscription of Gen. 1.1, the text reads, 'And Earth was...' After the opening announcement of Jn 1.1, the text reads, 'And Word was...' Genesis 1 is first of all the primal story of Earth (*erets*). John 1 is first of all the story of Word (*logos*).

John 1, by introducing Word, has moved the primordial back to a starting point where Word and God exist without any of the stuff of creation. This suggests a locus that is purely spiritual; it is a locus in which none of the material stuff of creation as yet exists. The Johannine description of the creation process implies a pre-creation spiritual world of the primordial and a post-creation world of the material—this is a division that is absent from the Genesis account.

There is nothing in the text of Genesis to suggest that the *ruach elohim* should be identified with Word of John's Gospel. The wind/spirit of God indicates God's presence in the world of primordial stuff, but this presence is not identified as an agent in the creation narrative in Genesis. The fact that a particular psalmist (Ps. 33.6) uses 'the word of the Lord' and the 'breath of his mouth' in parallel does not require that we read spirit in Genesis as the creative agent. Incidentally, according to Psalm 33, it is the heavenly hosts who are made by God's spirit, not the physical creation.

In John 1 the creation of everything (*panta*) in the physical world is covered in summary fashion in one verse (Jn 1.3). The text does not focus on the details of the seven-day creation scenario of Genesis 1. The bold story of Earth in Genesis 1 is ignored; the 'good creation' that God discovered is not even mentioned. The emphasis in John 1 seems to lie on what Word brings to creation rather than on creation itself.

What Word first brings to creation is life (*zoe*). While there is some difference of opinion about the division of words in Jn 1.3-4, it seems clear that the source or agent of life for creation is Word. Is this life to be understood as physical life, spiritual life, or both?

In Genesis 1, while God may be the ultimate source of life, Earth — including land, sea and air — is the domain from which life emerges. God summons Earth to bring forth life of all kinds, both flora and fauna. Life is latent in the physical universe and called into being by God. In Genesis, all the identified forms of life are physical and good.

Thus, while life ultimately derives from God, Genesis 1 and John 1 identify two discrete subjects as the sources or agents of life. Are they two different dimensions of life — one physical and the other spiritual?

Light and Darkness

When the text of John introduces the concept of light, the radical difference of orientation between Genesis 1 and John 1 becomes more apparent. 'Life' is explicitly identified as the 'light of humans'. This is presumably the same 'light of life' of which Jesus speaks (Jn 8.12), the light that Word brings to humans. Those who have this light need never walk in darkness. This light, it seems, it not physical but spiritual; it is light for humans not for Earth or creation.

The light in Genesis 1 is physical; light and darkness are identified as day and night, reflecting the basic pattern of life on Earth. The sun, moon and stars are created on the fourth day to shed light — quite explicitly — on Earth. If John 1 is a rereading of Genesis 1, light and darkness have been interpreted in terms of the spiritual. Have these elements of Earth been devalued in the process?

The character of darkness is reflected in its antithesis to light in Jn 1.5. The darkness seems to be presented as a subject that does not 'overcome' the light that has penetrated it. Here light and darkness are not complementary features of the cosmos (as in Gen. 1), but opposing spiritual forces. The light from Word is a spiritual force from outside the cosmos that penetrates the darkness in the cosmos.

The cosmos, it seems, is characterized by this darkness and in need of redemption by what enters from outside the cosmos (Jn 3.17-21). Light/ Son/Word is the redeeming power who invades the cosmos (Jn 1.9) from the outside. But is it the cosmos as a material domain that is to be 'saved' (Jn 3.17), or only the humans within that cosmos who believe (Jn 1.12; 3.18)? Is the intent of John 1 to identify that spiritual power from the outside who will rescue humans living in darkness — and only humans?

Carmichael, in his study of how John 1 interprets Genesis 1, maintains that:

> For John, the light that is Jesus is the light that appears on day one at the creation of the world... Not only does he, as the Word, create, but his light is the light that appeared at the creation (1996: 46-47).

Carmichael also argues that John the Baptist corresponds to the void (*tohu wabohu*) and the darkness of the primordial (1998: 43, 51). While I do not necessarily agree with this identification, Carmichael's study seems to confirm that John is not interested in the physical world of creation, but the spiritual reality that comes into creation with Word as revealed in Jesus.

The spiritual dimension of light and darkness is also indicated in the work of other interpreters; for example Francis Maloney, who suggests that John is alluding to an ancient battle — presumably in the primordial — between the powers of evil/darkness and the light. Contrary to what some readers may believe, the light was victorious and continues to shine in the world (1993: 33). No such conflict of spiritual forces takes place in Genesis 1; the darkness is not evil. To render it evil is to devalue it.

Above and Below

According to Painter (1996), the contrast between 'from above' and 'from below' or 'from the Earth' is distinctive to John's Gospel. This contrast further emphasizes the antithesis between the spiritual domain of God 'above' and the physical domain of the cosmos 'below'. In Jn 3.31 the one who is from above — from heaven — is contrasted with the one who is 'from Earth' who 'belongs to Earth'. Earth, it seems, represents the inferior physical domain that is enveloped in darkness and in need of the invading light from heaven.

When we look at the text of Jn 1.1-13 in context, it would seem to present a cosmology that devalues Earth and the physical cosmos. The superior realm is heaven, the domain 'above', from which Word/Son comes to create, to bring life and to redeem. The cosmos — and especially Earth — is an inferior domain 'below' clouded in spiritual darkness and in need of redemption. That redemption, however, is only for humans who believe.

Those humans who believe are born 'of God' and then belong, it seems, to God's domain. They are 'born from above' (Jn 3.3, 7) and ultimately no longer belong to the physical world below. The domain below, while it may have been created by the *logos*, is not accorded the same value as the domain above. And when the *logos* returns to redeem humans in the domain below, apparently the rest of the cosmos remains in darkness. Earth seems to be relegated to outer darkness.

According to Maloney, the reader is first told about the material reality of the created world (*cosmos*); this provides the context for the coming of Word. However, says Maloney:

> The reference to the negative response to the Word in v. 5 is now being developed further. There is a power at large that will not accept the revelation brought by the Word. That power of evil is also called *ho cosmos* (1993: 37).

In John 1, according to this analysis, the cosmos has been interpreted as an inferior domain — polluted by spiritual darkness — to which those who know the light do not belong.

Becoming Flesh

The text that I have always believed may suggest a redemption of the material world is Jn 1.14, the *locus classicus* for the incarnation. Here the invading Word from above 'becomes flesh'. 'Flesh' is explicitly identified in the previous verse as belonging to the domain below and incapable of making humans children of God (Jn 1.13). Flesh is the stuff of the living creatures of the physical world.

The 'entering' of Word into the cosmos reaches, it seems, to the very stuff of living creation. But does 'flesh' here mean more than human flesh? Is Word connecting here with more than humans or only with humans? Is Earth again relegated to the margin? Or is Collins right when he says: 'The doctrine of the incarnation literally means that God takes the flesh, matter and the world seriously — so seriously, in fact, that in Jesus the transcendent enters into the very processes of material existence' (1995: 243). The reference to seeing the 'glory' of the *logos* recalls the biblical tradition of the *kabod YHWH*, the mobile firecloud of God's presence that dwells on Sinai (Exod. 24.16), in the tabernacle (Exod. 40.34) and the temple (1 Kgs 8.11). The *kabod YHWH* is the visible presence of God, a presence that appears and disappears, a presence that is not necessarily permanent. Is the presence of the *logos* 'dwelling' in human flesh also a one-time entering of Word from above to redeem humans?

Are we to follow the lead of Käsemann who, when discussing the glory of Christ, declares that 'the world is for him (Christ) only a point of transit and humiliation simply means being in exile' (1968: 12).

Is flesh revalued by this action of God from above? Or is flesh but the temporary — and dispensable — abode of Word passing through from 'above' to 'below' and back to 'above' again? Even if the transcendent enters the material, does it continue there? Does it redeem the material world? Is the material accorded the same worth as the spiritual Word who enters human flesh?

The Challenge

This brief study is designed to raise questions about a text that has become a key passage in the ecotheology debate. Does the text support the ecojustice principles of the Earth Bible Project? Is Earth valued or devalued? Does Earth remain but a temporary residence of the very *logos* that once created it? Does the *logos* discover that flesh is good? And, if so, what does this mean?

I am conscious that scholars have raised serious questions about the form of dualism that Painter (1996: 348) asserts Bultmann viewed as determinative in the text. Nevertheless, after analysing the way John 1 reads Genesis 1, I would argue that, even if a Gnostic dualism is not present in John's Gospel, the text of John 1 seems to devalue the domain of Earth — the material world below — over against heaven, the spiritual world above.

I also note that Painter maintains that 'John sees the creation as still in process of attaining completion (Jn 5.17)', a process begun in John 1 (1996: 349). Nevertheless, my challenge still stands. Does the text of John 1 then begin with an incomplete, defective, darkness-dominated Earth below? Is that Earth, too, to be redeemed, revalued, restored to its primal state as 'good'?

Which Intertext? A Response to An Ecojustice Challenge: Is Earth Valued in John 1?*

Elizabeth Wainwright

Introduction

In his essay 'An Ecojustice Challenge: Is Earth Valued in John 1?' Norman Habel rightly draws attention to the Western dualistic framework that has shaped his reading of John 1. This is a framework that Val Plumwood has demonstrated had its origins in ancient Greek thought and which she calls the 'master paradigm' (1993). It could be argued, therefore, that it is not only a contemporary hermeneutical lens but one that would also have been shared by many first-century Christian–Jewish theologians or storytellers as well as those participating in the storytelling of the Johannine community. The Earth-denying perspective that Habel's essay draws attention to may have been a perspective that indeed shaped the very composition and reception of this early Christian poem.

Using this interpretive lens and the principle of intrinsic worth of the Earth Bible Project (Earth Bible Team 2000b), Habel's essay brings a hermeneutic of suspicion to the text of John 1. His challenge emerges from an intertextual reading of Genesis 1 and John 1. This brief response will take up his challenge: Is Earth valued in John 1? It will be a resistant reading, acknowledging the Earth-denying aspect already drawn to readers' attention by Habel, but also a reading against the grain of the text. This too will be accomplished by way of an intertextual reading but the intertext will not be Genesis 1 but rather three Wisdom texts: Prov. 8.22-31; Sir. 24.1-12; and Wis. 7.22–8.1.

I have shown elsewhere (Wainwright 1998) that the poem of John 1 may indeed have originated as a song praising Sophia/Wisdom or even Jesus/Sophia given the extensive intertextuality evident in it, an inter-

*   I wish to acknowledge the insights of members of a class in Biblical and Philosophical Hermeneutics—Susan Holm, Greg Watson, Jeanette Smith, Lyn Eastmure, Christine Lindsay, Mervyn Thomas, and John Treacy—who explored this response with me.

textuality steeped in the Wisdom tradition. Feminist scholarship has long recognized, however, that the Wisdom literature that provides a source of female imagery—even a female gestalt of the divine—also contains traditions originating in the male scribal community of Hellenistic Judaism (Schüssler Fiorenza 1994: 155-62). Interpreters need to read against the grain of the androcentric perspectives of the text resultant from these origins in order not to reinscribe them in their reclamation of Wisdom texts. Similarly, this same Wisdom literature manifests the dualism of the Hellenistic world and its master paradigm, separating reality 'into the domains of heaven and Earth, spiritual and material, mind and matter, humans and nature, flesh and spirit' (Habel, above, p. 77; Hobgood-Oster 2001: 35-36). The reading undertaken in this paper will be attentive to the necessary hermeneutics of suspicion or resistant reading necessary in this intertextual study but more particular attention will be given to the resistant voice of Earth that can be heard when John 1 is read intertextually with the Wisdom texts indicated above. It is to such a reading I now turn.

In the Beginning

Not only Genesis 1 and John 1 but also the poem of Prov. 8.22-31 begin with what Habel calls the 'primordial world of the beginning' (above, p. 78). 'Beginning' and 'in the beginning' marks the opening verses of Prov. 8.22-31, namely vv. 22 and 23. Both Genesis 1 and Proverbs 8 are therefore evoked at the beginning of the Johannine poem.

The voice heard in Prov. 8.22-31 is the voice of Sophia. She proclaims that she was created before the physical universe. She, however, locates herself both in relation to the creating one as well as in relation to Earth (*erets*; Prov. 8.23)—before the depths, the springs of water, the mountains and hills, the fields and the soil (Prov. 8.24-26). She then proclaims that she was there for the establishing of the heavens (*shamayim*) and of the depths, and of the separating out of the waters and Earth (*erets*). She was as one joined with the creating one (Prov. 8.30), delighting or rejoicing in the creator but also delighting in the *oikoumene*, the inhabited universe as well as in the human family. The delighting or rejoicing of Sophia links the creating one, the universe (even though it is not named as Earth and heavens but seems to encompass all that has been named in previous verses of the poem) and the human family.[1] The poem of Proverbs

1.   Shirley Wurst (2001: 57-60) also notes this phrase, and its use as a chiastic structuring device in Prov. 8. Citing Claudia Camp, she claims Woman Wisdom as mediator between G*d, Earth and Earth community, which includes human beings.

honours Earth and heavens as well as locating Sophia in what could be described as virtually a dance of relationship with divinity, the human community and the Earth itself.

One wonders whether, for first-century Christian–Jewish recipients of the opening of the Johannine poem, an intertextual reading of Prov. 8.22-31 was evoked. Would they have also heard echoes like the following:

> In the beginning was Sophia and Sophia was with God and Sophia was God. She was in the beginning with God and all things were made through her, and without her was not anything made that was made.

And would this not have brought to their imagination the dance of Sophia linking divinity, humanity and the Earth. Into the opening verses of John 1 through Sophian intertextuality are drawn Earth and the heavens, the depths and the heights. And even though the voice of Earth may have been dimmed for some and even silenced for others in the opening verses of John 1, today's resistant readers reading intertextually with Prov. 8.22-31 can let Earth's voice speak — to speak with the inter-connectedness that Earth evokes for contemporary readers.

Dancing beyond Discrete Subjects

The 'before' of Sophia in Prov. 8.22-31 is not the 'before' of the *logos* of John 1. Habel suggests that 'Word and God exist without any of the stuff of creation' in the Johannine poem whereas the five-times repeated 'before' of Prov. 8.23-25 is in relation to the stuff of creation — Earth: the depths, the springs of water, the mountains and the hills. Wisdom 9.1-2, however, hints at the move toward separation when it parallels *logos* and *sophia*:

> O God of my ancestors and of mercy
> Who has made all things by your *word*
> And by your *wisdom* have formed humankind (Wis. 9.1-2a).

Wisdom 9.1-2 links this parallel to a reiteration of humankind's dominion over the creatures of Earth community made by the divine hand (Wis. 9.2b). The ruling over of Gen. 1.26 as head or *archon*, becomes in Wis. 9.2b that of the despot or absolute ruler. We see emerging in this later Wisdom text, in quite a stark fashion, one of the dualisms charac-teristic of the Hellenistic world — human over material — and this 'power over' is associated with a paralleling of wisdom and word.

This intertext of Wis. 9.1-2 can, however, enable Sophia to dance

---

Significantly for readers of the Hebrew text, this relationship is also presented as a chiastic construction in the text (see Wurst 2001: 59).

between the supposedly two discrete subjects of Genesis 1 and John 1 that Habel notes, namely Earth and Word. When this dance is combined with an intertextual reading of Wis. 7.22–8.1 and Jn 1.4-5, readers find themselves being drawn into the dance. On the one hand, it has a tendency to take them into a spiritual realm that is, in accord with contextual Hellenistic dualism, superior to Earth (Wis. 7.29). Wisdom is more beautiful than the sun, and excels every constellation of the stars. Compared with the light, she is found to be superior. Yet, on the other hand, the dance tends towards interconnectedness by way of the 'all' that can include Earth even though Earth may not be explicitly named (Wis. 7.24, 27; 8.1). The Sophia of the book of Wisdom conducts readers on an interpretive dance that enables Hellenistic dualism to be critiqued so that the resistant voice of the 'all' of Earth interconnectedness can be heard. It can indeed be heard in the opening verses of the hymn of John 1, which praises not only Word but also wisdom evoked intertextually. Intimately linked with Sophia is Earth and so the attentive resistant reader can read the voice of Earth in the opening verses of John 1 however quietly it might sound.

Sophia is praised by way of a multiplication of adjectives in the hymn of Wis. 7.22, and one of the earliest is *monogenese*, generally translated as 'unique'. This same term is used of Word as the hymn of John 1 closes in Jn 1.18 – it is the unique one of G*d, the one being in G*d's very bosom who makes the generative one known. The hymn of John 1 from beginning to end evokes intertextual allusions to, and readings of, Wisdom literature. This unique one who can be interpreted as Word/Wisdom is, as Word, light for the human community (Jn 1.4) and, as Wisdom, a reflection of eternal light, mirror of the working of G*d and image of G*d's goodness (Wis. 7.26). Word, wisdom, human community and Earth are caught up in the dance of interpretation possible for contemporary resistant readers of Jn 1.1-5 so that Word as discrete subject is shattered by Wisdom intertextuality. Jesus, celebrated explicitly as male *logos* in John 1 can, at the same time, be imaged in a kaleidescopic way intertextually as Sophia/Wisdom and in this way can be linked intimately with Earth and Earth community, including human community.

Pitching a Tent Among One's Own

Sophia delights or rejoices in Earth and human community at the conclusion of the poem of Prov. 8.22-31 (Prov. 8.31). It is, however, the language of Jn 1.14 – Word pitching a tent among the 'us' of the human community – that evokes an intertextual reading of Sir. 24.1-12 and a response to Habel's questions: does the 'flesh' of this verse 'mean more than human flesh [and] is Word connected with more than humans or only with humans? Is Earth relegated to the margin?' (Habel above, p. 92).

Sirach's poem opens with Sophia telling her glory (not the glory 'as of the only Son of the Father' in Jn 1.14) in the midst of her people and in the presence of the hosts of the most high. As in the two previous Wisdom poems drawn intertextually into this reading of John 1, in this poem Sophia plays between Earth and the realm of the most high – and the hosts of the most high may well evoke the stars and the lights of the heavens as much as celestial beings (Sir. 24.1-2). And Sophia *comes forth* from the mouth of the most high (Sir. 24.3) just as Word *comes* among its own (Jn 1.11). The language of Jn 1.11b does seem to link Word with human community by its use of the term *idioi*, 'Word's own people'. Earth-attentive readers, however, note that in Jn 1.11a, Word comes among *ta idia*, generally translated as 'his own home' because of the human-centred focus of readers. But in light of the Wisdom intertextuality emerging in this poem, Jn 1.11a may well point to Word's coming among 'its own' or 'its related things' – the very stuff of the universe. The intertextuality of the poem in Sirach 24 affirms such a reading.

Sophia's coming forth from the mouth of the most high is intimately connected to Earth. She covers Earth like a mist (Sir. 24.3), stretching out between the vault of the heavens and the depths of the abyss (Sir. 24.5). Sea, Earth and all peoples belong to her (Sir. 24.6). Indeed one could say that such imagery suggests that these are the *ta idia* of Sophia. It is among all of these that she belongs. It is also among these that Sophia seeks a resting place (Sir. 24.7). The resting place given her – the place where the creating one bids her pitch her tent – is in Israel, among a people and at a place chosen to be holy (Sir. 24.8, 10-12).

For a few brief moments, the poet pauses to celebrate Sophia's pitching her tent among the human community, but even that brief pause is interrupted as she recalls in Sir. 24.9 her presence 'in the beginning' at the very work of creation, a work which we have already seen is profoundly Earth-centred. And as the opening of the poem (Sir. 24.12) saw Sophia dancing and stretching across the universe, so too it continues beyond to image her with metaphors drawn from Earth community (Sir. 24.13-22). An intertextual reading of Jn 1.11 and Jn 1.14 with Sir. 24.1-12 enriches not only these verses but the entire poem. Word/Wisdom, who comes among his/her own and pitches a tent there, is not one confined to the human community but one whom we can image stretching out between Earth and heaven and linking them in intimate communion, a communion that includes the human community but does not exclude Earth community. Sophia's dance continues into the poem of John 1 and moves gracefully and almost imperceptibly between Earth and heaven, divinity and humanity. What the master paradigm of Hellenistic Judaism and beyond into contemporary consciousness could divide, Sophian imagery can reunite.

In Conclusion

There are many issues at play amid first-century and twenty-first-century readings of John 1 that have not been addressed in this short response to Norman Habel's challenge in relation to John 1. This paper has had just a single focus as a reply — to hint at ways in which the intertextuality with three Wisdom poems evoked by a reading of John 1 displace and resist the male-(and human)-centredness of this poem. Word and Wisdom interchange by way of the language and imagery evoked and the human community interplays throughout with Earth community. Earth can, indeed, be valued in John 1 but it will be by way of a resistant intertextual reading that can shatter our deeply ingrained dualisms. Such a reading will be indeed, in the words of Val Plumwood, 'remaking the story', by taking inspiration from 'subordinated and ignored parts of western culture', namely the Wisdom traditions (Plumwood 1993: 195-96). And it is this new story that will shape a new religious imagination and will enable the human community, like Sophia, to dance between and among divinity, humanity and Earth community, honouring Earth, and recognizing Earth, the human and the divine as caught up in intimate communion.

John 1 – the Earth Bible Challenge:
An Intra-textual Approach to Reading John 1

Vicky Balabanski

In reading Norman Habel's essay 'An Ecojustice Challenge: Is the Earth Valued in John 1?', I had a profound sense of 'Fall'. What had been in Genesis a vision affirming not only the goodness, but also the agency of Earth, has in John 1 become a vision that is profoundly pessimistic of the stuff of creation. In this changed vision, the 'co-creative' action of God and the Earth has given way to a creation proceeding from a divine impulse extrinsic to physical matter. Rather than rounding out and broadening the vision of Genesis, John's prologue seems to be spiritualizing it in such a way that Word has left no room for the agency and intrinsic worth of Earth. Norman Habel's essay confronts me with more than a suspicion that John's Gospel's prologue may well be a 'Fall', an enforced *kenosis* that empties the Earth and physical matter of intrinsic worth.

In the face of this reading of John 1, Elaine Wainwright invites us to join with her in a resistant reading that draws its impulse from three Wisdom texts and catches us up in a dance of Sophian intertextuality. The following contribution moves to examine an *intra-textual* impulse that may be able to assist the reader of John's Gospel in resisting the cosmological dualism that is so much the horizon and backdrop of this Gospel. This impulse may be discerned through giving attention to the prominent, but shifting, term *kosmos* in John's Gospel.

The kosmos

It has long been recognized that John's Gospel is pessimistic about the *kosmos*, the world. Indeed, in the prayer recorded in John 17, Jesus even refuses to pray for the world, prompting one outstanding Johannine scholar to assert ominously that 'the only hope for the *kosmos* is precisely that it should cease to be the *kosmos*' (Barrett 1978: 506).

When we meet this term *kosmos* in John's Gospel, we are dealing with a very significant term – it appears no less than 78 times (contrast only 3 in Mark and Luke respectively, and 9 in Matthew's Gospel). However, in John's Gospel it is a term that has shifting semantic value:

First, it is the context into which Light (or humanity)[1] comes, and dwells (Jn 1.9, 10a).

Second, it is the totality of creation (Jn 1.10b, which parallels Jn 1.3: the world came into being through him/all things came into being through him).

Third—and most prominently—it is the world of human affairs, particularly referring to human beings who refuse to acknowledge their source (Jn 1.10c: 'the world did not know him').[2]

And fourth, it is 'this world', as contrasted with a world above (cf. Jn 8.23; 18.36).

Without specifying which aspect is being referred to, the *kosmos* is deemed to be sinful (Jn 1.29) and subject to judgment (Jn 9.39; 12.31). It is in need of a saviour (Jn 3.17; 4.42), for it is in the grip of a ruler who must be overthrown (Jn 12.31; 14.30; 16.11). Jesus has overcome the *kosmos* (Jn 16.33), and in Jn 17.9 does not pray for it, yet the *kosmos* is nevertheless the object of God's saving action in Christ (Jn 3.16), and the purpose of Jesus' ministry was that 'the *kosmos* may believe' (Jn 17.21) and 'may know' (Jn 17.23) that Jesus was sent by God and that God loves the world.

Where is the Earth in all this? When is it legitimate to equate the Johannine concept of the *kosmos* with the Earth? If we don't distinguish between the semantic layering here, we may find ourselves carried along in a maelstrom of dualistic impulses that almost inevitably invites the clarifying and systematizing of a framework. Such a dualistic framework cements the inferiority of the material and physical, as did the Gnostic frameworks of the second century.[3]

It was in the evangelist's interests not to systematize the symbolic speech of Jesus or indeed his own discourse, for the rich ambiguity and metaphor were 'language worthy of a deity' (Stibbe 1993: 236). This was

1.   With the editors of the United Bible Societies Fourth Edition of the Greek New Testament, I favour reading the participle *erchomenon* ('coming') as qualifying the true light.

2.   The order in which the first three are set out does not reflect their prominence in the Gospel as a whole, but simply their appearance in the prologue, Jn 1.9-10.

3.   Irenaus, quoting Valentinus, gives an example of this systematizing: 'For just as it is impossible that material substance should partake of salvation (since, indeed, they maintain that it is incapable of receiving it), so again it is impossible that spiritual substance (by which they mean themselves) should ever come under the power of corruption, whatever the sort of actions in which they indulged' (Irenaeus 1.1.11-12 Harvey; 1.6.2-4 Ante-Nicene Christian Library).

also a means of generating a cohesive group that defines itself over against the dominant society (Malina and Rohrbaugh 1998: 10). For the contemporary reader, however, the very richness and ambiguity of the language may lead to us identify the Earth with the *kosmos* that culpably refuses to acknowledge its source, or even more likely, with *this world*, as opposed to the world above.[4] We are therefore in danger of importing the cosmic dualism—that operates primariy in the fourth semantic category set out above—into all the other categories.

In order to locate which aspect, if any, of the four main categories of *kosmos* set out above may include the Earth, some brief points about the wider usage of the term are in order. The primary meaning of *kosmos* gives prominence to the order or system, so that in non-biblical usage and in the Greek text[5] of the Hebrew Scriptures', *kosmos* is not in the first instance a term that refers to the Earth as opposed to the heavens, but to the cosmic order of the universe (i.e. both heaven and Earth). In Jewish Hellenistic writings, it can be synonymous with 'nature' (*bios*) (e.g. in the Septuagintal book of Wis. 16.17). *Kosmos* is occasionally used to translate the Hebrew *erets* ('land') instead of *ge* (cf. Symmachus' translation of Job 38.4).[6] The four Johannine semantic usages of *kosmos* set out above all have parallels in other Hellenistic Jewish writings.

In the light of these brief observations, it is apparent that only the context, cosmology and theology of John's Gospel will show which of the four Johannine categories includes the Earth.

Category one, *kosmos* as the context into which Light comes, and dwells. The *kosmos* here includes the Earth, but not as subject or agent, rather as an arena in which the drama of salvation is played out.

Category two, *kosmos* as the totality of creation. This clearly includes Earth, as well as the heavens, and comes nearest to the interrelational and interdependant concept of Earth community that the Earth Bible Project is advocating.

Category three, *kosmos* as the world of human affairs, particularly referring to human beings who refuse to acknowledge their source. It is here that the Johannine notions of sin and judgment belong, for 'nonhuman

---

4. Some of the contemporary ramifications of viewing the Earth as temporary and dispensable have been set out by Harry Maier in his paper in this volume.

5. Also known as the Septuagint, abbreviated to LXX.

6. Given the diversity of meaning already present in the Johannine community's linguistic/conceptual environment, *kosmos* could be synonymous with *ge*. In Jn 3.31 ('the one who comes from above is above all; the one who is of Earth belongs to Earth and speaks about earthly things'), Earth is synonymous with the fourth category of *kosmos*, namely 'this world' as contrasted with the 'world above'; Jn 12.32 and 17.4 also foreground the dualistic cosmology.

creatures and the universe itself do not sin' (Edwards 1995: 145). Humanity is also the *kosmos* that presumably needs to come to believe (Jn 17.21). However, the saving action of God in Christ is not necessarily limited to the *kosmos* of human affairs, because the sinfulness of humanity impacts upon the entire Earth community, rendering Earth also in need of salvation.[7] In this sense, the Earth also needs to 'know' (i.e. experience) the purpose of Jesus' life and the fact of God's love. I therefore propose that wherever John speaks of the *kosmos* in relation to sin, judgment and belief, this is related only to human beings and excludes the Earth. However, where the reference is to salvation, though the primary reference is to human beings, Earth is also in need of experiencing this salvation, and is implicitly included.

Category four, kosmos as 'this world', and contrasted with a world 'above'. Here the world is in eschatological conflict with God. Here the *kosmos* is the realm in defiance against God. This is the clearest expression of a dualistic cosmology, and it is here that Barrett's comment quoted above most properly fits. This is the *kosmos* that is in the grip of a ruler who must be overthrown, a *kosmos* that Jesus has 'overcome'. This may also be the *kosmos* for which Jesus does not pray (Jn 17.9), given the strong dualistic perspective of this verse. Only this *kosmos* is by definition fully at odds with God and exclusive of the reign of Jesus (cf. Jn 18.36). This category is distinguished from category one—a passive or neutral arena—by its characteristic pessimism. I propose that this fourth category does not refer to Earth at all; Earth, as set out above, does not sin, and is evidence of God's creativity, and is not in opposition to God's purposes.

According to this endeavor to systematize the Johannine use of *kosmos*, categories one and two include reference to Earth. Of these two, only the second one approaches the sort of interconnectedness addressed in the Earth Bible principles. Category three, when referring to sin, judgment and belief, is related only to human beings and excludes Earth. However, when there is reference to salvation—even though the primary reference is to humans—Earth is implicitly included. The fourth category does not refer to Earth at all, but to those forces—human and angelic/demonic in John's cosmology—that are irredeemably in opposition to God.

Which of the four categories of *kosmos* is the recipient of God's love, as set out in Jn 3.16? Certainly not category four, nor, presumably category one. The human *kosmos*, category three, has been shown to be the primary recipient of God's love, for indeed humans are the ones who

7. See Denis Edwards's discussion of the salvation of the universe (1995: 145-52).

stand under judgment for sin and who are capable of belief. However, if category two refers to the totality of creation—as created and set in an interconnected order by God through Word—then not only humans make up the *kosmos* for which God gave the Son. The prominence of birthing imagery in John's Gospel is significant here. While the birthing/rebirthing of human beings is the focus of Jn 1.12-13 and the dialogue with Nicodemus (Jn 3), the fact that 'all things came into being' through Word (Jn 1.3) and 'the *kosmos* came into being through him' (Jn 1.10) means that the whole of creation/Earth community shares in the love of the one who gave birth to all things.[8] How could God and the creative Word through whom creation came into being/was birthed fail to have compassion on the whole world?

What difference do these reflections make to the interpretation of John's language of *kosmos* in practical terms? I would like to test them with reference to Jn 3.17, a verse in which there are three references to *kosmos*:

> Indeed, God did not send the Son into the world to condemn the world, but in order that the world might be saved through him.

These statements about the world can be reframed as follows:

1. God sent the Son into the world.
2. The purpose of sending the Son was not to condemn the world.
3. The purpose was that the world might be saved through him (i.e. the Son).

The first statement refers to the world as the arena of the drama of salvation, and thus corresponds to category one. The world is not deemed to be beyond the saving acts of God, and so the usage does not correspond to category four.

The second statement refers to judgment/condemnation, and so corresponds to category three, the *kosmos* of human affairs. However, by negating the assertion that the Son's purpose was to condemn/judge, category two is also a possibility.

The third reference is to the purpose of salvation; this would invite the primary reference being to category three, but a secondary implication also embracing category two, the totality of creation. The salvation of humanity by bringing about right relationship with God and one another would facilitate the restoration of the cosmic order.

No Johannine scholar whom I have read considers the possibility of

---

8. The verb *ginomai* can have the meaning of 'bringing into being by natural means' i.e. birthing.

God's saving acts embracing a broader horizon than that of humanity,[9] although it is in keeping with the trends of ecological theology.[10] This results in a resistant reading that refuses to systematize the various references to *kosmos* in John by means of the overarching dualistic framework of category four.

By examining the semantic range of *kosmos* in John's Gospel, and by offering an alternative means of systematizing the references, this contribution invites the reader to continue to move beyond dualistic categories towards a reading of John's Gospel that acknowledges our mutuality with Earth.

9.   Schnackenburg (1980: 401) writes of 'the universal salvific will of God', but by this means 'the well-being of all men [*sic*] and not just that of a privileged section' of humanity.

10.   Cf. Sally McFague (1993: 197): 'We have been *decentred* as the point and goal of creation and *recentered* as God's partners in helping creation to grow and prosper.'

Storing Up Death, Storing Up Life:
An Earth Story in Luke 12.13-34

Anne Elvey

In nature death is not an enemy, but a friend of the life process
(Ruether 1992: 53).

Introduction

From an Earth perspective the decay of dead organisms contributes to the life of others. But in so many ways (at least in the West) we deny death. One of the most potent examples of this denial is the practice of cryogenics by an elite few.[1] Rosemary Radford Ruether (1992: 53) connects a 'cultural avoidance of death' with 'the inability of some human cultures to create sustainable ecosystems', especially in the way waste becomes pollution. The irony is that by denying death we contribute to a material situation, characterized by overpopulation, overconsumption, and pollution, which promises death.

The recognition that death can be stored by Earth both as compost and as toxic by-product forms a contemporary context for my reading of Lk. 12.13-34, where the impending death of the rich person (Lk. 12.16-21) is juxtaposed with a well-known representation of the life-giving providence of the earth (Lk. 12.22-31).[2]

My starting point for reading Lk. 12.13-34 from the perspective of Earth is to affirm that the call to turn toward Earth requires a reorienta-

---

1.   That is, the freezing of all or part of a corpse in the hope of some kind of resuscitation in a technological future when 'we' will have conquered death.

2.   I distinguish between 'Earth', this planet and its multitude of constituents including ourselves, and 'the earth' which might be Earth as understood within a particular culture, such as that represented in the Gospel of Luke. I use terms such as other-than-human nature or non-human nature not to suggest that humans are outside of nature, but to distinguish between that part of nature which is human and that part which is other-than or not human. Such a distinction needs to be made in order to address precisely those situations in which other-than-human constituents of Earth are treated as other and lesser than the human.

tion on the part of the reader. Not only must I understand myself as part of the interconnectedness of Earth, but I am also challenged to regard the text as part of that same interconnectedness. I must take seriously the character of the text as an Earth product of paper or papyrus and ink and its debt to Earth through the reliance of its producers on other-than-human nature as well as other humans for their sustenance.[3] To respond to this call I employ a reading practice of attentiveness that has links with the ecojustice principles of voice and mutual custodianship. This practice of attentiveness resonates with the concept of Dadirri, a kind of contemplative awareness of country and story, of which Ngangikurung-kurr woman Miriam Rose Ungunmerr-Baumann (1993: 34) writes: 'It is inner, deep listening and quiet, still awareness.'[4] Attentiveness is also connected with the biblical concept of *shemah* in which hearing and obedience are intertwined. In the current context, it is a kind of listening that comes from and reinforces a reorientation of the reader toward Earth. Therefore, when the reader *attends* to Earth and its multitude of constituents as characters within the text, the implication is that something like the 'voice' of Earth is stored in the text.[5] Attentiveness to this 'voice' can be seen as a mutual engagement with an Earth of which the text and the reader are both part. In a small way this engagement —

3.   While there is need for further research on the nature of the Bible as an Earth product, such is beyond the scope of this paper. I am interested here in the way recognition of the debt to Earth (occasioned through both the production and the interpretation of biblical texts) entails a call to attend to Earth and its multitude of constituents in an interpretive engagement with the text. However, for a wonderful poetic description of a debt to Earth, incurred through both the 'use' of non-humans and the labour of 'subordinated' humans in the production of an illuminated prayer book, see Boisseau (2000). Her poem could very readily offer a model for considering debts to Earth incurred in producing ancient biblical papyri, contemporary Bibles, or indeed the Bible on CD-Rom.

4.   While I am conscious of the problems of non-Aboriginal appropriation of Aboriginal spiritualities, I want to acknowledge the way in which Miriam Rose Ungunmerr-Baumann's writing on Dadirri has shaped my sense of attentiveness to Earth. I was introduced to her writing of Dadirri during a retreat in the Barmah forest run by Marg Hill and Doug Smith for the Binnap partners of Aboriginal Catholic Ministry Melbourne. The retreat moved between listening to stories of the local Yorta Yorta people's struggle for justice especially in relation to their rights to land, both group and personal times of attentiveness to the land, and shared meals and rituals.

5.   I have concerns, like those expressed by Gene Tucker in conversation with the Earth Bible Team (2000a: 29), about the ascription of 'voice' to the Earth. I think that, as he also suggests, we can pay attention without necessarily ascribing a human- (or for that matter God-) like voice to Earth. Part of the challenge for me is to pay attention to the otherness of Earth as well as to human continuity with, and connectedness to, this otherness.

which focuses on the biblical bases of our ecological thinking and action—is part of the mutual custodianship in which we engage with Earth in its protection and healing.

But as a basis for our ecological thinking and acting, the biblical heritage is ambiguous. While this heritage might inform our ecological practice in life-giving ways, biblical texts can also be implicated in violence toward Earth, for example when Earth is characterized as other and lesser than both the human and the divine. In Lk. 12.13-34, a metaphor of 'storing' connects the two sections of the narrative (Lk. 12.13-21 and Lk. 12.22-34) and provides a contrast between the storing by the rich person and the providence of both the earth and the divine (Talbert 1988: 141). At one level a distinction is made between the storing of the excess by the rich person, which turns out to be a storing of death, and a divine benevolence that is stored by the earth for life. But when the Lukan presentation of divine providence relies on an overvaluation of the human with respect to other-than-human nature (Lk. 12.24, 28; see also Lk. 12.7), the distinction is not as clear as it seems. The metaphor of storing that occurs within the text of Lk. 12.13-34 becomes suggestive of ways in which the text itself stores both death and life. This ambiguous storing has ecojustice implications concerning the ways in which a text can be implicated in violence toward Earth.

The Metaphor of Storing in the Gospel of Luke

'Storing' is a key metaphor in Lk. 12.13-34. *Sunago*, 'to gather' (Lk. 12.17, 18), and *keimai*, 'to lay by', describe the activity of storing. *Apotheke* (Lk. 12.18, 24) and *tameion* (Lk. 12.24) mean storage areas, such as treasuries, warehouses, barns and pantries. *Thesaurizon*, 'one who stores up treasure' (Lk. 12.21), and *thesauros*, 'treasure' (Lk. 12.33, 34) come from the same root as *apotheke*. Within the Lukan narrative the heart (*he kardia*), which is the 'seat of thought, memory, [and] affectivity' (Meyer 1964: 45) and the site of Mary's keeping activity (Lk. 2.19, 51), is a storehouse or treasury (Lk. 6.45; cf. Lk. 12.34). In Luke 6 and 8 a metaphorical link is made between what is stored in the heart and what is stored in plants or in the earth itself (see Lk. 6.43-45; 8.4-15, esp. 8.15). Through an analogy with trees and earth, the moral capacity of humans is transferred to the earth and its constituents. 'Badness' and 'goodness' as descriptors of human intent and behaviour are confused with a reasonable judgment about the fitness of the produce of earth for human consumption or the fitness of parts of earth for the production of crops.[6] This confusion between what

6.   Interestingly, the description of earth (*ge*) in Lk. 8.15 as good (*kale*) recalls the

is judged good in a moral sense and what is judged good as a resource for humans has resonances in a perspective that sees Earth only as a resource and uses it up accordingly. There is an inherent violence in displacing the intrinsic worth of Earth in favour of an instrumental evaluation of Earth. Approaching Earth principally as a resource has in practice led to the violence of, for example, overfishing seas, over-farming land, and indiscriminate logging of old growth forests.

Divine Providence and the Providence of Nature

The principle of intrinsic worth, which resists such violent practices as those described above, could be understood as drawing our attention to a goodness stored by Earth independently of any human need or agency. In the Septuagint, the metaphor of 'storing' is used to describe the divine harnessing and release of the potentially unruly elements of storm, wind and sea (see Pss. 32.7; 134.6-7; Job 38.22-23). In the context of the faith-fulness of the creator to the creation, the earth is a store of divine mercy or compassion (*eleos*; Ps. 32.5). The relationship between God and crea-tion involves a mutual storing up of creative elements and compassion. This mutuality has affinities with the interplay of natural and divine providence described in Lk. 12.22-31, especially Lk. 12.24-28:

> Consider the ravens: they neither sow nor reap, they have neither store-house nor barn, and yet God feeds them. Of how much more value are you than the birds! And can any of you by worrying add a single hour to your span of life? If then you are not able to do so small a thing as that, why do you worry about the rest? Consider the lilies, how they grow: they neither toil nor spin; yet I tell you, even Solomon in all his glory was not clothed like one of these. But if God so clothes the grass of the field, which is alive today and tomorrow is thrown into the oven, how much more will he clothe you—you of little faith!

The picture that emerges in Luke 12 of a provident natural order sub-sisting as part of a divine providence is, however, more complex than it seems. At one level non-human nature is idealized as unambiguously provident: God provides for nature and through nature for humans. What happens, however, when in conditions of drought or severe flood ravens perish or the grasses of the field die off prematurely? Is this bad

---

divine assessment of all aspects of creation in Gen. 1, where there is no suggestion that earth or its constituents might also be 'bad'. But as Norman Habel (2000b: 47) points out, in Gen. 1 this story about the goodness of Earth, which exists before its revelation in creation, is already being subordinated to a story about humankind and its own subordination of Earth.

'nature' as opposed to the good 'nature' which receives and mediates divine providence? In the characterization of nature as unambiguously provident, what is stored in the text?

Divine Providence and Earth Limits

In general, droughts and floods are indicative of limits that are proper to nature.[7] As Garrett Hardin (1980: 66) argues, we live in a world of limits in which 'not all things are possible'. From an Earth perspective attention to the limits within which an ecosystem functions and remains healthy is a good. Movements, such as those advocating permaculture use knowledge of ecological limits to design food-growing practices that protect and renew the soil. Sharing of possessions is seen as a counter-consumerist strategy for living within Earth limits. At the same time, in contemporary Western urbanized societies, the perpetually stocked shelves of supermarkets open 24 hours a day suggest a world without limits. The produce of Earth is available to those who can afford it in seemingly limitless amounts. For some, everything is available instantly; nothing is impossible. This limitless providence has disturbing resonances in the Lukan characterization of a God for whom nothing is impossible (Lk. 1.37; 18.26).[8] When considering the interplay of divine and natural providence in Luke 12, I am suspicious, therefore, of a characterization of nature as unambiguously provident, especially in relation to a characterization of a providential God for whom nothing is impossible.

The Lukan God, for whom nothing is impossible, is the subject of an expectation that is expressed in the longing of characters such as Simeon (Lk. 2.25). Within the Lukan narrative this expectation is being realized in the person of Jesus. But this realization is characterized in ways that

7.   This is not to deny that human activity can also contribute to the impact of so-called natural events such as floods and droughts. But the fact that this can occur serves to highlight that there are 'natural' limits. When at the end of winter snow melts in the highlands of Victoria, for example, the flow of water may well flood creeks and rivers downstream. This apparent excess describes a limit to the behaviour of snow as it melts. The characterization of this as exemplifying an Earth limit does not mean that either snow or Earth need be seen as passive with respect to 'natural' limits; rather these limits describe the parameters of Earth's agency.

8.   In Luke the divine purpose is a central concern frequently expressed as a divine necessity (*dei*). This necessity describes relationship between the human and the divine as being subject to a kind of providence which differs both from Greek notions of fate and Jewish scriptural notions of divine election (see Green 1997: 22; Cosgrove 1984).

are problematic from an ecojustice perspective. In Lk. 3.3-6, the imminent 'salvation of God' is accompanied by a violent homogenization of nature:

> Every valley shall be filled,
> and every mountain and hill shall be made low (Lk. 3.5a).

In Lk. 8.22-25, the authority of Jesus over the chaos of evil is imaged as a power to rebuke the natural elements of sea, storm and wind (Lk. 8.24). In Lk. 17.5-6, if they have sufficient faith, the apostles are capable of exhibiting mastery over nature. While we should not take these instances literally, in each case elements of non-human nature serve a Lukan characterization of divine power. This power, which has resonances in the authority of Jesus and the potential authority of the apostles, is characterized with reference to aspects of nature deemed either evil or subject to mastery both human and divine.

Nevertheless the God for whom nothing is impossible is also in Luke the God who creates the possibility of a change in relationship to possessions with a potentially different relationship to Earth and Earth limits. The portraits of community in Acts 2.42-47 and 4.32-35, for example, offers an early Christian model for holding possessions in common as a shared resource. The question of possessions (*ta huparchonta*), which resonates throughout the Gospel of Luke (see esp. Lk. 14.33; 18.22; 19.8) and is connected with the motif of reversal (see esp. Lk. 1.52-53; 6.20-26; 16.19-31), frames Lk. 12.13-34 (see esp. Lk. 12.15, 33). Early in Luke 12 fear of God suggests attentiveness to a particular limit of human existence, namely death. The authority of God in relation to death (Lk. 12.5) is of a different order from the authority of the persecutor to kill the body (Lk. 12.4). In Lk. 12.8 the shift to a focus on the Lukan Jesus and the title *ho huios tou anthropou*, 'the Human One', recalls those moments throughout the Lukan Gospel where the anticipated passion, death and resurrection of the Human One is related as a divine necessity (Lk. 9.22; 17.25; 24.7; cf. 22.37 and 24.26). The threat of persecution and death for the 'friends' addressed (Lk. 12.4) is repeated here (Lk. 12.11). The theme of fear turns to one of anxiety. Worry about strategies for survival in the face of the threat of persecution forms a context for addressing anxieties about everyday survival (Lk. 12.22; see Ellis 1981: 177). Divine authority and providence in relation to these issues of survival and death will put human relationship to nature into perspective through the lens of human attitudes to possessions. From an Earth perspective, it is as if Luke asks: How does our attitude to possessions reflect our respect for Earth limits?

Luke 12.13-34 opens with a question concerning inheritance (Lk. 12.13). Earlier, in Lk. 10.25-37, a lawyer's question about inheritance (Lk.

10.25) evokes in the parable of the Good Samaritan, a narrative representation of passionate compassion.[9] This passionate doing of compassion by the other is recalled when in Lk. 18.18-30 a rich ruler approaches Jesus with the same question about inheritance: 'What must I do to inherit eternal life?' (Lk. 18.18). Here, the issue of possessions is explicit. The ruler is instructed: 'Sell all that you own and distribute the money to the poor, and you will have treasure in heaven; then come follow me' (Lk. 18.22). The invitation to follow comes after the imperative to dispossess oneself. But dispossession, here, is not for its own sake; its focus is relief for those who are already dispossessed.

When in Lk. 12.14 the Lukan Jesus refuses to answer a question about inheritance, he issues a warning against greed, which concludes, 'for one's life does not consist in abundance of possessions' (Lk. 12.15). A question is implied: if one's life (*zoe*) does not consist in abundance of possessions, in what does it consist? That is, what sustains life? Discussing this passage in the light of ancient Greek and Latin writings on greed and covetousness, Abraham Malherbe (1996: 129) quotes Dio Chrysostom's *Oration* 17: 'Nature and the gods may have given us the entire earth to enjoy, but we are not to use everything...but only such as each of us needs most.' Is this what Luke also intends?

Providing the background for a response in Lk. 12.22-34 is an exemplary tale, designated as a parable, about a rich person whose land produces abundantly (Lk. 12.16).[10] In order to store the excess produce of the land, the person determines: 'I will do this: I will pull down my barns and build larger ones, and there I will store all my grain and my goods' (Lk. 12.18). The self-directed words, 'Soul, you have many goods laid by [or stored] for many years; rest, eat, drink, rejoice' (Lk. 12.19), reflect the style of the narrator in Ecclesiastes 2 (esp. 2.1), where the speaker engages in building and planting, acquires slaves, possesses herds and flocks, and gathers treasures, amassing a great fortune (Eccl. 2.4-8). In the face of human mortality, the narrator considers even these activities that he judges wise, to be futile (Eccl. 2.3, 9, 12-23).[11] The best response for humans is to eat, to drink and to show to one's soul the good of one's labour (Eccl. 2.24). Luke deliberately echoes the reflections

---

9. For a more detailed ecological feminist reading of this passage see Elvey (2001).

10. On the designation of this parable as an example or exemplary story, see Fitzmyer (1985: 971).

11. Seow (2000) discusses the meaning of the Hebrew term, *hebel*, traditionally translated as 'vanity' in Ecclesiastes and usually rendered by the Greek, *mataiotes*, in LXX. Seow (2000: 3) argues that *hebel*, associated with air, wind, steam, dust and so on, suggests not so much vanity or futility, but that which is 'beyond mortal grasp'.

of Ecclesiastes on human mortality.[12] The rich person's words also recall Isa. 22.13b: 'Let us eat and drink, for tomorrow we die.' Indeed, in the Lukan story God addresses the rich person: 'Fool, this very night your life (*ten psuchen sou*) will be demanded of you. And the things that you have prepared, whose will they be?' (Lk. 12.20).[13]

This question, 'whose will they be?', not only emphasizes the folly of the rich person, but invites the reader to respond.[14] From an Earth perspective the reader might consider the deep resonances of the meaning of property: each thing that is considered as a possession already bears a debt to Earth to whom it owes its being. It is of Earth before it is 'mine'; and its supposed being 'mine' does not erase its prior and persistent Earth-ness. So the question 'whose will they be?' suggests the further question of my responsibility toward that which I would presume to possess and to store as property.

In Luke 12 the impending death of the rich person forms the horizon against which to consider the attitude to possessions displayed in storing the excess. As the narrative unfolds, gathering the excess into stores for personal use promises not life but death for the rich person. But where Ecclesiastes focuses on the fragility of human existence in the face of the limit that is death, Luke invites the reader to consider human life and death in the context of divine providence. For Luke the human limit of death shows up not so much the futility of any action whether wise or foolish, but the folly of the activity of the rich person. While soul (*psuche*) and body (*soma*) require material goods for survival, excess of goods, far from being necessary to the abundance of life (*zoe*), is inimical to it. The promise of imminent death to the rich person becomes an analogue of his or her storing the excess. The rich person stores death, not as part of a cycle of germination, growth, death, decomposition, germination and so on, but as an interruption to and withdrawal from that cycle.[15] Just as

12.   In fact, in Eccl. 8.15a (LXX), the verbs used, 'to eat and to drink and to rejoice', match those used in Lk. 12.19.

13.   While *psuche*, 'life or soul', has the nuance of a 'more-than' material life that might be valued above the material, the emphasis here is on physical life rather than a spiritual life thought to be in opposition to the materiality of the everyday (see Fitzmyer 1981: 788; 1985: 970, 978).

14.   I am grateful to an anonymous reader for bringing the potential resonances of the question, 'whose will they be?', to my attention.

15.   Something analogous to the rich person's storing up can be found in Martin Heidegger's (1993) notion of *Bestand* or standing-reserve. When humans treat nature as a store for their present and future use, they encounter nature as *Bestand*. *Der Bestand* which might have implied the continuing existence of nature instead signifies nature as corpse (cf. Merchant 1990).

contemporary Western patterns of overconsumption can be seen as storing death for both human and non-human others if not also ourselves, the rich person's storing the excess is a storing of death. This storing up for oneself forms a contrast in Luke to a storing of riches in relationship to God (Lk. 12.21). In this contrast Luke poses the question: what constitutes riches in relationship to God?

The words of the Lukan Jesus that follow in Lk. 12.22-34 are grounded in this contrast.[16] The attention of the disciples (and the reader) is directed toward the ravens, which are characterized as not storing up anything: they have neither storeroom (*tameion*) nor storehouse (*apotheke*). The disciples are likewise to eschew such storing and to seek instead God's *basileia* (Lk. 12.31-32).[17] For Luke *he basileia tou theou*, traditionally translated as 'the kingdom of God' but also as the rule or reign, commonwealth or kindom of God, is a divine gift. The *basileia* is a present reality, characteristic of the Lukan today and evident in the community around Jesus, but it is also the content of an expected future. In both present and future aspects it is marked by the hospitality of God.[18] In seeking and receiving the divine hospitality of the *basileia*, the disciples must respond appropriately. Their commitment to receiving God's providence on a daily basis (cf. Lk. 11.3) will be tested. Commanded to sell their 'possessions and give alms' (Lk. 12.33), they must dispossess themselves of what they have stored as property. Like the rich ruler in Lk. 18.22, they are assured that such dispossession will produce a different kind of store: they will find treasure (*thesauron*) in heaven (Lk. 12.33).[19] The promise of 'treasure in heaven', suggestive for Luke of an inner disposition, namely what is stored in the heart (cf. Lk. 12.34), returns the reader to the question of what constitutes riches in relationship to God. That is, in relationship to God, what is one storing up? From the perspective of Earth, the question is not only what am I storing up for Earth and its

16. Jesus' words in Lk. 12.22 begin with *Dia touto*: 'Because of this' or 'For this reason'. The speech of the Lukan Jesus is here directly related to the question of storing up for oneself and the contrasting issue of what constitutes riches in relationship to God.

17. I prefer to leave the term *basileia* in its Greek form rather than translate it. There are problems with the traditional language of kingdom which reinscribes the kind of hierarchy I am critiquing here. To use terms such as 'kindom' or 'commonwealth' tends to hide the problem completely. But it needs to be noted that the notion of the '*basileia* as gift' creates an opening in the text for upsetting a hierarchical logic.

18. On the hospitality of God as a significant theme in the Gospel of Luke, see Byrne (2000).

19. But, as in Lk. 18.22, such dispossession is directed toward the claims of the human other who has already been dispossessed.

constituents in my attitude to possessions, but also what is stored in the text: life or death, toxin or compost?

Divine Providence and the Overvaluation of the Human

In the text of Luke 12, the characterization of divine providence rests on an overvaluation of the human with respect to the other-than-human which is at odds with a sense of the intrinsic worth of Earth. There are three instances where humans are represented as of more value than other-than-human nature (Lk. 12.7, 24, 28). Each occurs within the context of human responses to concerns about survival. The first instance, where the verb *phobeomai*, 'to fear or be afraid', occurs five times (Lk. 12.4-7), seems to be informed by the context of waves of persecution of the early Christians. Fear occurs in relation to death; addressed as 'friends', Jesus' disciples and also the early hearers or readers of the text are admonished not to fear the one whose only power is to kill the body (Lk. 12.4, cf. 12.11). A second type of fear is recommended, namely fear of the one who has authority after killing to consign one to Gehenna (Lk. 12.5).[20] The one who has authority to enact such judgment after death is not Satan but God. The fear then to be cultivated is not fear of death nor of persecution leading to death, but fear of God.

In the biblical Wisdom tradition, fear is 'the beginning of knowledge' (Prov. 1.7) and 'the root of wisdom' (Sir. 1.20). Such fear is a deep respect or awe of the divine other, set here in the context of a divine remembering of and concern for creatures such as sparrows (Lk. 12.6) and of the detailed knowledge the divine has of the human (Lk. 12.7a).[21] The affirmation of divine concern for sparrows, however, does not wholly mitigate their description here in economic terms (Lk. 12.6). Judith Lieu (1997: 99) makes the point: 'Perhaps it is particularly as disciples and not just as members of the human race that Jesus can affirm their greater *worth*, known to God in each personal detail.' But the characterization of relationship between the divine and the human disciple rests on a comparison between humans (does it matter that they are also disciples?) and sparrows, which inscribes a superiority of the former over the latter (see Fitzmyer 1985: 960). While this comparison occurs within

20.   Gehenna was a place that had historical links with sacrifice and fire. It was an unclean place, a rubbish dump, which then 'came to be associated with the fiery judgment of eschatological punishment' (Green 1997: 482).

21.   Emmanuel Levinas (1998: 149) reads the Hebrew biblical tradition such that fear of God is defined by the ethical injunctions of care for the other; in this way 'fear of God' becomes 'fear *for* another'.

the rhetorical style of the Hebrew *qal wachomer*, 'and how much more so', such that divine attentiveness to humans parallels rather than supplants divine attentiveness to sparrows, the effect is to suggest a hierarchy which privileges the human.

In Lk. 12.22-31 a pattern of human anxieties about everyday survival contrasted with an assurance of divine providence is established on the basis of such a hierarchy.

Human Anxiety	Divine Providence	Valuation
v. 22		v. 23: 'life is more than food, the body is more than clothing'
	v. 24a: God feeds ravens	v. 24b: 'Of how much more value are you than the birds!'
vv. 25-26	vv. 27-28a: God clothes the lilies	v. 28b: 'how much more so will he clothe you...'
vv. 29-30a	vv. 30b-31	

According to this pattern, the comparison, in which life and the body are more than food and clothing respectively, is carried over into a comparison between the human hearers and the fauna and flora of the earth. As earlier, in Luke 12, the disciples may be the implied addressees within the narrative.[22] Their intimacy with the Lukan Jesus should distinguish their relationships to other-than-human nature from those of 'the nations of the world' (Lk. 12.30). But their relationships to other-than-human nature are already infected by the relative devaluation of the flora and fauna in Lk. 12.24, 28.

This devaluation also infects the description of divine attentiveness that is a key point of the passage. The disciples are invited to share a similar attentiveness when they are commanded to consider, observe carefully, or contemplate (*katanoesate*) other-than-human nature to learn of God's attentiveness (Lk. 12.24, 27). When considered in conjunction with Lk. 12.4-7, these verses imply that the hearer is to hold in awe the one with the capacity for such attentiveness. Divine attentiveness ensures that the disciples need not fear refusal when they seek the *basileia* (Lk. 12.31). The gift of the *basileia* is based in but not limited to divine attentiveness to human material or vital needs (see Lk. 12.31-32).[23]

22. Here, the appellation 'little flock' (Lk. 12.32) echoes the affection of the earlier vocation, 'my friends' (Lk. 12.4).

23. The use of the aorist *eudokesen*, 'has been pleased', emphasizes the *already* and perhaps also the interruption of the gift of the *basileia*, in the context of which God will attend to the disciples' material needs as well (Lk. 12.31-32). This verb also recalls the proclamation of peace on earth 'among those whom God favours' (*en anthropois*

At the same time, the force of Lk. 12.22-32 is to subordinate these vital human needs to a desire for the *basileia*. This subordination tends to devalue the body in a way that reflects the devaluation of the other-than-human with respect to the human.[24]

This divine attentiveness is moreover an assurance of a paternal care (Lk. 12.32) that is ambiguous. On the one hand this paternal care is expressed in a divine providence made explicit in Lk. 12.22-31 and dependent on the providence of Earth not only to humans but also to sparrows, ravens and lilies. This Earth providence is at best implicit in Luke 12. Further, as Turid Seim (1994: 73-74) suggests, the providence of non-human nature is in effect mediated to Jesus and the (male) disciples of the narrative, as well as to the ministers of the Lukan community, through the labour and providence of women such as those described in Lk. 8.3. The mediation of nature through the labour of women (and I would add slaves) is forgotten in the text of Luke 12. At the same time, the *agency* of Earth in the provision of human life and sustenance is backgrounded. On the other hand Lk. 12.22-32 offers a model of the paternal based on divine attentiveness to the vital needs of others, both human and other-than-human.[25] In the wider narrative of Luke–Acts, this concern for human vital needs is set within the context of an early Christian community where property is held in common and no one is in need (see Acts 2.42-47; 4.32-35). Providence is therefore characteristic of community. But supporting this communal ideal is a general forgetting of the provisioning labour of women and slaves and of the agency of a provident Earth.[26] This forgetting continues to reflect a hierarchical logic in which the privileging of the paternal stands beside an overvaluing of humans with respect to other-than-human nature. The suggestion of a hierarchy, which privileges human over other-than-human Earth constituents, however subtle, undermines the assertion of a valuation that resists such hierarchies. Moreover, the privileging of humans over other

eudokias; Lk. 2.14). Both attentiveness to material needs and the promise of peace suggest a kind of earthly flourishing. Chris Cuomo (1998: 62-80) suggests that an ethic of flourishing might describe the goal of an ecological feminism.

24.   There is already a hint of this devaluation of the body in the reference to the persecutor's power to destroy the body and the privileging of a divine authority beyond death (Lk. 12.4-5).

25.   This fatherly providence has, moreover, an association with the maternal. In Lk. 12.24 the divine activity of feeding the ravens is described by the verb *trepho*, which is used in Lk. 23.39 to describe a woman breastfeeding her child.

26.   Even the Lukan emphasis on receiving hospitality, e.g. in Lk. 10.7, tends to elide the material conditions for that hospitality, namely the transformation and consumption of Earth products and the provisioning labour of women and slaves.

animals and plants is one element of a system of hierarchical dualism which has affinities with patriarchy and in which Val Plumwood (1993: 41-59) has rightly identified a logic of human colonization of nature.

Conclusion

In the Lukan narrative, where both Earth and heaven are figured as treasuries, the most common understanding of 'treasury' is that of a storehouse for grain and goods; that is, a storage area for provisions. The metaphor of the treasury is directly connected with divine providence, whether that be concerning provision of vital material needs to non-humans and humans or of the *basileia*, which could itself be understood as given in response to a certain vital need. Likewise, the critique of the rich person's storing of the excess, the motif of dispossession in favour of the already dispossessed other, the model of divine attentiveness to other-than-human nature, and the challenge to participate in this atten-tiveness, are textual motifs that promise much for an ecotheology.

But the storing of the rich person, which is in effect a storing of death not as compost but as toxin, stands also as a metaphor for a storing of death in the text. This occurs in a particular way through an over-valuation of the human with respect to other-than-human nature. We cannot claim the ecotheological benefits of the text without also taking into account the textual violence that supports these. When it inter-weaves a motif of divine and human attentiveness toward other-than-human nature with a preference for the human, the text is ambiguous in such a way as to support an anthropocentrism that is at odds with the pressing need to be reoriented to an Earth of which we are already one of many interconnected parts.

Reconnecting with the Waters: John 9.1-11

Oyeronke Olajubu

Introduction

The connection of religion and water dates back to the beginning of human life. Water is first a significant element of the universal order. Wherever they are found, waters are often bound up with divine powers (Rudhardt 1987: 351). Water, in all religious traditions—from the most ancient to the most contemporary, in Indigenous and the world-famous religions—has been noted to transcend its scientific explanations. Its primordial significance is of no less value than its present sacred quality (Eliade 1958: 188). Most disciplines—theology, cultural anthropology, and history of religions alike—conceive water as a sacred element and as a symbol of cosmic harmony. Its primordial existence is entrenched in most religious mythologies as it affects nature and human life.

Across cultures, human reactions to water stem more often than not from its utilitarian benefits rather than its intrinsic worth. The biblical tradition is no exception to this, as water has been presented as an avenue for political encounters (Red Sea and River Jordan) and sites of healing (Pool of Bethseda, Pool of Siloam and River Jordan). Some references to water's intrinsic worth are also discernible in biblical texts.

Although Jesus' use and recognition of water as a healing element derives more often than not from his authority embodied in the spoken word and not from the essential qualities of the water bodies involved, there are some instances where a different understanding of water is implicit in the text. John 9.1-11 is an example of a passage where Jesus' use of water in a healing miracle is fused with his personality as the 'living water' and thus suggests a recognition of the intrinsic worth of water: water is an integral element of all living things on Earth.

In this paper, I will attempt an interrogation of Jn 9.1-11, using the Yoruba cosmic perception of water. In this quest, I will also use two Earth Bible Project principles: the principles of intrinsic worth and inter-connectedness. My choice of the text of Jn 9.1-11 rather than John 4 is underscored by the different representations of water discernible in Jn 9.1-11. The passage provides examples of water in literal and symbolic forms: as a pool and spittle as well as a metaphor for Jesus, who is depicted as being 'living water' in this text. As we shall see shortly, multiple ways of perceiving water are also integral to the Yoruba world view.

Crucial to my investigation of Jn 9.1-11 is the Yoruba perception of water: the Yoruba not only validate the intrinsic worth of water but also recognize water as a significant part of a whole design where the prevailing principle is interdependency as opposed to hierarchy and/or custodianship. This motif has been grasped by practitioners of Christianity in Africa and is manifest in what is now known as African Christianity.

Interrogating Jn 9.1-11 from the Yoruba perspective raises questions that invite reflection in relation to the Earth Bible Project's ecojustice readings of the Christian Scriptures. Do Jesus' use of water as spittle and instructions to wash in the pool of Siloam reinforce or deny the intrinsic worth of water? Is the recognition of water's intrinsic worth exclusive to its utilitarian value, or could the two perceptions coexist and at the same time uphold positive ecojustice principles?

Water in Yoruba Cosmic Experience

The contemporary Yoruba people are located in south-western Nigeria and parts of the Benin Republic, but the Yoruba belief system extends beyond these boundaries. Yoruba religion is practised in Yoruba land and other parts of Africa, in Brazil and Cuba, and in the United States of America. The Yoruba thought system is pervasively religious since no aspect of people's lives is outside the spectrum of religion. In the Yoruba perception of the world, nature is interlocked with the supernatural realm and humans are dependent on both.

The Yoruba ascribe primal existence to water: water existed before anything else. Hence the cosmological accounts in Yoruba mythology begin with waters covering Earth. This primordial character of water also informs the agency of some gods and goddesses in the Yoruba pantheon, who derive their functions and sanctity from water.[1] The Yoruba stance on the intrinsic worth of water is thus rooted in the primordial qualities of water. Ritual prescriptions and taboo safeguard this intrinsic quality of water for the Yoruba people: water in its many manifestations is revered and its sanctity guarded by ritual regulations and taboos, proverbs, and sometimes through worship practices.[2]

1.   One of such deities is Obatala, the Yoruba arch-divinity who is in charge of molding human physical figures, a job for which he needs water. Water is also used to effect healing and to give children to the barren in his cult.

2.   These include stipulations barring people from fishing in some waters; farming is prohibited in landscape surrounding these sacred waters.

The Yoruba interact with water in different ways because water is symbolized in a variety of contexts among the Yoruba: mythical, mystical, natural, metaphorical. The mythical aspects of water may be perceived in Yoruba cosmological accounts where water preceded everything else. Mystically, water is regarded as the abode of spirit beings especially goddesses; at the same time, water as a natural element satisfies human domestic needs. The liquid contents of some plants and fruits, such as coconuts and oranges, have additional metaphorical connotations because of their water-like qualities. In some situations, these liquids are employed for ritual and medicinal purposes (Ogungbile 1997: 21). Manifestations of water include rivers, streams, rain, spittle, flood, teardrops and dew. To the Yoruba, water is a basic element on which all life depends. No life could survive without water as is apparent in this section from the wisdom corpus of Ifa:

> *A se gbere w'aye*
> *Omi lo maa gbaa*
> *Arinrin gbere lo s'ode orun*
> *Omi lo maa gba*
> *Omi l'abuwe*
> *Omi l'abu mu*
> *Enikan ki i b'omi s'ota*

> The one who comes to the world
> Will be received by water
> The one who slowly goes back to heaven
> Will be received by water
> It is water that we bath with
> It is water that we drink
> No one makes enmity with water.[3]

Water is one of the three prime elements by which humans are sustained and the Yoruba assume it therefore has intrinsic as well as utilitarian worth.

Among the Yoruba, healing is an inherent value of water. This is especially true of waters that are attributed to goddesses. Curative and preventive healing in addition to regeneration are the inherent properties of such waters. This essential quality of water informs its use for healing purposes. This also underscores its use for healing purposes in some religious groups in African religion and in African Christianity. An example of such a religious group among the Yoruba is the group associated with the Osun Osogbo goddess, personified as the Osun

---

3. Interview with Iyanifa (Ifa Priestess) Doyin Faniyi at her residence: Osogbo, Osun State, Nigeria, 20 September 1999.

River. Her waters, according to the Yoruba belief system, are imbued with therapeutic qualities, and bestow health, and children, to barren women. Her waters are sacred and their properties are ritually preserved and guarded daily, as well as being protected through prescribed weekly, monthly and annual worship practices. The healing qualities of the waters of the Osun River are predicated on the intrinsic worth of water rather than its utilitarian value—though at the same time the Yoruba do not deny its use in medicinal preparations. The goddess Osun Osogbo's *oriki* (praise poem) reflects the intrinsic healing qualities of her waters:

> Her eyes sparkle in the forest,
> Like the sun on the river
> She is the wisdom of the forest
> She is the wisdom of the river.
> Where the doctor failed
> She cures with fresh water.
> Where medicine is impotent
> She cures with cool water (Beier 1980: xiii).

The use of water is a prevalent feature of postnatal care among the Yoruba—for the mother as well as for the child. Hot water is often preferred for these purposes due to the conviction that it soothes and relieves tense muscles in the body. Hence newborn children are usually cleansed with warm water to make their bones strong. The mother's body is also cleansed with hot water (*jo ara*) to enable blood to flow freely within and from her body.

Conversely however, there is a group of individuals in Yoruba land on whom hot water may not be used, and who may not consume hot foods, in many cases, from their childhood to their old age. This is known as the cold-water practice, and is another example of Yoruba beliefs about water. Known as the *Olomitutu* ('cold water') postnatal care practice among the Yoruba, this practice gives a prominent and exclusive place to the use of water. *Olomitutu* underscores the Yoruba appreciation for water's intrinsic qualities. During the first week of the birth of a new child it is customary among the Yoruba for elders of the family to find out the identity of the new child. The process, done through the aid of Ifa divination, is known as *Mimo Ori Omo* or *Mimo Esendaye Omo* (knowing the 'head being' of the child or knowing the way the child comes to the world). This process would reveal, among other things, which of the prominent deceased members (heroes/heroines) of the family has reincarnated in the child (this is described among the Yoruba as *Ta ni o ya a*) and returned to the world through the newborn baby. It is believed and fervently prayed that, after death, valiant men and women should reincarnate in the form of new children. Such children are automatically believed to inherit all the attributes — including habits, dos, don'ts — of the persons of whom they are reincarnations.[4] The *Mimo Ori Omo* or *Mimo Esendaye Omo* process would also reveal details of how the child should be nurtured, particularly during infancy. For instance, the consultation would confirm whether hot water should be used on the child or not. If the divination forbids the use of hot water for the child, the child becomes an *Olomitutu* (i.e. a 'cold-water child'). This means that no hot water is required for the child's bath and the child may not be fed with hot food and drink. Many *Olomitutu* never eat hot foods or drinks and never wash with hot water throughout their lifetime.

It is also a taboo for an *Olomitutu* child to take any medicine when sick. Whatever illness may afflict these children, they should only be treated with cold water. Furthermore, the mother of the child procures a small water pot with a firm lid known as an *oru*, and a small calabash (cup). Every morning, at dawn, before any other woman gets to the stream or river to fetch drinking water and water for other needs in the family, the mother of the *Olomitutu* child will carry the *oru* on her head and make for the stream. On her way to and from the stream, she will not talk to any one or respond to any greeting; however, she sings the praises of the river deity throughout the journey to collect the water:

> *Baba Omo akaaki agbo o*
> *Agbo kori o gbo*
> *Agbo kara o le o*
> *Agbo jedi inu*
> *Agbo jedi o ode*
> *Baba Omo mi lo ni*
> *N ma b'elewe sere*
> *Baba Omo mi, lo ni*
> *N ma ma b'elegbo igi sore*
> *Elegbo igi subu loja*
> *Mo berin si*
> *Baba Omo mi t'okunrin*

The father of my child maker of complete infusion
Infusion[5] that makes the head strong
Infusion that makes one well
Infusion for haemorrhoids

---

4.   Names given to reincarnated heroes and heroines include Babatunde ('father has come again'), Iyabode ('mother went away but is here again'), and Yeyejide ('mother has woken up again').

5.   These infusions (*agbo*) are known for their efficacy in curing different types of illnesses. They are usually made up of herbs (*ewe*) and roots (*gbongbo*).

Infusion for piles
It is my child's father who said
I should not play with retailer of herbs
It is my child's father who said
I should not befriend retailer of roots
A peddler of roots fell down at the market place
I burst into laughter
My child's father is indeed a man
My child's father is indeed a man.

On getting to the stream, she identifies the part of the stream where the water is clearest and cleanest — usually close to the source. It is from here she gets the water for her *Olomitutu* child. She does not dip the pot into the river as normally done by other women. She uses the little calabash (*aha*) to collect the water and pour it from the cup into the pot. She examines critically each cupful of water to make sure that it is perfectly clean before pouring the water into the pot. It is a very slow and painstaking process. She should not be in any hurry. As she is fetching the water she continues to recite the lyrics. When the pot is full, she will cover it, put the pot on her head and head for home, singing all the time and making sure she does not talk to any one. Should anybody meet her at the stream such a person should wait for her to finish. No one should approach the stream while she is there.

On reaching home she sets the pot in the corner of her room away from the reach of anyone. She will use this water to bathe the baby, and it is this water the baby drinks. If the baby is sick it is the water from the stream that serves as the only medicine. Many *Olomitutu* children carry the practice throughout life, abstaining from any drug or medication, and never using hot water for any thing. The *Olomitutu* practice was common among the Ijesa and Igbomina people of Yoruba land in western Nigeria until about 1950. Names like Olubu, and Lomi were generic names for children who are nurtured under this practice.[6] Other examples include Omisade ('water is my crown'), Omifunmi ('water gave me'), Omigbodun ('water advocates my cause').

This Yoruba conviction of water's intrinsic worth is translocated into African Christianity. An example of this is the place of water in the healing activities of the Christ Apostolic Church in Nigeria and abroad. Water is regarded as possessing essential healing qualities, which could eliminate any disease or misfortune. Apostle Babalola, the founder of the Christ Apostolic Church, emphasized the fact that God gave him water to effect healing of all kinds for his followers. To date, this practice is a

---

6.   Interview with Professor Oludare Olajubu, a retired Professor of Yoruba Studies, University of Ilorin, Nigeria, on 8 September 2000.

significant aspect of the church's doctrinal stance on healing as people attend services with containers filled with water that is taken home after the worship service and used for various healing and restorative purposes. In fact, in some of these churches, members are discouraged from using any type of drug (both Western and traditional) for healing but to depend on the essential healing qualities of water.

The Yoruba do not, however, deny the utilitarian qualities of water. Water is valued for its social as well as ritual use. It is employed for domestic purposes and as a symbol in ritual activities. The use of water is a prevalent feature of an individual's life — from birth, through initiation to death.[7] This practical use of water is, however, predicated on the Yoruba perception of water as an element with intrinsic worth. The intrinsic and utilitarian values of water thus fuse in the Yoruba experience.

The Yoruba need to protect water from contamination and pollution is informed by their perception of water as being sacred and imbued with 'power'. This is described in proverbs, rituals and socio-religious activities. This may also have informed the establishment of groves where fauna and floral should remain intact (Ilesanmi 1996: 158). The people's dependence on waters around them for drinking and other domestic purposes contributed to the imperative to preserve nearby water sources. Despite the introduction of pipe-borne water systems, however, this awareness of water's sacredness and its intrinsic worth persists among the Yoruba and is underlined and ensured by ritual parameters put in place to ensure its cleanliness and purity. This underscores the fact that the Yoruba perception of water is embedded in the people's notion of the partnership between humans and nature as an interdependent relationship.

The Text: John 9.1-11

The central motif of John 9 is healing. In reading this healing narrative from a Yoruba perspective I will focus specifically on three agents of healing evident in the text: the person of Jesus, the saliva-mud formula and water.

The significance of the person of Jesus is linked to one of the symbol systems employed by the author of the Gospel of John. According to

---

7.   Water is used for bathing and naming ceremonies for newborn babes because it symbolizes resilience among the Yoruba. It is used for washing the feet of a new bride before she is admitted into her marital home; this signifies the new beginning for her and the marital family. In addition, corpses are ritually cleansed with water before burial to ensure a smooth journey to the abode of the ancestors.

Koester (1995: 4), the Gospel of John employs a fundamental symbolic structure that refers to Christ as a primary level of meaning and discipleship as a secondary level. In Jn 9.1-11, for example, Jesus is portrayed as the 'light of the world', which explains why he restored the sight of the man born blind. On the primary level, the miracle of sight is christological; on the secondary level, however, the miracle is about discipleship, and this chapter explores what it means to 'see the light' physically and through the eyes of faith (Koester 1995: 4).

Similarly, like the other images in the Gospel, water can also be understood christologically. Jesus describes himself as the 'living water' in Jn 4.10, but also instructs the man born blind to wash in the pool of Siloam and only then does the man receive his sight. Worthy of note, however, is the meaning of Siloam, which is revealed later in the Gospel: Siloam means 'sent' (Jn 9.6). The author of John apparently supplies information about the meaning of Siloam to enable his readers to connect the pool with Jesus, the prophet and Messiah 'sent' from God (Koester 1995: 180). We are presented, it seems, in this 'restoring of sight' miracle in John 9 with a fused portrait of Jesus as the 'living water' and the one 'sent' (represented by the pool of Siloam; Towns 1990: 20).

This symbolic dimension points to Jesus as the agent of the healing. The story, however, incorporates two other significant agents that need to be considered—the saliva-mud formula and the water itself. The importance of these two elements becomes apparent when we recognize that the healing does not take place through a simple word from Jesus. Jesus does not declare the man healed. On this occasion, Jesus first anoints the eyes and then directs the man to wash in a pool. The use of the saliva-mud formula points to Jesus as a typical folk healer, as is apparent from the work of Malina and Rohrbaugh (1998: 175).

Malina and Rohrbaugh (1998: 175) identify three overlapping systems of healing and health in antiquity: the professional, trained and socially credited healer who approaches sickness philosophically and propagates theories to explicate symptoms; the popular healer who perceives healing as embracing the individual, the family and all social networks in the community, and prioritizes the entrenchment of health and its maintenance above the healing of sicknesses; and folk healers who possess the ability to restore people to health. As a folk healer, Jesus heals by command—sometimes by touching his patients, sometimes at a distance (Jn 9.6; 5.8; 4.50). As is true of folk healers generally, Jesus' interactions with his patients are suggestive of possible familiarity. Moreover, Jesus' use of saliva in the process of healing the man born blind (Jn 9.1-11) may indicate a subscription to the belief in antiquity that saliva may protect from the evil eye (Malina and Rohrbaugh 1998: 170).

Priests and priestesses in Yoruba religion as well as in African Christianity do prescribe similar formulae for healing purposes. Sometimes eggs are smashed against stones to signify the defeat of the enemy; and prayers may focus on the water in a coconut, because of its connotations of invincibility. Just as no one can explain how water got into the coconut, so no one would be able to harm the supplicant for whom this prayer is said. Such prayer sessions often end with a ritual bath in a flowing river to effect physical and spiritual cleansing and regeneration.

Jesus' use of mud and saliva in this Johannine passage has been interpreted in various ways by scholars. The mixing of mud and spittle is listed as one of the forbidden tasks on the Sabbath and thus Jesus could have been challenging the authority of the traditions of Judaism. Also, Jesus' action could be a reminder to humans that they originally came from the dust and to the dust they will return. The spittle-mud formula links the healing to the life juices of Jesus the folk healer and to Earth, the very stuff of which humans are made.

Given the person of Jesus the healer and the use of spittle and mud as agents of healing, it is striking that a third element — water — should be introduced. The man is not healed by the initial words and actions of Jesus. The man is only healed when he bathes in the water. This suggests that the water is the final — and perhaps key — agent of healing in this John 9 narrative. Clearly water here has value as a healing agent; the pool of Siloam is not just a bathing pool but also a healing pool. The healing is not complete without the water. The instruction of Jesus and bathing in the water may be complementary acts, but water remains integral to the act of healing. The intrinsic worth of water, it seems, is affirmed in this healing narrative.

The intrinsic worth of water especially as pertaining to healing is a theme replete in Yoruba religious consciousness as is displayed in the Indigenous and Christian traditions. In addition, this same fusion would point to another way of viewing the principle of interconnectedness. Not only are all the living components of the web of creation interconnected; this passage suggests an interconnection between the natural (water, spittle, mud) and the spiritual (Jesus, word, presence) in the healing process.

When placed within the literary context of Johannine writings, this passage reinforces Jesus' position as the Son of God in whom and from whom all things were made and fulfilled (Jn 1.3). Jesus is presented as the light of the world, a stance that negates darkness and by implication blindness. In John 9, however, Jesus is also portrayed as connecting himself as the light and the water of life with the very stuff of life — with mud and water themselves.[8] In so doing, he is affirming the worth of these components of creation.

The implications of the miracle of restored sight in Jn 9.1-11 are manifold. One, the prominent place occupied by healing in Jesus' ministry fulfils the central aim of his life on Earth. Healing is the confirmatory aspect of the three activities that make up Jesus' earthly ministry and through which his role as the anointed and promised one is entrenched. Also, healing glorifies God (which was Jesus' main concern) and replaces the kingdom of darkness (manifest in diseases, drought and hunger) with the kingdom of light (exemplified in healing and restoration). Moreover, though Jesus used other methods for his healing miracles, his use and prescription of water for healing suggest that he recognized water as a genuine healing force. Further, Jesus' status as the 'living water' substantiates his recognition of water as an element of healing (Jn 4.7-13). Further, embedded in this healing event is the notion of an intertwined link between humans and nature: both are a part of a whole and both are involved in the healing process. Clearly, the role of water in this narrative is not confined to its daily utilitarian functions; water in John 9 also has an intrinsic value.

Water in Contemporary Times

Appraising water and its importance in contemporary times, using the lenses of religion, presents us with a disturbing picture. In the past, human beings' relations with water were marked by reverence; water's inherent value as spiritual and restorative was apparent in people's conduct. Water's utilitarian values did not obstruct the people's view of its intrinsic essential qualities.

Moreover, as water was considered crucial to survival, its preservation and cleanliness were of primary concern to everyone in the society. Expressions of the intrinsic value of water are apparent across cultures, in religious activities including ritual practices, ceremonies, festivals and a variety of regulations relating to the use of water. The actions and reactions of people towards water demonstrate a conscious sense of responsibility that was underlined in a variety of ways. Reasons for this responsible attitude towards water may range from the fear for survival to the need to preserve water because of its sacredness. On the whole, however, these practices also suggest a more general awareness of the need to guard and maintain nature.

8.   See Gen. 2.7, 19; water is implicit in the process of forming of humans and other living things from the ground/*adamah*.

The advent of the Industrial Age, and its ramifications for the whole Earth community, significantly altered this perception of the essential interconnectedness between humans, nature and the divine. Industrialization opened the way to pollution. The lead content of much industrial waste is now the main source of water contamination. Water is contaminated by pipeline leakages, asphalt and chemical plants, mining and toxic spills. Effects of water pollution may be immediate, as in the death of fishes when oil is spilled in the ocean; or remote, as is the case when chemicals are washed into rivers and streams. The example of Minamata Bay, Japan, seems apposite here. In the 1950s and 1960s, many people living near the Minamata Bay developed nervous disorders, tremors and paralysis. The mysterious epidemic claimed four hundred lives before the cause was discovered: a local industry was releasing mercury into Minamata Bay.

Since the early 1970s there has been a worldwide focus on combating water pollution but the overall success of the attempts remains largely controversial. This is understandable since the world's population is on the increase. The import of this has been an increase in the overall demand for water for domestic, industrial and agricultural purposes. For instance, between 1940 and 1990, withdrawals of fresh water from rivers, lakes, reservoirs and other sources have increased fourfold. The demand for fresh water rises continually as the world's population increases. The situation is compounded by the contamination of ground water by the wastes of primarily human activities, especially in developing countries.[9]

The contemporary situation in relation to the limited availability of water suitable for use by all members of Earth community is a consequence of a human attitude to water particularly, and for the ecosystems and Earth community generally. I would argue that this attitude stems from a utilitarian perception in which the prominent concern relates to how water is useful to humans, and what benefits they can gain from it. If water were regarded as an Earth element with intrinsic worth, people worldwide would demonstrate a more 'care-full' attitude towards it. They would put in place practices that would ensure its ongoing purity, and prevent its flagrant contamination and abuse.

The need to reverse the present situation is underscored by the Earth Bible principle of interconnectedness. Due to the complex relationships between many types of organisms and ecosystems, any type of environmental contamination may have far-reaching consequences that are not immediately obvious or that are difficult to predict. All members of

9.   See the Ground Water website for more Information: www.danpatch.ecn. purdue.edu/~epados/ground/src/sources.htm.

Earth community are ultimately interconnected, intertwined in a variety of ways, some of which are complex and hard to discern in the short-term. As a consequence, ultimately all members of Earth community are affected, often adversely, when any part of the ecosystem is violated and degraded.

Applying the Yoruba Model

The prevailing principle in Yoruba cosmic experience is that of inter-dependency and complementary relations between humans, between humans and nature, and between humans and the supernatural and divine forces. This prevailing principle entails complementary connec-tions, a concept that Jn 9.1-11 presents as being significant for under-standing Jesus' healing miracles. This Yoruba conception of human-nature–divine interconnectedness is reflected in their respect for every part of nature. Every aspect of Earth is crucial to the whole design of Earth community in their world view. For the Yoruba people the prin-ciple of intrinsic worth is inextricable from the principle of intercon-nectedness in the exploration of any ecosystem. This underlying philosophy is apparent in Yoruba people's sense of responsibility in relation to water; humans are not dominant, they are not in a 'higher than thou' posture in relation to water. Rather, there is a mutual inter-connection that reflects their understanding of nature's interdependence with humans. In this investigation of Jn 9.1-11 through a Yoruba lens, my conclusion is that contemporary societies in both developed and developing countries would do well to emulate this philosophical stance. Worthy of mention is the fact that the situation in relation to the availability of water in cities and urban centres in Yoruba lands is not different from that in other urban centres worldwide. My argument therefore rests on the importance of the way water is valued intrinsic-ally, and that industrialization has affected the attitude of people towards water even in indigenous communities where, in the past, because the people respected water's intrinsic sacredness and healing powers, they guarded and restored its purity through religious practices and rituals that had implications for the way water was used every day.

Efforts at arresting water pollution could incorporate an awareness of the intrinsic value of water, and argue for its essential role as one of the elements in a complex multifaceted design, in which humans constitute merely one part among a multitude of others. Biblical scholars' inter-pretations of water passages will need to be cognizant of this shift in order to be part of the development of a balanced and responsible global eco-consciousness. The development of this changed consciousness has

implications for individual Christians as well as the individual ecclesiastical bodies as members of a global community of Christian believers.

The eco-friendly credentials of other passages of the Bible will also need
to be examined in order to achieve a holistic re-evaluation of the matrices
available for Christian interpretations of the Christian Scriptures.

John 9.1-11 interpreted from a Yoruba ecoperspective will connect the
healing of the blind man through his washing in the pool of Siloam with
the belief that Jesus is the 'living water'. Connected with the words of
Jesus, the man's healing is a result of his washing himself in the pool of
Siloam and the touch of Jesus' spittle mixed with earth, and the authority
and touch of Jesus as the 'living water' and the 'sent one'. This connection is replicated in an African Christian ritual where prayers in the
name of Jesus are said into water to be used for healing. Here, too, the
authority of Jesus as the 'living water' is combined with the intrinsic
qualities of water to achieve healing.

It could be argued, therefore, that in this narrative, healing could be
construed as deriving also from the intrinsic worth of water.

The pragmatic experiment of appropriating Yoruba perceptions
relating to the intrinsic value of water by African Independent Churches
of Nigerian origin is a profitable place to begin an assessment of the
effectiveness of this appropriation. Popularly referred to as *Omi Iye*
(meaning 'water of life') in these churches,[10] water is employed for
healing purposes. Some of these churches, for example the Celestial
Church of Christ and the Cherubim and Seraphim Church, also recommend ritual baths in flowing rivers, which is believed to remove both
seen or unseen impediments to the well-being of the individual.

My intention in this paper is not to dislodge the centrality of Johannine
Christology, but to reinforce it with the Yoruba cosmic perception of
water as sacred and regenerating; because of these attributes, water
possesses intrinsic worth. This connection is strengthened with the symbolic presentation of Jesus as the living water in the Gospel of John.

Jesus' use of spittle and mud can also be readily accommodated as
both elements, and the process of kneading them together, are familiar
from events detailed in Yoruba cosmogony, notably the moulding of
human bodies by the arch-divinity, Orishanla. Moreover, as Jesus is male
and Earth elements are understood in many traditions to be female,
Yoruba beliefs in gender complementary relations are also reinforced by
Jesus' actions of mixing fluid from himself with soil from Earth in
performing this miracle.

---

10.   Examples of waters used in these rituals include water from the River Aayo,
located at Oke Oye, Ilesa, Osun State, and the River Oni, at Efon-Alaye, Ekiti State.

Conclusion

In this paper I have attempted to interrogate the way water is presented in Jn 9.1-11 with Yoruba beliefs about water. I focused on two Earth Bible Project ecojustice principles: the principles of intrinsic worth and interconnectedness. My interrogation revealed a fusion of the physical and symbolic representations of water in this Johannine passage, which in turn underlines water's intrinsic worth to the writer of the narrative, or to Jesus as the person who demonstrates that water has an integral role in making the man able to see. This paper therefore concludes that entrenching a philosophy that elevates water's intrinsic worth and the interconnectedness of water with other elements of nature, humans and the divine, is an important step in the successful implementation of global strategies to preserve water's purity, and protect it from con-tamination. Integrating a philosophy that focuses on water as valuable in and of itself would result in more responsible stance towards water that recognizes it is a component of the design of Earth. It would also result in more sensitivity to the implications of the interdependency in Earth community, a network of complex relationships in which humans are only one part of the whole.

A Footstool or a Throne?
Luke's Attitude to Earth (*ge*) in Acts 7

Michael Trainor

Introduction

In a previous essay in this series I examined the text of Lk. 2.14: 'Glory/ among the highest to God/And upon Earth peace/among human beings/of good will' (Trainor 2000: 174-92). I was primarily attracted to this text because it has been a centrepiece of reflection for generations of Christians, especially at Christmas time. In this earlier essay, I concluded that care is needed in preaching or teaching about this hymn and in its appropriation for worship at Christmas time.

A cultural–literary study of Lk. 2.14 revealed that the Lukan author reflected an attitude typical of a person living in the first century CE around the Mediterranean. Through a careful reading of this text in the light of the Earth Bible ecojustice principles of intrinsic worth and inter-connectedness (Earth Bible Team 2000b: 42-46), I came to suspect the idealism with which Luke seems to lavish Earth in this angelic hymn. The first principle allowed me to read the biblical text from a hermen-eutical stance that considered Earth and Earth's components as having intrinsic value in themselves and not simply for their utilitarian value to human beings. The second principle helped me to read the biblical text from the perspective of Earth as a mutually interdependent and con-nected living entity. An application of these principles to Lk. 2.14 con-firmed how the evangelist maintained a dualistic attitude that separated heaven from Earth. Earth seemed to Luke, in a word, functional.[1]

From one perspective, the birth of Jesus had important anthropo-logical and cosmic effects that spilled out to grace Earth. Luke affirmed that Jesus' birth brought about a renewal that enhanced the whole of the created cosmos. The fruits of this were evident in human beings of 'good will'. On the other hand, we also saw that Luke held an attitude to Earth

---

1. The juxtaposition of Earth and heaven is interpreted by Kretzer (1990: 246) as reference to Earth's eschatological and universalistic perspective derived from the First Testament.

that was dualistic and ambivalent. The evangelist reinforced a hierarchy between heaven and Earth. This hierarchy reflected the relationship between God and human beings: God was the supreme benefactor who graced the cosmos and humanity. The presence of God's agent, Jesus, breached the eternal divide between the sacred and secular, the divine and human. This is celebrated in the birth of Jesus and reflected in the angelic hymn of Lk. 2.14.

The hymn and the wider literary context of the story that framed it had been shaped by something else: Luke's purpose. It seems that Luke's agenda was to encourage a social renewal among members of the Christian community addressed by this Gospel. They represent a socially, ethnically and economically diverse mix. Luke's intent is to encourage them to overcome barriers of social, racial and economic distinction as they find ways to live out their discipleship together in the Graeco–Roman world of the late first century CE. However, in the hindsight of a sensitivity sharpened by a contemporary ecological keenness, this encouragement comes at an apparent cost. It seems that Luke presents Earth as an object of domination and subjugation.

Focus on Acts 7 in the Light of Ecojustice Principles

Is Luke's attitude to Earth revealed in this early chapter of the Gospel typical of the whole Lukan corpus? This is my interest in what follows. I have framed this interest by drawing on an image of Earth Luke uses in Acts 7.49, and asking: Does Luke see Earth as a footstool or as a throne? Is Earth a footstool upon which the feet of God or human beings can rest? Or is the Earth regarded as a throne, with intrinsic dignity and worth? Put simply, does Luke regard Earth as an object or subject? While it is impossible to study the context of every Lukan usage of 'Earth' language in the space of this brief chapter, I would like to turn to one chapter in Luke's second volume, the book of Acts – Acts 7, and to three texts in this chapter: 7.3-7, 33, 49-50. As in the earlier study, I will reflect on these texts in the light of the ecojustice principles of intrinsic worth and interconnectedness. Both of these hermeneutical principles offer a way of reading and critiquing Luke's appreciation of Earth reflected in Acts 7 and of identifying any alteration or inconsistency from Luke's attitude already discerned in the Gospel, demonstrated by my earlier chapter in this series.

My reasons for focusing on Acts 7 are threefold. First, noteworthy in Acts is the function that Earth plays in terms of geography and location. The geography that Luke presumes is panoramic. It embraces the whole Mediterranean world from Cyrenaica (Acts 2.10) and Ethiopia (Acts 8.26-

39) to Rome, from the most south-western and south-eastern corners of the Levant to the principal city of the world (Robbins 1991: 314-15; Johnson 1992: 154-55). This world needs to be travelled around and over. From this perspective and depending on the interpretative perspective of the audience of Acts, Earth is either a *barrier* to the spread of the gospel or a *vehicle* for the growth of early Christianity. Whatever perspective one takes, geography is at the service of Luke's theology. Place becomes a revealer of Luke's Christology and ecclesiology, and provides a portrait of authentic discipleship.

Second, a third of the occurrences of 'Earth' (*ge*) found in the Second Testament occur in Luke–Acts (Trainor 2000: 190 n. 14). Over half of the occurrences of these (25 out of 33) occur in Acts, and of these almost half (10 out of 25) are concentrated in Acts 7. This chapter of Acts naturally invites particular investigation into the function and attitude of the writer towards *ge*. This should either confirm or nuance the results of my earlier study on Lk 2.14.

Narrative and Thematic Importance of Acts 7

A third reason for my focus on Acts 7 stems from its importance in the narrative and thematic plot for the book of Acts (Wiens 1994: 44-53). An overview of both is necessary to contextualize the more detailed study of Luke's Earth language that follows.

Acts 7 is strategically placed in an important section of the book of Acts concerned with the overall growth and development of the Christian movement despite the apparent frustration and difficulties experienced. This motif is central for Luke's narrative development in the book of Acts. The chapters that lead up to this story narrate how the Christian community in Jerusalem, though decimated and fledgling, is reconstituted and flourishes beyond expectation. This theme of unexpected growth despite opposition offers a tangible ecclesiological expression of the Gospel's parable of the sower (Lk. 8.4-8), in which seed flourishes and an extraordinarily rich harvest results despite setbacks and failure. The abundant harvest of the word through the preaching of the community of disciples is evident in the large numbers of converts that are baptized on the day of Pentecost (Acts 2.37-47). The fruitfulness of the disciples' preaching is also evident through the summaries that dot the early chapters of the book of Acts (4.32-37; 5.12-16, 42; 6.7; 8.1b-8). All this encourages optimism in the audience addressed by Luke and establishes the future theological agenda that will unfold in the remaining chapters of Acts: God is faithful and can be trusted; God's word will be fruitful ultimately and eternally unstoppable; the Christian community

will flourish despite civil opposition and religious persecution (Njoroge
Wa Ngugi 1997: 64-71).

These themes seem to coalesce in the story of Stephen in Acts 6–7; the
value of this event for Luke's theology is inestimable. Stephen is presented as a wisdom figure of grace and power, a revealer of God's word,
and a worker of 'signs and wonders' (Acts 6.8). With what has preceded,
the reader can be confident that Stephen's preaching and martyrdom
will result in the growth of God's word. Throughout the whole Stephen
narrative, echoes of and thematic parallels with the story of Jesus continue and find expression. Stephen's speech at his trial also becomes a
summary of Lukan theology and orthopraxis. It reveals to Luke's
Graeco-Roman Christian audience a way of living in the present and into
the future. The story of Jesus is not something lost to the past. It finds
continual expression in the lives and deeds of individuals who — Luke's
audience would still remember.

Through this narrative dynamic and the thematic interplay between
the stories of Jesus and Stephen, the evangelist encourages the Lukan
audience to continue to express the life and ministry of Jesus in their
own lives (Dockery 1990: 423-37).[2] For them the story of Jesus must
become a rich source of reflection that influences their present life.
According to Luke, they must live like the Stephen depicted in Acts 7:
imbued with the spirit and compassion of Jesus, committed to the cause
of God, and confident in God's support, especially at the most powerful
of moments — a martyr's death. It is from this appreciation I move now
to consider specifically the structure of Stephen's speech and Luke's use
of 'Earth' language in the speech.

The Structure and Purpose of Acts 6.8–8.1a

From a literary perspective, Stephen's trial and speech (Acts 6.8–8.1a) are
framed between two summary statements (Acts 6.7; 8.1b-8).[3] These reinforce the themes of Christian growth in the midst of persecution. In
this typical framing technique, these summaries prepare for and speak to
the story of Stephen, which in turn illuminates the reason for the suffering that accompanies the Christian mission. The Stephen story itself
(Acts 6.8–8.1a) has a literary balance. Two scenes (Acts 6.8–7.1; 7.54–8.1a)
surround the central feature of the narrative, Stephen's speech (Acts 7.2-

---

2.   I see a clear christological agenda influencing Acts 7 and Stephen's speech,
contra Kilgallen (1989), who argues that Christology is not the overt theme of Stephen's
speech.

3.   For an alternative structure, see Légasse (1992) and Wiens (1996).

53); these framing scenes contain strong echoes of Jesus' trial and execution as depicted in Luke's Gospel. The first scene focuses on the public religious trial that stems from Stephen's ministry of grace and power (Acts 7.8). The second concludes the Stephen story with his public execution and becomes the opportunity for Luke to introduce the principal actor for the remaining chapters of Acts: Paul.

summary	Acts 6.7
Stephen's trial	Acts 6.8–7.1
speech	Acts 7.2-53
Stephen's execution	Acts 7.54–8.1a
summary	Acts 8.1b-8

Figure 1. *The Structure of Acts 6.7–8.8.*

The Stephen story is obviously important for Luke. The speech that Luke creates for Stephen is the longest in the book of Acts[4] and the events that flow from what happens to Stephen precipitate the Christian missionary movement away from Jerusalem, into the Gentile world and towards the West (Witherington 1998: 252). At one level Stephen's speech helps to establish the reason for the Christian movement beyond Judaism through Luke's reinterpretation of Israelite history (Duschulnigg 1988: 195-213). At another level, Stephen becomes Luke's mouthpiece responding to a charge of blasphemy laid against him (and by inference, against Luke's audience) of misrepresenting Moses and the Torah, and attacking the essence of Jewish life. Reading between the lines of the speech, it seems that the writer is dealing with a very sensitive issue for Luke's Christian, and predominantly Gentile, community: how faithful can a Gentile Christian be to the Jewish origins of Christianity? Can Christians legitimately move away from Judaism and Jewish cultural practices as the Christian community attracts more Gentiles and God-fearers? Are Luke's people faithful to God's plan or are they renegades? (See Johnson 1992: 119; Kilgallen 1989: 173-93.)

Stephen does not seek an acquittal of the charges of blasphemy. Rather, Luke portrays Stephen using the accusations as a way of indicting his accusers (Tannehill 1990: 84-5). The speech addressed to the Jewish leadership offers a Deuteronoministic view of history that reveals the positive understanding of Israel's past and a negative judgment on its present leaders. It is this view that also frames the attitude that Luke adopts towards Earth and expresses through Stephen's speech. Through Stephen, Luke's principal concern is not to argue against the importance

---

4.   Stephen's speech occupies 365 verses out of about 1000 verses used for speeches in the book of Acts; see Soards (1994: 1).

and function of the temple (Duschulnigg 1987: 195-213; Weinder 1987: 88-90) but to underscore the purpose of Jesus' mission.[5] This christological motive is revealed in the last verses of Stephen's overview of Israel's history: Israel silenced and persecuted its prophets who 'foretold the coming of the righteous one, and now you have become his betrayers and murderers' (Acts 7.44). Stephen's interpretation of Israel's history, inspired and interpreted through the lens of Israel's prophetic tradition, leads to this final invective against Israel's leaders and shapes Luke's use of 'Earth' language. The location of this language, especially in Acts 7.3-7, 33, 49-50, is significant in the overall development of Stephen's selective presentation of the story of Israel.

'Earth' (ge) Language in Acts 7

'Earth' (*ge*) occurs in Acts 7.3, 4, 6, 29, 33, 36, 40 and 49. The importance and understanding of Earth for discerning Luke's 'ecological' sensitivity already identified in Lk. 2.14 will be discussed in greater detail below.[6] There I shall focus on three main sections of Stephen's speech where *ge* appears: (1) the introductory part of the speech (Acts 7.3-6); (2) the directive which God gives Moses as he approaches the burning bush (Acts 7.33); and (3) Luke's adaptation of Isa. 66.1 towards the end of the speech (Acts 7.49-50). However, I hope it is clear from what I have already said in identifying the overall importance and context of the Stephen episode that Earth, for Luke, holds a secondary almost subservient function. The author's central message concerns Israel's history. Stephen's speech becomes a paraenetic reflection on God's promise, care for the Jewish people, and the importance of Israel's prophetic tradition (Duschulnigg 1987: 195-213). It is also a story of rejection.

Stephen's speech is in three parts and Earth features in each. The first (Acts 7.2-19) begins with the story of Abraham, Joseph and the other patriarchs. The second and major part (Acts 7.20-34) focuses on Moses, the great leader and prophet of the Jewish people, and highlights God's concern to liberate the people of Israel and consolidate their salvation. This positive portrait of God's redemptive plan is contrasted to rejection of God by the current leaders of Israel, which occupies the third part of

5.   For a similar assessment that considers Luke's assessment of Judaism as positive, see Ravens (1995).

6.   I do not pretend that the writer of Acts had the ecological appreciation we have today. With this caveat always in mind, my associating the book of Luke–Acts with an 'ecological sensitivity' is a way of investigating this first-century CE writer's attitude to Earth and considering the possibility of how much readers since then have unwittingly adopted this attitude.

the speech (Acts 7.35-53). Their continued resistance to this plan is reflected in their criticism of Moses (Acts 7.35-43) and persecution of all the prophets (Acts 7.52). Through this speech, Luke's Stephen lays the ground for the way Jesus and those who follow him will also be rejected. In essence, Stephen becomes Luke's mouthpiece for understanding the failure of the Jewish mission.

Given the writer's overall purpose and perspective, Earth plays a minor role in Luke's nuanced presentation of Israel's history. Read from the perspective of the ecojustice principle of intrinsic worth, s-e[7] functions in a rhetorically utilitarian way. This comes to the fore in the opening verses of the speech that now deserve closer examination (Acts 7.3-6). Half of the times *ge* is found in Acts 7 are clustered in these verses.

1. *Acts 7.3-7*
The speech begins with Stephen's account, drawing from Gen. 12.1, of God's injunction to Abraham.[8]

> 'Go out from your land (*ge*) and from your kin and go into the land (*ge*) which I shall show you'. Then going from the land (*ge*) of the Chaldeans he [Abraham] lived in Haran. And from there after his father died God removed him into this land (*ge*) in which you now live. And he was not granted an inheritance in it, nor so much as a pace, and God promised to give it to him as a possession for him and his posterity after him, though he had no child. God spoke in this way, that his descendents would be aliens in a land (*ge*) belonging to foreigners who would enslave and oppress them for four hundred years. 'And the nation which they serve I myself will judge', says God, 'and after these things they shall come out and worship me in this place' (Acts 7.3-7; my translation).

These verses are packed with either explicit 'Earth' language or references to Earth, and reveal Luke's opinion of *ge* as unredeemed, devalued, disconnected from human beings and in need of divine rescue. Reading the text from the perspective of the ecojustice principles

---

7.   The search for an appropriate pronoun for Earth is challenging. The use of a personal pronoun is preferred, rather than the conventional 'it'. This would help me to be sensitive to the Earth as subject and more obviously interpret the Earth texts of the writer of Luke–Acts from the point of view of the two ecojustice principles of intrinsic worth and interconnectedness. I am tempted to use the feminine pronoun 'she' to refer to Earth. While this use would acknowledge and preserve the feminine form of the Greek, *ge*, it would in fact also serve to reinforce a patriarchal, oppressive attitude that reifies the feminine. Consequently I have chosen to use 's-e' and 'h-r' in reference to Earth.

8.   Acts 7.3-6, though, is Luke's reflection on the Greek text of the Hebrew Scriptures, esp. on Gen. 11.31-32; 12.1-4; 15.13-19; 16.1; 48.4; Deut. 2.5 and Exod. 2.22.

of intrinsic worth and interconnectedness heightens this evaluation of Luke's ecological viewpoint. The poetic parallelism of the first two verses belies the pragmatic disregard in which *ge* is held.[9]

In Acts 7.3, *ge* is dissociated from Abraham's family. The Greek clearly brings out the separation between the two entities ('Go out from your land *and* from your kin'). In other words, *ge* is an object of settlement and from where the principal actor and representative image of the faithful person, Abraham, can easily leave. There is no sense of integration, compatibility or harmony between human beings and Earth. The tension that is incipient or implicit in this verse surfaces more clearly in the next few. The second half of v. 3 ('go into the land which I shall show you') further underscores how *ge* is the object of divine action. God will direct Abraham to h-r. S-e is incapable of self-determination or independent existence. S-e cannot act as a partner with Abraham, the great patriarch of the Jewish people, and — by inference — with all human beings. Earth is not considered an indispensable collaborator in human growth or community and s-e needs God's decree and declaration to enable h-r to participate in the unfolding of Israel's salvation history.

In Acts 7.4, Earth is regarded as a boundary that marks off one cultural group or nation from another (Sasse 1964: 677-78). S-e is a particular geographical locale and becomes the dwelling place for Abraham and his family. This perspective of *ge* as a place of human habitation is reflected in other parts of Stephen's speech (Acts 7.29, 36, 40), and intimately connected with the well-known locations associated with Israel's story of salvation: Midian and Egypt. In Midian Moses encounters God, and Egypt provides the important geographical focus for Moses' liberating leadership.

In Acts 7.4, God's initiative and plan is at the forefront of the writer's mind and *ge* is again the object of divine action. God acts to move Abraham from one place to another. God 'removes' Abraham from 'the land of the Chaldeans' to settle in the 'land in which *you now live*'. Here,

---

9.   The ways Acts 7.3 and 7.4 are constructed illustrate a close poetic parallelism that reflects a theological insight that Luke seeks to explore in the figure of Abraham. In Acts 7.3, Abraham is instructed by God to go from his place of birth into a land that will be pointed out to him. There are two main actions commanded by God and both actions are focused on *ge*. Acts 7.4 shows how Abraham faithfully executes God's command. As God instructs Abraham in two actions in Acts 7.3, so in Acts 7.4 Abraham responds in two actions. He leaves the security afforded by his original place of settlement, and finally arrives under God's direction to the place in which the present audience of Stephen's speech live. The theological import of the sentence could not be clearer: Abraham is God's envoy and faithful respondent, modelling the kind of response and openness indicative of Luke's community.

Luke's Stephen makes links with his present audience. They are identified with a specific location. They are associated with and can be identified with *ge*. This identity assumes literary and thematic importance. As the next verses seem to suggest, *ge* takes on the same potentially destructive characteristics of the implied audience addressed by Stephen. As God can act upon *ge* to bring about Earth's liberation so too can the Jewish leadership imbue *ge* with evil intent and destruction. In both instances *ge* is a passive victim affected by the qualities of the one/s acting upon the victim. Earth is theologically and anthropologically defined.

While it might seem that *ge* is connected to a salvation-oriented geography, overall Luke adopts a conventional, almost disparaging understanding. Earth is not the *fruit* of God's salvific intent but a negative geographical symbol. S-e represents the arena of occupation from which people leave or to which God directs them (Acts 7.3, 4). Theologically, s-e moves between being a passive, voiceless object in need of redemption to becoming an agent of oppression requiring exorcism or liberation.[10] In terms of the ecojustice principle of intrinsic worth, the writer of Acts devalues Earth. This development becomes more obvious in the verses that follow Acts 7.4.

In Acts 7.5, *ge* is considered owned by God and disconnected from human fertility and communion. She now has degenerated into becoming an article of divine trade to ensure perpetual human security. *Ge* is described as a 'possession' for Abraham and his clan, without voice in h-r own destiny. Earth is neither protected nor safe. S-e can be exploited at human whim with divine blessing. All this leads to Acts 7.6 where the theme of the Earth's domination continues, expanding to a reflection on what might be considered ecological abuse.

In Acts 7.6, *ge* is presented as the cause of alienation coopted by foreigners to enslave and oppress God's people: 'God spoke in this way, that his descendants would be aliens in a land (*ge*) belonging to foreigners who would enslave and oppress them for four hundred years' (Acts 7.6). *ge* becomes the place in which God's people are alienated; this expands on the negative possibilities that Earth is capable of producing in human beings. Luke acknowledges that this is a place of slavery and oppression. Though these characteristics are not directly linked to Earth, it is because of Earth's association with 'foreigners', people not belonging to God, that *ge* can be indirectly the cause of tyranny and ill

---

10.   In those other texts in Acts 7 where Earth appears but is not explicitly dealt with, Earth is depicted as being in need of a miracle (Acts 7.36), and as a place from which God's people seek to be liberated (Acts 7.40).

treatment. Through Earth's association with those who do not actually belong to this place, God's people – already alienated from the land – are now persecuted. These attributes reflect the same oppressive characteristics of Jewish leadership that Stephen's speech is intended to address. In other words, it could be argued that Earth – like the religious leadership that occupies h-r – is an indirect cause for the crushing disaster experienced by God's people. The alienation and hardship which *ge* brings about in God's people is further realized by comparing Earth's description in Acts 7.6 ('a land belonging to foreigners') with the source from which Luke drew, Gen. 15.13 in the Septuagint ('a land not their own'). In other words, the writer of Acts, drawing on an Earth tradition from the Septuagint, focuses on the negative possibilities contained in this early tradition and heightens the contribution that Earth makes to the personal estrangement experienced by human beings.[11]

The final verse of this first text under examination, Acts 7.7, offers a redeeming and balanced picture associated with the place in which Abraham's descendants live. Though *ge* language is absent it is implied. Through God's agency Earth becomes a place of divine encounter and worship. This liturgical association, a reminder of the angelic hymn of Lk. 2.14 in which a similar correlation is made, continues to uphold the initiative of God who determines the value of all created things. This includes Earth. Acts 7.7 effectively sums up the way Earth is perceived in this opening section of Stephen's speech and this perception is reinforced by reading the verse from the point of view of the ecojustice principle of intrinsic worth: Earth is a passive, valueless object that affects human beings. Earth's quality is determined by the worth of those who dominate h-r – whether God or foreigners. What seems clear in the mind of the writer of Acts 7 is that Earth can be both dislocating and alienating to human beings (Acts 7.3-6), and a revealer of God's presence and holiness (Acts 7.7). What is implicit about *Earth* in Acts 7.7 – that *ge* can be sanctified by God's will or judgment – becomes explicit in our remaining two focus texts, Acts 7.33 and 7.49-50.

2. *Acts 7.33*

As Stephen continues to trace the story of the patriarchs after Abraham, he moves to consider Moses whose story occupies much of the speech. After Luke reworks the story of Moses from the Septuagint in Exodus 2 and 3, he arrives at the moment when Moses encounters God in the burning bush. God directs Moses: 'Remove the shoes from your feet, for

---

11. For a discussion of the use of the Septuagint in Luke's Gospel, see Van de Sandt (1991).

the place upon which you stand is holy Earth (*ge*)' (Acts 7.33; my translation). This is a defining moment in Moses' encounter with God and his commission to liberate the enslaved Israelites. In the context of Moses' commission and his sacred encounter, Earth is described as 'holy'. This is the only time in the whole Lukan corpus that *ge* is explicitly invested with sacredness and described in language normally reserved for God. Here Luke expands on the vision of Earth implied in the previous verse, and evidenced earlier in the birth narrative and the angelic hymn of Lk. 2.13. In Acts 7.33, Earth is considered so intimately connected to God that s-e reflects the sanctity of God's very being. For this reason, Moses is asked to remove his shoes. This request should not be passed over lightly. In Exod. 3.33 and in Luke's reinterpretation of the event here, the same meaning is given. Moses' body, the consequence of the God's creative act in Genesis, must touch the very substance from which it was made. This is Earth (*adamah* in Hebrew) from which God creates *Adam*, the 'Earth creature'. The act of removing the shoes is an act of reverence. Earth becomes the location in which human beings, represented in Moses, offer obedience to God. S-e is the place where humanity's relationship to God, disrupted by the Earth creature of Genesis, is fully restored.

Further, Earth becomes a reminder to Luke's audience of the prim-ordial vision of human freedom and communion of Genesis. Acts 7.7 presents *ge* as offering the possibility of communion with God and reminding Luke's audience of the loving creative act of God that first fashioned human beings. As Stephen presents the central memorable features of the story of salvation, Moses can now be God's agent of liberation. He has encountered the liberating holiness of God experi-enced by Earth upon which he has walked. This positive and religious regard in which *ge* is held in Acts 7.7 is further explored in Acts 7.49-50 towards the climactic end of Stephen's speech. It is in this final section that we are able to understand more clearly why Earth can be considered holy. I will argue, using the ecojustice principle of intrinsic worth, that this comes from an inherited cosmological duality that permeates the Mediterranean world of Luke's audience and the Septuagint version of the First Testament.

3. *Acts 7.49-50*

The final section of Stephen's speech acts as an apologia that interprets history from Moses to Solomon (Acts 7.44-53) and accentuates the part Moses plays as prophet and a type of Jesus (Johnson 1992: 136-7). Moses is presented as one like Jesus, exiled yet empowered through the Spirit to lead God's people. Stephen also reflects on the place of the temple in an attempt to argue for God's transcendence (Sylva 1987: 261-75). In this reflection is found another perspective of Earth consistent with what we have already seen: Earth is regarded as object of divine action and dependent on God. This estimation also emerges from a cosmological dualism that interprets Earth only in reference to heaven.[12]

Stephen recognizes that Solomon built a house for God (Acts 7.47) but argues that God does not dwell in houses made by human hands (Acts 7.48). What looks like Luke's critique of a temple-centred theology is rather a judgment on a form of human conduct that seeks to control God's action. The temple is the narrative symbol or metaphor for human activity. The temple structure is of human origin and intent but, as Luke argues through Stephen, God is not dependent on such a structure. The argument which Luke marshals at this juncture through quoting from the Septuagint Isa. 66.1 seeks to reinforce this point of view.

> 'Heaven is my throne,
> Earth my footstool,
> What house will you build for me?' says the Lord
> 'Or what place for my rest?
> Surely my hand has made all these things?'
> (Acts 7.49-50; my translation)

Luke's reworking of the Septuagint original adds 'says the Lord' into the two questions and 'surely' into the final line of the quotation to render interrogative what was originally declarative (Johnson 1992: 133). In Acts 7.50 Luke inverts Isaiah's 'For all these things my hand has made' to 'my hand made all these things'. This emphasizes God ('my hand') rather than human beings as the agent and initiator of creative activity. These Lukan redactions serve to reinforce Stephen's argument. They emphasize divine judgment on the human endeavour to create a place for God and to locate and confine the divine presence.

Luke uses a conventionally inherited understanding of Earth from the Septuagint Isaiah that can be illuminated through an application of the ecojustice principle of intrinsic worth. In Luke's view, Earth is created by God. S-e is a creature whose existence is determined by God (Sasse 1964: 679) and subject to God's power and judgment. Together with heaven, Earth constitutes the total cosmos, and is dependent on God's will. They represent two parts of creation: connected, though distinct. In this duality heaven is considered hierarchically superior and the place of God's throne. Earth is inferior: Earth is God's footstool and the place

---

12.   For another angle on how dualism is interpreted in the First Testament see Schmidt (1992) who discusses Stephen's encounter with God as an example of 'divine penetration', the breaching of the barrier separating heaven from Earth.

where God's feet rest (Earth Bible Team 2000b: 44). S-e is imperfect and in need of subjugation. Luke's use of Isaiah reinforces a cosmic and ecological dualism that serves to distinguish Earth from heaven, and depicts Earth as inferior and separate. This echoes the Earth–heaven duality identified in my earlier study of Lk. 2.14 (Trainor 2000: 185-87).

Earth (ge): Footstool or Throne?

I am now in a position to answer the question posed by the title of this chapter. Does Luke regard Earth as a pedestal or a throne? The answer that I have come to is: 'both'. The reasons for this, however, are not simple and are further complicated by the fact that whether Earth is a pedestal or a throne, these images can have both positive and negative associations.

It is clear from reading Luke's use of *ge* language in Acts 7, using the ecojustice principles of intrinsic worth, that Earth is definitely God's footstool in a negative sense: the Earth is need of redemption and subjugation. S-e is a passive object, like a footstool, upon which the power of God acts and over which the key figures of Israel's story of salvation travel. In this Earth Bible reading, Earth is the arena of human activity and habitation, inhospitable and out of step with h-r habitants. Only God has the power over *ge* to move, guide and relocate the principal figures of Israel's story.

Read from the perspective of the ecojustice principle of interconnectedness, Earth is separate from creation and humanity and has the power to act. From this perspective, then, Earth is like a throne, again in a negative sense. S-e can exercise an authority. But h-r ability to act is not the royal activity of protection and justice building, rather of subjugation, oppression and maltreatment of human beings. I have suggested that a possible cause of this connection lies in the very attitude with which *ge* is viewed: as a receptacle of action and object of exploitation, whether from God or humans, disconnected from h-r dependents. As Earth can be shaped by divine action; s-e can also be influenced by human activity. I suggest a further possibility that could be implicit in Acts 7.6: by inference, it is possible that *ge* could be oppressive by absorbing and reflecting the overwhelmingly oppressive spirit of Luke's interlocutors.

If I am correct in this reading of Luke's ecological viewpoint in Acts 7.6, then this verse also contains the seed for an alternative reading and offers the potential to interpret Earth positively. This is not to redeem Luke's utilitarian regard for Earth but to offer a way in which a relevant hermeneutic might be reclaimed today. If Earth, according to Acts 7.6, can be influenced negatively by those seeking the oppression of Luke's community (and this is reflected in the trial and subsequent martyrdom of Stephen), s-e can also be influenced positively. This opens the possibility of a synergetic or symbiotic relationship between Earth and humanity that critiques the hierarchical cosmology maintained by the author of Acts. It is this possibility for such a harmonious relationship that opens the door to see Earth not in anthropological, voiceless and victimized terms, but as a cooperative agent and collaborator in the story of liberation. From this point of view, s-e can be a throne in a positive and creative way, reflecting the royal protective agency associated with God in the First Testament. This insight is supported in Acts 7.7, 33 and 49, and links us back to the Gospel verse: Lk. 2.14.

This study has nuanced the conclusions derived in the earlier examination of Lk. 2.14. There, the angelic hymn affirmed how Earth was caught up in God's declaration of universal peace brought about through the birth of Jesus. This overwhelmingly positive image of Earth's potential expressed through the hymn affirms how Earth can act in collaboration with God for peace. From this point of view, the Earth can be regarded as a footstool in a positive sense. The Earth can allow the presence of God to rest or alight upon h-r. For this reason, the Earth, as a throne, shares and participates in God's royal desire for human, social and cosmic wholeness (*shalom*).

In summary, a reading of Acts 7 from the perspective of two ecojustice hermeneutical principles confirms my earlier view that Luke regards *ge* with ambivalence, with negative and positive associations. It is this ambivalence that can be dangerous for contemporary readers and proclaimers of Luke–Acts.

Negatively, the writer of the Gospel of Luke and the book of Acts sees Earth in essentially the same way: as part of a hierarchical and dualistic cosmology; the object of divine or human action and in need of liberation; voiceless and capable of exploitation with divine blessing. Earth is the place of human habitation where people can be alienated. Earth is the footstool on which God's feet can rest and s-e is enthroned with a power that can oppress.

Positively, Earth is blessed with God's presence, empowered with God's attributes to become the arena for the blessing of peace. This blessing can permeate the cosmos and bring human beings into harmony and communion with God. In this perspective, Earth is the footstool that can carry the presence of God and reflect it into the cosmos. In representing God's throne, s-e can also share in the beneficence and goodness of God that liberates and empowers creation, including human beings.

While the negative sense contained in the footstool and throne images dominates, it is possible for contemporary readers to reclaim the positive potential inherent in both, though this reading is masked by Luke's ambivalent ecological attitude.

Finally, it would be important to repeat here the caveat voiced in the earlier study. It is necessary for contemporary readers of the First Testament, especially of Luke–Acts, to recognize the first-century CE ecological perspectives reflected in the text. While there is a sense of Earth's goodness celebrated in the Christmas Gospel reading, Lk. 2.14, a goodness brought about by God's action, there is also a view of how Earth has been infected by the actions of dishonourable human beings. Both perspectives are held in tension. As we are part of the web of interconnectedness and seek to value Earth it is important to recognize how our attitude to this planet has been influenced—however unwittingly and subtly—by the attitudes of the Bible's writers. We need to continue to find ways of reading the Bible's Earth texts in a way that supports us in our quest for cosmological liberation.

The Cosmic Christ and Ecojustice in the New Cosmos (Ephesians 1)

Elmer Flor

Explanatory Preface

The following article is a paper by Elmer Flor from Brazil with annotated comments — responses and questions — posed by Norman Habel (on behalf of the Earth Bible Team). The focus text of the paper, Ephesians 1, is frequently cited in current ecotheology discussions. To further debate on the problematic nature of this text and its contribution to ecotheology, we have, with the concurrence of Elmer Flor, raised questions that respect the scholarship of Elmer but open the way for further postcolonial research on the text. Both Norman Habel and Elmer Flor are descendants of immigrants to their respective colonial countries, Australia and Brazil; both are seeking now to understand the biblical tradition about Earth from a postcolonial perspective. Norman Habel's comments are presented in shaded boxes to differentiate his commentary from the words of Elmer Flor.

Introduction

Major celebrations had been prepared by Brazilian authorities for April 2000 to mark the fifth centennial of the country's discovery by the Portuguese navigator Pedro Alvares Cabral on 22 April 1500. In order to re-enact the original scene, 13 caravels or sailing ships left Portugal to cruise the Atlantic Ocean, as the navigators did five hundred years ago. On Discovery Day they were due to arrive at Porto Seguro, the spot at the north-eastern state of Bahia, where the discoverers first landed. On the day this re-enactment was about to happen, the coastal land was occupied by Aboriginal peoples of South America, their kin and environmentalists, in a huge demonstration of protest against what they said was the origin of a state of affairs in the so-called new world in which they were taken from their own land.

This negative reaction to the European discovery of the American continent over five hundred years ago is a result of hundreds of years of nationalistic opposition to what has been called the 'uncovery' or 'invasion of the new world'. This explains why local Indigenous peoples did not participate in the celebrations planned by the officials. The presence of the South American Aborigines was tantamount to an outcry of Earth, whose soil had been taken from them centuries before.

The 'uncovery' may have precipitated enormous human tragedies and devastation of nature in South America, but it also began a greater revolution. It created the disciplines of science, geography, philosophy, agriculture, law, religion, ethics and government—the sum of what was known in the sixteenth century as Western culture. There are even those who see Cabral's journey as a triumph of human progress toward completeness and fulfilment. This kind of colonial reading has been part and parcel of history books as well as part of the teachings of the Christian Church on the American continent. Whether this reading is in conflict with the ecojustice principles of the Earth Bible Project is a question to be explored in the present study of Ephesians 1. Does the work of the Cosmic Christ in Ephesians 1 ultimately value or devalue Earth?

Issues Facing the Ephesian Church

Completeness and fulfilment are two of the main themes in the epistle to the Ephesians. A central motif of the epistle is the movement of all things from creation through redemption to an ultimate purpose: their unity in Christ. Father and Son are mentioned together in the initial salutation and blessing (vv. 2,3). All of creation is a 'joint venture' of Father and Son. In this way creation begins, develops and ends with Christ. He is, together with the Father, *pro kataboles kosmou*: 'from the foundation/beginning of the cosmos'; they both work to its ultimate fulfilment by ways that seem to anticipate a universal restoration. Even if various ancient philosophers had already considered matter evil, and even if a basic issue behind the book of Ephesians was a search for freedom and redemption from the material world, it becomes clear that through Christ and his incarnation the created world is highly valued.

I contend that the writer attempts to counter a dualistic approach to redemption, which erroneously proposed a movement from evil to good, from darkness to light, from matter to spirit, from Earth to heaven. Against this world of dualism much of what is said in Ephesians 1 becomes clearer. The *mysterion* mentioned in Eph. 1.9 is not used in the ordinary way in which we understand the term today: as something we know exists, though we do not know how it exists. In this text the 'mystery' is not the hiddenness of God's will but its manifestation that is emphasized. The term is probably used here in contrast to the use in the religions of the time of the writer, according to which hidden things or concepts would be made known only to selected individuals who had been initiated in their ritual. In the text of Ephesians 1, mystery is rather a truth that might not have been known before, which is now being revealed. This mystery of God's will, described later in the epistle as the 'mystery of the gospel' (Eph. 6.19), is what the writer seeks 'to make proclaim' ('make known/to proclaim?'). The proclamation of the mystery of God's will 'according to his good pleasure' has special importance at the beginning of the epistle. This mysterion is not revealed through visions or rites, but through the power and insight given by the Holy Spirit and holds a power of its own, the 'pledge of our inheritance'.

Comment: The force of the *mysterion* as a plan of God for creation before the foundation of Earth raises the question of whether this divine purpose is in harmony with the ecojustice principle of purpose. Is the divine *mysterion* a strictly spiritual force at work—or does it also embrace the biological and non-biological forces for life at work in the cosmos?

The initial aim of the writer is to declare Christ a co-participant of the creation and to make known this mystery to those who believe in him. Thus the time of this revelation of the mystery of God's will is also stated. It is to be put into effect at the *pleromatos ton kairon* ('fullness of times'). *Kairos* is not chronological time, but a space of time in which something is to happen, an opportunity. It will be up to God always to decide when things should happen. This time goes back to the times before the creation of the world, when it is said that God already chose or predestined the elect according to a purpose of love. *Kairos* ('the opportune time') also exists at the time of the writing of the epistle and will continue until the *pleroma* ('fullness') is attained. This fulfilment, however, is anticipated in the climax of Eph. 1.10.

The event at the heart of the divine *kairos* is 'to *gather up* ['sum up, gather together'] all things in him [Christ], things in heaven and things on Earth'. The Greek word for 'gather up' is *anakephalaiosasthai*, whose literal translation is 'to be re-set under one head'. The full meaning of the expression, particularly gained by paying attention to the prefix *ana*, is 'to gather *again* under one head' people and things that had been originally one. As the parallel passage in Col. 1.16-20 puts it: 'by him all things were created...and in him all things hold together...and through him to reconcile to himself all things, whether things on Earth or things in heaven'.

The same apparent dualism of Earth and heaven and the need for an alienated creation to be reconciled is displayed in both texts. The conjunction 'and', however, links heaven and Earth to one another, without necessarily establishing any opposition or hierarchy. Both are mutually connected. Black's comment is appropriate:

> By this language Paul imports a specifically Christian content into the contemporary cosmology for which there was no more pressing question

than the source of harmony in a world of diversity and freedom. That immanent power of God which providentially guides the universe is identified with Christ (Black 1962: 983).

Another element to be considered in the term under study is the Western understanding of headship, which is usually read as hierarchical. The main idea of *anakephaleo* (*gather again under one head*) is that of unity attained in the midst of — and in spite of — previous diversity. The head is vitally connected to the rest of the body, so that it cannot say to other members, 'I don't need you!' (1 Cor. 12.21). By following this line of Pauline thought, it seems that the headship of Christ as expressed in the text is one of interconnectedness with his believers and, as the same verse affirms, with all 'things in heaven and on Earth'. Therefore the ecojustice principle of interconnectedness reclaims ancient dimensions of the text when the Cosmic Christ reunites and reconciles all things. Christ fills all in all. Christ restores an original interconnectedness of creation. God's power works in and through Christ and equalizes/ neutralizes all (unjust and undue) power and dominion, all rule and authority (Eph. 1.21). Putting 'all things under his feet' and making him 'the head over all things' need not be read in terms of earthly or colonial oppressive power.

Comment: Linking the verb *anakephaleo* ('gather again under one head') with the principle of interconnectedness presents us with a new challenge. Does the argument of the text imply that nature was originally a biologically interconnected and balanced whole that later became disconnected? If so, why did this disconnection happen? Is it a result of the ecological sins of humanity? Or is the alienation and disconnectedness of nature in Ephesians to be understood quite differently?

The text also introduces the concept of *oikonomia*, ('household management'). *Oikos* had for the Greeks an importance and value similar to what the concept *bet* ('household') means in the Hebrew Bible. The term's meaning ranged from the house as a dwelling place for the family to a king's palace or even to the temple as God's habitation. In 2 Corinthians 5 the writer calls the human body our earthly house or tent, for which we are responsible to the Lord. The term 'ecology', derived from the same root, refers to the pattern of interrelationships between living things and their 'house' or environment. In the text of Ephesians 1, *oikonomia* seems to refer primarily to the eternal counsel or plan of God for human salvation. In a wider sense it points to the office of trust or stewardship, which has been handed down to people of all ages, and involves acting economically with creation and interacting with God as the preserver of all things in taking care of this inheritance.

> This is the destined issue of creation, the end for which the universe was brought forth; in this the mind of God is at last revealed and his glory manifested in the Grace which planned and is carrying out so great a design (Buttrick 1954: 621).

To the Colossians (Col. 1.20) the writer declares that the creative and redemptive work of Christ embraces or reconciles all things in heaven and Earth.

Comment: Assuming *oikonomia* does refer to the divine plan/manage-ment of all creation, does it not reflect a decidedly hierarchical model? In the *oikos* of Earth, it seems, Christ is Lord and the Church is Christ's steward over the household of creation. In the household codes of Ephesians 5–6, however, the master–slave household model is retained. Does the unity of the *oikos* of Earth under Christ imply anything like equality of respect for all (*ta panta*) in creation? Does it not rather imply a hierarchy of household power and status under one cosmic head/master?

The Cosmic Christ

Before Columbus first arrived on the shores on the American continent in 1492, he had set for himself the aim to attain the sea route to India by heading west. For this reason the Aborigines in the new lands were mistakenly called 'Indians'. The explorers' trips to the west were an obvious expression of the thought and hope of many people at that time that Earth was round and that these immense, sparsely populated continents were part of a *kosmos* that was at their disposal and had not been known nor taken over by existing Western civilizations. The process of discovery fundamentally enriched and altered the old world from which the navigators had come.

There is no room here to enter the debate between those who see the discoverers' journeys as events that shaped the modern world and drove human progress toward fulfilment (in many senses) and those who view the same events as hemispheric rape. During the 'discoveries', the Western church

> was part of the Iberian project of conquest and gave its backing to the social system imported from the peninsula; the result was a semi-feudal regime in which the Aborigines became dispossessed of their lands and subjected to the service of their conquerors (Flor 1992: 151).

This was the outcome of a particular understanding of the biblical cos-mology on the part of the Church. To the conquered people, the Chris-tian God looked like a great landowner administering new estates. Colonial readings of this text, for instance, interpreted the term 'inheri-tance' (Eph. 1.11) as the allotment of land that had been designed to those 'who were the first to set our hope on Christ' (Eph. 1.12), which is to say, the European Christians of the developed world. By sailing west, Columbus tried to prove that Earth was round, producing at first hand what could be called a 'global theory' and the grand march of the West in search of cosmic power.

Comment: Clearly the great 'discoveries' of the era in which Columbus lived challenged the Western church's understanding of the extent of the cosmos and hence of Christ's role as Lord of the cosmos. Is it not therefore understandable that the new world would be viewed as an accessible part of that cosmos? And is it not plausible for the church of the time to believe that bringing all things together under one head, namely Christ, would encompass discovering and redeeming new lands and their peoples? How this was done may be a separate issue.

I would argue that in Ephesians 1 the focus lies on the role of Christ in creation and redemption, rather than on Christ's role in conquest and rule. The writer, first of all, puts Christ right in the centre as the synthesizing force in the process that formed the world and gave it intrinsic worth. God predestined and adopted the believers through Christ, in accordance with God's pleasure and will (Eph. 1.5). Human beings were created to be holy and blameless, and there is no talk about the fall into sin. Nevertheless, a clear reference is made to the need for redemption and forgiveness. The restoration of the entire universe in Christ is a dominant theme of the epistle. 'All structural lines of the world converge upon Christ and are knitted together in him, who gives its consistency to the entire edifice of Matter and Spirit' (Chardin 1970: 101).

There is no single way of speaking of God in the cosmos and in Christ. Joseph Sittler was one of the first Christian theologians of the last century to talk seriously about the ecological implications of Christian theology long before the recent awareness of the plight of Earth. He asserts it is 'legitimate to see a growing magnitude in the christological utterances of the New Testament and...an ever-widening orbit of Christological meaning, scope, and force' (Sittler 1972: 11). The cosmic dimensions of Christ's lordship expand the scope of redemption to include the whole creation. Based on these premises, Creede (1977: 242) concludes that 'so closely, then, do the functional and ontological christologies come to one another that they seem interpenetrating rather than parallel'. This view also states the interconnectedness of Christ with Earth-bound humans and that our understanding of this relationship should be functional as well as ontological. To this end Sittler articulates his 'cosmic christology' and embraces ecology as a theologian—though not by relying on labels and stock terminology on the subject. He strove to speak of the close relationship between faith and nature as well as between creation and redemption.

The 'plenitude' or fullness of Christ, his *pleroma* (Eph. 1.10), represents in the Apostle's mind the extension of Christ's work as co-author of creation, his work of redemption of humankind, as well as the liberation of the whole cosmos, 'things in heaven and things on Earth' (Eph. 1.10). The term *pleroma* was quite common in the vocabulary of the time and

> designated God's penetration and envelopment of the material world. In Colossians and Ephesians Paul strips this term of its stoic pantheism and gives it a content familiar to the Old Testament, that of the cosmos filled with the creative presence of God (Mooney 1988: 97).

At this point he places the locus of Christ's cosmic reign in the Church, in which he exerts not only and primarily his rule, authority, power and dominion, but the riches of his grace.

Comment: If the cosmic reign of Christ is located in the Church, then the Church is apparently the body that rules for Christ in creation. And if so, is that 'rule' to continue the work of the cosmic Christ in bringing all things together in Christ—both in heaven and Earth, in the realms of both the spiritual and material? Does that 'rule' also mean working with Christ to bring all things under his feet? And does such a process not imply a devaluing of those things that are under foot?

Ephesians 1 describes God's plan of salvation as a 're-establishment', a 'summing up' of all things in Christ. The Latin translation reads: *instaurare omnia in Christo*, which points to a cosmic framework into which it fits a 'Body-of-Christ' theme when referring to the Church. The redeemed are to be united, as Christ and the Father are one (Jn 17.21). In the same way Christ's power unfolds in the development of the physical world, giving it meaning and direction. This leads to the belief in the unification of the world—including the material world—by God through Christ's incarnation.

The epistle writer finds in Christ and in 'the summing up in him all things' (as Eph. 1.10 can also be translated) the fundamental principle by which Christ is raised to a 'cosmic' position according to his humanity. This principle has been further defended as follows:

> Christ is precisely he who stands at the head of the world, but the vast majority of theologians show themselves to be absolutely incapable of understanding him in this position. If, on the contrary, according to the Scripture itself, we give to the Christ all his attributes, if our faith recognises in him the totality of everything that belongs to him, then everything changes (Crespy 1968: 82).

When seen from this angle, the whole creation ought to be respected and valued, first of all, by believers in the cosmic Christ—namely those who were predestined and chosen before the foundation of the world. The term *ta panta*, moreover, embraces all components of the cosmos, physical and spiritual. This 'summing up' of 'all things' in Christ ultimately implies this intrinsic worth extends to all creatures, and therefore the need for those who know the Cosmic Christ to reflect the same attitude towards creation, working with Christ to redeem 'all things'.

Comment: The references to *ta panta* may be taken to embrace all components of the cosmos—material and spiritual. That would mean that the Church as the agent of Christ would be involved in reuniting the broken cosmos, ecologically as well as spiritually. The difficulty we face when reading Ephesians, however, is that the writer's discussion about the work of the Church focuses on human beings—especially those who are Jews and Gentiles—and their being united into one humanity. Does Ephesians really offer an impetus for restoring Earth in ecological terms?

Earth Interconnected with Heaven

Ephesians 1.10 refers to Earth, *ges* together with *ouranos*, without, however, establishing any opposition: 'to gather up all things in him, things in *heaven* and things on *Earth*'. As said before, the idiom used here suggests an additional sense—literally 'gathering' all existing creatures. This points to the ecojustice principle of *interconnectedness* between heaven and Earth, and among all creatures with each other, integrating thereby the entire Earth community. Even though this aspect is not actually stressed in the text, it becomes evident that the writer opposes any belief that God is pure abstraction. God is involved in the concrete activities of creation and predestination. These acts are performed according to the divine *boule* (will), which depicts God's decision expressed through action in favour of *ta panta* (all), a neuter plural that is all-inclusive and connects all things and living creatures according to God's eternal 'good pleasure'.

Ephesians 1 is a so-called 'cosmic text', whose aim is to determine Christ's relationship to the material world and the redemption he *epirisseusen* ('lavished') on his believers. The writer establishes the fact that all things in heaven and things on Earth—including human beings—are to be gathered up and reunited in Christ as their head. The writer adds that in Christ we—the believers—have obtained an inheritance. I contend that this *kleronomia* ('inheritance') implies a mutual commitment to the *custodianship* of creation by all human beings in general and as a specific task for the chosen ones: to be partakers of the heritage and to be taken into it through Christ. This new spiritual and social order will recognize the leadership of Christ. God the Father, by giving his Son great power (Eph. 1.19) and by seating him 'at his right hand in the heavenly places', introduced an era in which believers will be co-rulers with Christ of *ta panta*. This divine act of power and grace makes Christians partners with the Creator and Redeemer.

Comment: If this text implies that the believers (the Church) are made co-rulers with Christ over *ta panta*, then the hierarchical nature of the new cosmic order under Christ is apparent. The hierarchy in descending order would then seem to be Christ, Church, humanity, all (other) things. If this is so, this order is in conflict with the principle of mutual custodianship. This principle also affirms that Earth and all things in Earth community have been custodians of human life from the beginning and that this model of mutual dependency/custodianship reflects a world view that is in tension with traditional concepts of 'ruling' and 'stewardship' suggested in Ephesians 1.

A Postcolonial Understanding of the Cosmic Christ

As noted above, the writer in Ephesians 1 makes Christ a co-participant of the creation and makes known this mystery to those who believe in him. In addition, the writer places the *locus* of Christ's cosmic reign in the Church, where he exerts not only and primarily his rule, authority, power and dominion, but the richness of his grace. The final aim and purpose of Christ's cosmic reign is to make him 'the head over all things for the Church, which is his body, the fullness of him who fills all in all' (vv. 22-23).

The church established on the Iberian Peninsula at the end of the fifteenth century had a distinct concept of power and a limited sense of purpose as it joined the discovery expeditions. Columbus sailed off for his discoveries sponsored by the Catholic Monarchs Fernando and Isabel of Spain in a joint political, economic and religious venture. Eight years later King Manuel of Portugal sent the Dominican friar Henry Soares along with other religious workers on the Cabral's expedition. It set out for India, but because of calm winds they ended up at the Brazilian coast. Four days after their arrival, the first Catholic mass was celebrated on South American soil. A huge cross was then erected to symbolize the conquest and possession of the newly discovered land. No flag, but a cross!

What then followed under the sign of the cross was an ordeal of devastation and slavery. The land was despoiled of its riches, especially so by felling the *pau brasil*, a very hard and precious type of red wood, which was shipped to Europe for the making of furniture. There are no exact records of the huge amount of gold, silver, diamonds and other riches carried away, nor of all the ecological deprivation to which the new lands were submitted. The Aborigines had to serve as slaves on farms and as guides and gravel washers on expeditions called *bandeiras*, in the search of precious stones and metals. The temporal order and the ecclesiastical divine order, as structured in scholastic thought, were now being coordinated and enforced. The influential religious order of the Jesuits was put in charge to Christianize the natives in the so-called 'reductions' or Missions and at the same time transform them into obedient colonial subjects. Theirs was an understanding of mission as a territorial expansion of Christendom. The conquerors' action was derived from their view of the cosmic Christ and his unifying power of the universe as they knew it.

The original inhabitants of the so-called new world/new cosmos were dispossessed of their heritage by followers of the Cosmic Christ. They were despoiled of their liberty in the name of the Liberator they were expected to accept. Instead of being 'gathered up' in Christ as part of *ta panta*, however, they were indoctrinated to believe in a conquering and subduing Christ, far away from the outreaching Redeemer of the Christian message. Human beings created and redeemed with a high purpose had been downtrodden and marked with a *sphragis* (seal) much different to that promised to them in our pericope, the seal of the Holy Spirit, 'the pledge of our inheritance toward redemption as God's own people' (v. 14).

Comment: The irony of the colonial conquest, it would seem, is that those who were conquered and became Christians — and hence part of the Church — ought therefore to be made co-rulers of *ta panta*. These colonized and converted humans, however, became another rung in the hierarchical ladder of the new cosmic order and servants of the Church in conquering/exploiting *ta panta*.

If the gospel is to be used in bringing justice to the suffering colonized people of Brazil, it needs to focus on both their spiritual and material needs so that they may obtain the inheritance that has been allotted to them 'according to the purpose of him who accomplishes all things according to his counsel and will' (v. 11). A postcolonial reading of this text would demand that the conquered would inherit all that the cosmic Christ has won for them — both in heaven and on Earth — according to the 'immeasurable greatness of his power' (v. 19). Such a reading would also demand that *ta panta* participate in that same inheritance and be part of 'an inclusive vision of mountains and marmots, lakes and loons, human black, white, red, and brown as lying within the scope of God's embrace' (Bouma-Prediger 1995: 214-15). It should be said that not all is lost. The Aborigines of the Kaingáng tribe still remaining in the Brazilian hinterland, for instance, have been able to retain their original language 'in spite of the attempt of the colonising language to stifle it' (Becker 1999: 145). Here it is impossible to mention the many ways in which minorities, racial, religious or social have survived oppression in the South American context. Conquest of these peoples in the name of the Cosmic Christ was far from total.

Conclusion

Every time power and dominion escape the purpose well established by God in Christ there will be chaos. For this reason one must come to the conclusion that Christ fulfilled his Father's purpose when the *mysterion* was revealed to all people and accepted by those who believe in Christ at all times and in all places. He superseded every human or superhuman seat of power and glory as he fulfilled the position ascribed to anyone or anything and *panta en pasin* (all in all) were put under his feet. This includes all rule and authority and power and dominion, be it on the part of angels or of other forces to date or to come. The final purpose of this overall authority is to strengthen the Church, 'which is his body, the fullness of him who fills all in all'(v. 23). This fullness also includes the presence of grace within nature; creation should therefore be respected as the tent in which human beings live respectfully as the redeemed people of the Cosmic Christ.

Comment: A postcolonial reading of Ephesians 1, already initiated by Elmer Flor, is perhaps the very process that highlights a language of rule and power in the text. This language does not seem to promote justice for Earth or the colonized people of Earth. Such a reading also confronts us with the way in which the Church, as part of the colonizing process, was often implicated in forms of injustice grounded in a belief that the Church was the agent of power and conquest for the Cosmic Christ, a conquest that rendered the rest of Earth community vulnerable to all kinds of abuses. Reading against the grain, the challenge is to discern whether it is rather the suffering Christ of the cross (Eph. 1.7; 2.16), as distinct from the Christ of cosmic power, who is the healing force that 'fills all in all' and 'reconciles all', including *ta panta* and the Church.

Earth as Host or Stranger?: Reading Hebrews 11 from Diasporan Experience

Alan H. Cadwallader

Hebrews 11 has a carefully constructed elevation in the movement of the writing. Traditionally it has been interpreted as a collation of traditional heroes who are exemplars for the contemporary community. Ernst Käsemann inverted the standard paradigm by accenting the resilience of faith through the vagaries of Jewish history (Käsemann; cf. Eisenbaum 1997a: 186). This broached the second major line of interpretation: a retelling of Jewish history such as to authorize the new community and new patterns of thinking over against the old. The language of 'new covenant' became unrelentingly supercessionist. It was dismissive of Jewish institutions; and it exiled Earth as well.

Pilgrim through this Barren Land

The hegemonic presumption in interpretation and translation is a Platonic dualism between heaven and Earth. The 'new' belonged to heaven; the 'old' belonged to Earth — that which was growing old and poised to vanish (Heb. 8.13). '*The* fatherland' was a 'heavenly one' where, it was deduced, God had prepared 'a city'. Earth as a whole was nothing more than 'a foreign land', a contrastive backdrop to the 'strangers and exiles' in its midst 'of whom the world was not worthy' (Heb. 11.16, 9, 13, 38).[1] 'Believers know', wrote Simon Kistemaker, 'that this earthly scene is transitory and their heavenly home abiding. Therefore, they fully recognize their temporary stay on earth and long for their eternal dwelling in heaven.' And again, 'The Bible warns us not to attach ourselves too firmly to this earthly scene. Scripture tells us that this earth really is not our home' (Kistemaker 1984: 325, 329). Thus Heb. 11.13-16 becomes the hub of the whole chapter, and Earth nothing more than a '"motel" for passing pilgrims' (Earth Bible Team 2000b: 43).

Here, heaven becomes reified and literalized in spatial terms. 'New' is

---

1. A turn of phrase itself indicative of heaven: see Philo, *Embassy to Gaius* 347.

interpreted as replacement and alternative. A two-worlds dyadic conceptual heuristic is reinforced by contextual alignment with Philonic and
Septuagintal parallels and transmitted through a long line of improviza-
tions that has left Earth and its dependents gasping at their marginalization before the 'spiritual realities'. Of course, one needs must become
apologetic about the affirmation that God created Earth. It survives as a
residue (at best) — 'the Christian's workshop' (Kistemaker 1984: 325) of
preparation for the greater reality awaiting our (or Earth's) passing.

The Offence to Earth and to the Pilgrim

On such a reading, Earth loses any inherent value (warranting either
disdain or abuse). Similarly, any socio-historical investigation of Hebrews
becomes irrelevant. This would merely signal an effort to overturn the
document's teaching of disconnection from the spatial, temporal and
therefore transitory, realm. Earth becomes nothing more than a useful
object to think with, to be manipulated, spoken of and ultimately trashed
once the real (read: spiritual) meaning is revealed. The offence to at least
two guiding principles of the Earth Bible Project is palpable: any intrinsic
worth of Earth is denied and any mutuality (actual or potential) between
Earth and human beings is dissolved.

The goal of this essay is to recover the inherent value of Earth and of
the pilgrim's mutual relationship with it, through a 'countercoherent'
reading of Hebrews 11.[2] As Heather Eaton has argued: the question is
no longer *what* or *why* the Bible means, but *how* it means (Eaton 2000: 59).
As neglected elements of context and text are made pivotal in order
to establish a new Earth reading, previous interpretations that have
rendered Earth obsolete become exposed as reading *choices* transmitting
disastrous ecological consequences and ethical immunities on their
perpetrators.

Pilgrim to Jerusalem?

One lone voice stands out against the total renunciation of Earth. George
Buchanan's reading of Hebrews, much disputed and even maligned,
argued that Hebrews belonged to a Maccabean-style aspiration for
restoration of the key elements of Jewish identity. Most particularly, it

---

2.   The term 'countercoherent' was explained in volume 1 of the Earth Bible as
'describing alternative readings of the text that both make sense — cohere — and
challenge the dominant reading and/or the tradition of interpretation associated with
this reading' (Earth Bible Team 2000b: 40).

envisioned the reconnection of a people with the land of its ancient foundation. Reformulated upon the surety of a high priest who would purify the temple from its pollutions, Hebrews, claimed Buchanan, was written to justify the return of diasporan Jewry to Jerusalem and to exhort their continued perseverance in the face of opposition from the 'old priesthood'. For Buchanan, then, Hebrews announces a restoration to one particular land, the 'Holy Land', and particularly its heavenly city whose ultimate architect and builder is God, namely, Jerusalem (Buchanan 1985: 253-63). The heavenly home is the earthly Zion.

On this view, the 'love of the fatherland' is, in Luther's words, not merely 'numbered among the greatest virtues of the heathen'[3] but becomes the faithful and anticipatory sign of the reconstitution of Israel. Unlike the apostolic encourager, Barnabas, who liquidates his place in the inheritance of God's people (Acts 4.36-37), diasporan Jews, in Buchanan's conception, sell up their possessions and return to their homeland to live in sanctified communities (Buchanan 1985: 258-59).[4]

The land thus becomes a backdrop again, though this time a backdrop to the restoration of ethnic (and 'spiritual') identity in the world. The advantages of Buchanan's analysis are that he resists a dehistoricization of the text, and emphasizes the importance of the land as the proper home for the people the text addressed. He rightly objects to the (Gentile) Christian spiritualization of hope that makes the search for a heavenly home antagonistic to Jewish earthly aspirations (1985: 265).[5]

The Offence to Earth and the Pilgrim: Reprise

Consequently, we are left suspended between two utilitarian approaches to Earth. At one end we find Earth interpreted as the umber shadow of heaven. At the opposite pole, Earth is partitioned into a hierarchy of holiness that privileges Jerusalem as the crown, and the land of Israel as its consort. The language of 'heaven' is summonsed to augment this importance. *This* land becomes sacred; the rest of Earth is profane (Earth Bible Team 2000b: 41) or 'the Diaspora'. Either way, however, Earth is merely an object mined for a larger return, a victim of a contrast with heaven or of a narrowed colonialist identity elevated above all its

---

3. Martin Luther, in Pelikan (1968: II, 238).
4. Buchanan is influenced by the hegemony of the monastic interpretation of the Essenes and the Qumran community, but this is not essential to his basic argument.
5. Luther held that the loss of the land of Canaan (presumably after the Jewish war against Rome in 70 CE) signalled the cessation of the Law and all its key concerns: kingdom, priesthood, Sabbath… See 'Lectures on Genesis', in Pelikan (1968: II, 362).

surroundings. It is either disowned or owned but never granted a contribution to or disengagement from the decision. Earth has neither inherent value nor any mutuality of relationship with humanity.

Rehistoricizing the Text, the Pilgrim and Earth

Buchanan's experiment invites a reconsideration of method. Instead of looking to a dematerialized philosophy for the explanation of Hebrews, the return to the exigencies of earthly existence may be the necessary first step in breaking the hold of nearly two millennia of spiritualized pedagogy that has incessantly presumed to deliver guidance 'through this barren land'.

Hebrews itself provides a number of prods to question a flight into the realm of ideas divorced from material life. There is a concentration on the hard-suffering humanity of Jesus (especially in Heb. 2; 5), a recognition of imprisonment, property loss, public humiliation, threat/memory of bloodshed (Heb. 10.32-34), interior dissensions and collapse of nerve (Heb. 6.4-12; 12.15-17). Again, the blind assumption of persecution of *Christians* ought be questioned. Rather, given the repeated utilization of Maccabean traditions in the writing, diasporan (and Christian) Jewry provides a fuller, more probable resource for re-establishing the historical groundedness and realistic cut of the reconfigured Jewish lineage of Hebrews 11 (cf. Eisenbaum 1997b: 391-96).

Diasporan experience—of the Jews in the particular context of Hebrews, and of diasporan communities more generally—affords the opportunity and rationale for disintegrating the dualisms infecting the interpretation of Hebrews and the dismissive attitudes to Earth distilled from its text. Oddly enough, few scholars have turned their attention to such issues for Hebrews 11. David de Silva is one exception. He recognizes that one's native land is critical to a sense of identity. The configuring of identity in relation to a land where one no longer dwells has significant impact on the quality of life in a new country. Reproach and dishonour are commonly the accompaniment to diasporan identity. There is no citizenship conferring rights and enfranchisement; property and status are fragile; one is prey to abuse and attack with reduced mechanisms of redress (de Silva 2000: 394-95).

He might have added that instability threatens the cohesiveness of the diasporan community itself. Divisions in sociopolitical fabric and alignments in the homeland (and these were plentiful at this time; Razak 1983: 65-77, 104-43) can be exacerbated by the tensions of diasporan life as disputes arise over patterns of relationship with the immediate dominant authority (Honigman 1983).

The Jews in Alexandria: A Growing Fragility of Existence

The Jewish Diaspora figures prominently in all analyses of the origin of Hebrews, whether it is perceived to be Alexandria, Rome or Jerusalem. Although argumentation about provenance cannot be pursued here, certain terms in Hebrews 11 invite a reconsideration of the Alexandrian connection. This language is found in crucial political and legal constructions of connection with city and land. Hebrews operates with this cartography.

The gathering of Alexandria (and the granaries of Egypt) under the imperialist control of Rome spun a new complexity into the web of tense racial, class and status relationships in Alexandria. Alexandria lost its exalted place in the Mediterranean. Though its Greek population retained citizenship and gymnasium, they were denied their ruling council (*boule*), unlike two less prominent Greek cities in Egypt (Naukratis and Ptolemais).

Egyptians continued as the colonized people, stigmatized in popular stereotypes and in legal position.[6] The succession of conquerors had squeezed them down the status scale. Their ignominious position was exacerbated by the presence of Jews.

Jews are found across the gamut of class, status and occupation. A few (such as Philo) held citizenship (Lewis 1983: 18-35; Haas 1997: 95-98; Modrzejewski 1993: 77-80) and could exercise leadership and influence at the pinnacle of government. Moreover, in their own 'quarter' of the city[7] Jews exercised their own authority through a council (*gerousia*). Certain exemptions from tax (especially the poll tax) made citizenship most attractive (Tcherikover and Fuks 1957, I: 60-62) but ethnic criteria

---

6.   This fraught position stretched across centuries. An Egyptian living in the third century BCE complains that (the colonizing) Greeks 'have treated me with contempt because I am a barbarian'. Significantly he writes a letter in Greek, knowing that Demotic will not secure a hearing for his request to be paid regularly so that 'I do not die of hunger'. He bemoans that 'I do not know how to *hellenizein* (to behave as a Greek)' (P. Columbia Zenon 66). Over four centuries later, the Roman Emperor Caracalla denigrates Egyptian pretensions at urbanity, noting their distinctive and despised speech, appearance, dress and manners (P. Giess 40). Philo records how ethnic and status distinctions affected even scourging—different implements of scourging were accorded different peoples as a respect for (or confirmation of) their standing (Philo's, *Against Flaccus* 78-80).

7.   Called the 'Delta'. Philo claims that two of Alexandria's five quarters were considered Jewish (*Embassy to Gaius* 124, 132; *Against Flaccus* 55). There has been resistance to the suggestion of a Jewish ghetto in Alexandria, even though concentrations of Jews are evident. Certainly Jews were found throughout the city, as well as across Egypt.

(i.e. the restriction of exemption to Greek or Roman citizens) were difficult to bypass. Considerable offence resulted from the use of the poll tax to designate race — most Jews paid it, and therefore were 'Egyptian'.[8]

Greeks and Egyptians harboured grievances against Jews, against each other and against the all-conquering Romans. However, the Jews were softer targets, readily set upon with a vehemence intensified by a hatred of the Romans and by the position Jews had engineered with Roman support.[9] Dislodging Jews from their position (and aspirations) in Alexandria and from their favour with Rome were bound up together.

Violent ethnic eruptions dot Alexandria's history. Jews were often embroiled both actively and passively. Each successive fracas added to mutual suspicion and calculating memory. Around the turn of the second century, the Jewish historian, Josephus, and the imperial orator, Dio Chrysostom, both testify to the festering poison of relationships.[10]

Predictably, there was no single Jewish response or direction. Those with citizenship, status, longevity of habitation and wealth argued for rapprochement with Rome. Some adopted a more complete assimilation to Graeco-Roman mores (the famous example is Tiberius Julius Alexander the nephew of the renowned Jewish civic philosopher Philo). Others urged a radical rejection of any perceived compromise of Jewish identity (as in *3 Maccabees*). Diasporan experience promoted a Jewry far from monochrome (Barclay 1996).

The Land as Platform of State Power and Influence

Quietly lying in the background is Earth, silent witness to the bitterness of the ethnic and religio-political conflicts, and impotent drain for spilled blood. But land is also grasped as the ground of the political and legal structures of councils and authorities. Here — in terms of ownership, security of tenure, wealth from production, currency of philanthropic contributions to the life of the city, sites of meeting and contention — a

8.   So the vehemently anti-Jew Isodoros in the popularized account of his claim before Claudius: *Acts of Isodoros* (ll. 26-27). The persistent reference to Egypt and Egyptians in Heb. 11 (vv. 26, 27, 29) may indicate this friction. Certainly Heb. 11.29, though based on Exod. 15.4, shifts the language from 'Pharaoh and his force' to the more general, and more contemporary, 'Egyptians'.

9.   In the *Acts of Isodoros*, one of the popular pamphlets grouped together as *The Acts of the Pagan Martyrs* by moderns, Isodoros (a known leading Greek citizen of Alexandria) calls the Emperor Claudius 'the cast-off son of the Jewish Salome', and accuses him of caring for a 'cheap-skate Jew like Agrippa'.

10.   Josephus, *Antiquities* 19.278-292; Dio, *Oration* 32. The bloody climax came in late 414/early 415 CE (Haas 1997: 91-92).

person's own place and display of position were located.

This is no conceptual game. The period is heir to a century of land privatization in Egypt. The Ptolemaic rulers had preserved the received tradition of the concentration of all land in the 'crown'. The erosion of this singular possession into private holdings was accelerated after Roman rule formally began in 30 BCE. Earth quickly became a commodity and not merely the extended domain of Pharoah's person (Green 1986: 102-109). Land ownership became the mechanism of social mobility, if not status enhancement. A piece of paper defined 'property'; an imperial bureaucracy enforced proprietary rights. This strengthened dependence upon the state, and the state thereby had its claim for increased productivity (in goods and tax) underwritten. For those fortunate enough to receive grants of crown land, ties to the emperor were layered in political, social, geographic and economic terms. They became 'interested' participants in the cause of empire.

Jewish Arguments for Security of Place

It is no coincidence that Philo's philosophic discussions frequently contrast Abel and Cain. Abel is the husbandman (*georgos*) of Earth, Cain its mere worker (*ergates tes ges*). Cain is unsophisticated, lacking in refinement of knowledge and the ability to distinguish and regulate things (Hamerton-Kelly 1976: 53-56). Philo, the learned, urbane civic dignitary, manipulates Earth as the ground on which to grade humanity. The Egyptians, more concerned for the body than the soul, were automatically Cain's descendants.[11]

He designates Abel as the one who value-adds and Cain as the one who fritters away.[12] This is the very language he employs to criticize those who attacked the Jews in Alexandria (*prostithemi, aphairo*): 'you are not adding to but taking from the honour given to our masters'.[13] Philo arrayed the proud cultural 'Abelesque' credentials of Jews in Alexandria in his contention before the Emperor Gaius Caligula following the destruction of Jewish life and property in 38 CE. The desecration of Jewish synagogues with statues of the emperor had accompanied the 'Cainite' rampage.[14] The Roman prefect of Alexandria, Flaccus, supported this clever ploy to flatter the emperor's fantasies. These places

---

11. *Posterity and Exile of Cain* 62; compare the more elaborate denigration of the Egyptians in *Embassy to Gaius* 166 and *On Agriculture* 62-63.
12. *The Sacrifices of Abel and Cain* 1.
13. *Against Flaccus* 49.
14. *Embassy to Gaius* 132-33.

became off-limits to Jewish religious gatherings.[15]

This expropriation of place effectively and symbolically denied Jews control over their own affairs. Though sometimes mistaken as a plea for restoration of Alexandrian citizenship, the focus of the Jewish delegation to the emperor under Philo was the reinstatement of the ethnically based civic authority and rights (*politeuma*).[16] The loss of independent decision making threatened their overall place within the vast metropolis.

The Linguistic Constructions of Relationship to Earth and Roman Enforcement of Pilgrim Status

Philo's descriptions of both the delegation and Flaccus are significant. He concentrates on the city and an individual's relationship to it. He carefully describes the outrages upon Jews as akin to the sacking of a city (*halosis*). Implicit here is a claim to Jewish identity and standing in Alexandria. Elsewhere he defends Jewish loyalty to their diasporan locality as to a 'fatherland' (*patris*) without demeaning Jerusalem as their 'mother city'.[17]

Flaccus's efforts had been geared to undermining this place – his terminology is critical. According to Flaccus's proclamation, Jews no longer held any authorized position; they were 'strangers and foreigners' (*zenoi kai epeludes*).[18] This classification carried the full weight of Roman authority, rendering the Jewish cause indefensible. They were left without ground on which to stand – precisely the security that citizenship and/or customary (limited) political autonomy provided.

Philo unequivocally denounces the decree as 'tyranny',[19] that is, the denial of legitimate rights and protections which are the mark of good government. He proceeds to recount in lurid detail the devastating cruelties that ensued (cf. Heb. 11.35b-38). Those who could, escaped 'outside the city' into desert(ed) places (*eremiai*).[20]

The argument against the status reduction of Jews to 'strangers, foreigners, without a fatherland or city' is at the heart of Philo's contention. He delights in recounting Flaccus's later fall from grace,

---

15. Philo claims that there were numerous synagogues spread throughout Alexandria's five quarters (*Embassy to Gaius* 132).

16. A similar distinction is actually made in the letter of Agrippa to Gaius Caligula supposedly reproduced (invented?) by Philo; see *Embassy to Gaius* 287.

17. *Against Flaccus* 46.

18. Cf. *Embassy to Gaius* 123: 'outcasts and refugees'.

19. *Against Flaccus* 54. He is as free in recording the same for the Emperor Caligula as well (*Embassy to Gaius* 350)…after he too has died!

20. *Embassy to Gaius* 127.

manifest in his deportation to a remote Aegean island—which was, gloats Philo (decorously, of course), to be called his 'new fatherland' (*patris kaine*).[21]

The demise of the Emperor Caligula three years later heralded the opportunity for Jews to recover their despoiled synagogues. Vengeance accompanied the 'recapture',[22] and was mirrored in other parts of Egypt. Even Judaea lent help. Rome intervened to restore order and yet another set of delegates travelled to argue their case.

The result was the *Letter of Claudius to the Alexandrians*, dated November 41 CE;[23] it reveals that the Jewish community had become fractured at a deep level. The new Emperor, Claudius, castigates the Jews of Alexandria for sending two embassies to Rome. Long-standing tradition authorized one representative body for each ethnic group. Consequently, the Jews were portrayed as representing two cities, rather than one. This decisively undermined any Jewish claims to Alexandrian citizenship.

A significant turn of phrase occurs in the course of Claudius's decree. He deems the Jews of Alexandria to be 'of a foreign city' (*allotria polis*—line 95). That telling characterization spelt the collapse of Jewish hopes for a more secure standing and more elevated status in Alexandria (Schäfer 1998: 146). The consequence of the application of *allotria* to Jews was that a 'foreigner' could never have legal and political roots in the land.

The Jews' place in Alexandria, their particular locality and status in relation to Earth, were governed by this lexical field. 'Stranger', 'exile', 'foreigner' were all terms whose referential sweep and exaction of authority depended on land, or better, by a measured estrangement from it. The mandarins behind this verbal system were the Romans. Their words created a visible world, a tangible *kosmos* that encroached powerfully on Jewish aspirations for security of place.

The Clash of Historical Exigencies and Spiritual Exegesis

The poignant irony is that this is no innovative language field for Philo. Earlier, in his philosophical reflections, Philo had liberally applied such

---

21. *Against Flaccus* 159. Compare the same topos (of Jason and Antiochus) in 2 Macc. 5.8-10; 9.28.

22. Josephus, *Antiquities* 19.278-279.

23. The importance of this letter is indicated by the frequency with which it appears in collections. The most detailed analysis, with provision of Greek text and English translation remains that of Tcherikover and Fuks 1960 §153. The letter was plenteously copied and sent to various cities and towns throughout Egypt. Our extant copy comes from the Fayyum district.

terms to the life of pious relationship with the God of the universe. He even countered the accusation that such pursuits were conducted in Egypt, 'the land of the body'. He responded that Egypt was only for sojourning not settling, and avowed *heaven* was his 'fatherland' (*patris*).[24]

James Thompson linked Philo's works with the cosmological eschatology of Hebrews. Here, he argued, is spawned the thoughtworld of Hebrews 11—strangers, exiles, heavenly fatherland and city, the recognition of the invisible, the pursuit of a spiritual country and impatience with one's sojourning. All these are the trigonometric points of guidance for the pilgrimage of the soul. It is 'a world-renouncing vision' exemplified in the faith of Abraham and Moses (Thompson 1982: 56-61). Earth has no inherent value and nothing to contribute to the pilgrims.

Thompson's seduction by Philo's spiritual allegories left him oblivious to Philo's rejection of this language *when it attacks the actual material welfare of his people.* Two millennia of spiritualized interpretation have left their mark. The assumed meaning of Hebrews blankets countervailing materialistic evidence, and Philo's warnings against 'hyper-allegorization' have been ignored.[25] Spiritualized semantics may provide heuristic tools for religious formation, but Philo never intended the negation of Jewish interests. The actual disconnection of the spiritual quest from Earth turns out to be a chimera. Philo presumed and later defended land possession with its superstructure of political and legal securities. 'Stranger' and 'exile' might explain aspects of the journey of the soul, but for Philo they were not to be applied literally to a relationship with Alexandria!

Resisting the Dominant Linguistic Construction of Earth

Henry Green's exploration of the origins of Christianity in Egypt posited two sociological perspectives. The first was to see a sectarian movement within Judaism that 'provided normative values and behavioural patterns' for the socially unintegrated that might establish a place in the Roman world. The second was to see it as 'a response to fluctuations in a political economy in which social groups have lost status' and are trying 'to compensate for their anomie' (Green 1986: 101). While he appears to prefer the former (1986: 109-10), it is the second that is closer to Hebrews (which he does not address). In the light of the analysis above, it also

24. *On Agriculture* 64-65.
25. Hyper-allergorization devalued deference to the Holy Land, the temple and the sociopolitical infrastructure built thereon by divorcing the 'spiritual' meaning from material recognition: *Confusion of Tongues* 2-14; *Migration of Abraham* 89-93.

satisfies his salutary call for the identification of 'critical juncture points', that is, the institutional or actual life connections.

Here lies warrant for an alternative reading of Hebrews 11. The presence of similar key terms and concepts to those found in Philo *and* Roman edicts is no invitation to play other-worldly language games. The terminology impacts the immediate practical lives of people. In the historical particulars, these people are Alexandrian Jews.[26]

Granted this operating presumption, the writer of Hebrews is no theosophist. His[27] address is to Jews who have suffered massive up-heavals in their experience in this part of the diaspora. Their hopes for stability, security and status had been destroyed. *This* experience — not the cost of being a Christian *per se* — lies at the heart of the references to adversity in Hebrews. Hebrews is another Jewish attempt to deal with the corrosion of legal and political support for a place for Jews on Earth.[28]

Clearly, Hebrews is informed by a Jewish commitment to Christ. This vision of 'in Son' (*en huio*; Heb. 1.2) provides an encompassing unity that remembers the fragmented connections of the past (the 'many and manifold ways of old' Heb. 1.1) and radically realigns a sense of place and providence (Übelacker 1989: 76-104). Earth *as a whole* becomes the place of connection for the writer, not some particular place that has been documented, surveyed, bureaucratized and defended. Earth is thereby released from partitioned ownership, and affirmed as the place of God's creative providence, inherently valuable in its own right. Unlike Philo, Hebrews accepts withdrawal of legal and political ownership. The author discerns that a new way of relating is opened up involving a mutuality of respect for discrete identities and their worth.

In spite of the assistance of Philo in locating Hebrews, the author's position is quite distinct. The emphasis on the unity of all things in Christ — one priest, one sacrifice, one temple — extends to Earth. In Christ, Earth is now one, and not fragmented into 'many and various' parts to

---

26. Corroborative evidence is not slim. Certainly not enough has been made of the singular parallel of the etymology of Salem as 'peace' rather than Jerusalem (Heb. 7.2). This is only attested in Philo and Hebrews (Horton 1976: 48-50, 86).

27. As Harold Attridge argues (1989: 5), the use of the masculine participle in Heb. 11.32 is decisive.

28. Debate continues as to the date of Hebrews. A key focus of discussion is the use of the present tense for the temple/tabernacle operations (e.g. Heb. 9.6-10, noting especially 'the present time' in Heb. 9.9). One might also point to the grammatical indication of the present in the condition contrary to fact in Heb. 7.11, along with the preferred reading of the perfect tense *nenomothetetai* rather than the variant pluperfect *nenomotheteto* in the same verse.

be allotted or colonized. Indeed, given that the Son's work is for the whole creation (Heb. 12.27-28) Earth and Heaven are viewed as parts of the total aeon (Heb. 11.3). A house of God as indicative of heaven and located in a specific place—whether Great Synagogue in Alexandria, or fortified temple at Leontopolis or Jerusalem—is deemed secondary and derivative if existent at all because the writer asserts 'we are his house' (Heb. 3.6).

Earth is thereby released from hierarchical allotment and can freely engage people wherever they may wander. These pilgrims constantly recognize the liminality of existence as the heart of relationship with both God *and* Earth, *not* as the movement from one to the other.

A Countercoherent Reading of 'Strangers and Exiles upon Earth'

'Strangers and exiles upon Earth' (Heb. 11.14) is traditionally taken to indicate not only an other-worldly anchor but also the Abrahamic lens for the entire parade in Hebrews 11. David de Silva (2000) considers this 'confession' to be an amalgamation of Gen. 23.4 and 24.7 LXX. He takes the expression 'upon Earth' as a modification of 'in their land' to create a contrast between heavenly and earthly countries (de Silva 2000: 399). He does not entertain the possibility that the expression 'upon Earth (*epi tes ges*)' might indicate a *different* relationship to Earth, one that is built neither upon ownership, possession, colonization and documented protection, nor upon a transitory stage to something 'higher'.

Hebrews' choice of 'upon Earth' over 'in their land' (as per Gen. 24.37) is deliberate. It evokes the creation focus begun in Gen. 1.11 where Earth is fecund host for the seed. A new nuance is therefore placed upon the earlier reference to Abraham in Hebrews. God's concern is with the 'seed of Abraham' (Heb. 4.16). Now Earth's mutuality with God in the bearing of salvation becomes clear. The whole Earth promotes the well-being of the seed, not some exclusive parcel of land.

Hence, the story of faith in Hebrews 11 cannot culminate 'in their land' with Joshua but 'upon Earth' with one who *continually* occupied a liminal relationship to it, namely Rahab. Neither Joshua nor the colonized land had delivered the 'rest of God' (Heb. 4.8). Hence Abraham's model is not that he looked to a space beyond Earth but rather that the pattern of being 'upon Earth' is *not* about owning it, even in the 'land of promise'. In first-century Alexandria, this was clearly to be 'foreign' to the land (*allotria*; Heb. 11.9). 'Foreign' in the political and legal framework of the time denies ownership of, and control over, the land. This is the demonstration of faith that is called for from Abraham.

The clue to where Hebrews is travelling in ch. 11 is actually in the phrase 'strangers and exiles'. It is a commonplace axiom in scholarship upon Hebrews to note both the writer's meticulous and deliberate care in lexical, grammatical and rhetorical construction, and his dependence on the Septuagint. And yet the obvious absence of the use of 'stranger' (*xenos*) for Abraham escapes notice. Some manuscripts show their transcribers were alert to the inconsistency because they restored the Genesis terminology: 'sojourners' (*paroikoi*).[29]

In fact, 'stranger' (*xenos*) only occurs as the Greek translation of Hebrew *ger* in Job 31.32. 'Stranger' is absent from the patriarchal stories. The first use of 'stranger' (*xenos*) in the Septuagint is therefore laden with significance. It is Ruth's self-designation (Ruth 2.10 for Hebrew *nakri*, usually translated as *allogenes* or the more familiar *allotrios* 'foreign/ foreigner'). As a *Moabite* she has no claim to the land. The only position she enjoys is that of guest.

Significantly, she does not explicitly do obeisance *to* Boaz, but 'upon Earth' (*epi ten gen*) unlike, for example, the brothers do to Joseph (Gen. 42.6, cf. 24.52, 43.26, 48.12, where it is made clear that obeisance is made 'to him [with face] upon the ground'). Earth enters into a mutuality of provision of salvation, notably for Abraham, Lot and Jacob (Gen. 18.2; 19.1; 33.3), and is honoured for it. Hidden in the background, Ruth's relationship with the land informs Hebrews' portrayal of the patriarchal models. Faith demands an encounter with Earth that is built not upon ownership but rather upon Earth's hospitality.

This introduces a semantic arc of *xenos* that has been absent from the discussion. The Job reference (31.32) indicates that *xenos* has the sense of 'guest': 'the "stranger" did not pass the night in the courtyard but my door welcomed everyone who came'. This usage is found elsewhere in the Septuagint, albeit rarely (1 Sam. 9.13; 2 Sam. 12.4). Indeed the phrase usually translated as 'strangers and exiles' could as readily be understood as a hendiadys with the force of 'travelling guests'.[30] It taps into an ancient debate about hospitality built on whether distrust or welcome of strangers is the wisest course.

Certainly, Earth's hospitality to the 'stranger' is predicated upon the stranger possessing no recognized rights over it. It is xenophobia that leads to defensive bureaucratization of Earth, the hierarchization of land into protected parcels from which others are repelled. But it is precisely as 'stranger/guest' that a new relationship with Earth occurs.

---

29. The pleonastic restoration is found in the interface codices D, E.

30. The combination of words, unknown in the LXX, is familiar enough in Hellenistic texts: Polybius, *History* 26.1a.2; Diodorus Siculus 4.18.1, 4.27.3; Athenaeus, *Deipnosophists* 13.42.16-17, 13.44.3; see also Justin Martyr, *Apology* 1.67.6.

The references to 'city' and 'homeland' in vv. 14 and 16 are deliberately anarthrous. Grammarians often lament that English translations fail to recognize the significance of the absence of the Greek definite article. As Stanley Porter reminds us, 'The quality rather than particularity of a substantive may be referred to in structures without the article' (Porter 1994: 105). This option, granted for anarthrous *ge* in Heb. 6.7, is refused by commentators here. Once entertained, the sense is not spatial ('a city/a homeland') but qualitative ('city/homeland'). The explicit use of the definite article for 'Earth' in v. 13 thus focuses attention on 'Earth' as a particular entity. The specific relationship hosted by it to 'travelling guests' is what grants to those pilgrims-in-relationship the character of 'homeland' and 'city-zenship'. In other words, what God confers to such 'guests' (v. 16), as distinct from the emperor, is *Earth* as 'homeland' and 'city'.[31] The adjectives 'better' and 'heavenly' are therefore inseparable from Earth and descriptive of a different encounter with it. This is lost in translation where 'country' is all-too-rapidly supplied to establish an opposition to Earth and remove the ambiguity of reference in the Greek (*ekeines…af'hes*).[32] 'That from which they had passed' (v. 15) was governed by ownership understood as a possessing of benefits.[33] As 'strangers and exiles' they discovered God and Earth open to them. Here, as guests, they discovered 'homeland' and 'city', 'better' and 'heavenly'.

Earth as Host

The view of Earth as host in Hebrews recovers a forgotten 'ideology' of the land, one where it is viewed 'as a host country and its inhabitants as potentially friendly peoples' (Habel 1995: 115). Hebrews turns the focus of the Abraham encounter with Canaan into the engagement with Egypt, the one national territory named in Hebrews 11 (Heb. 11.26, 27). This can be achieved because the ground of his argument is creation itself, within which any particular place provides a typological indication of the whole. Hence even Salem indicates the broader notion of 'peace' and is exemplified by the welcome extended by Melchizedek to Abraham as 'guest' (Heb. 7.1-10) (Habel 1995: 126-27).

---

31. Here, the ancient philosophical asides about 'citizens of the world' become relevant.

32. Ellingworth (1993: 596-97) acknowledges the ambiguity but uses the traditional schema to remove it.

33. The translation of *me labontes* in v. 13 as 'received' fails to recognize the negative use of *labontes* in v. 29b. The variant reading in v. 13, *me komisamenoi*, 'not having carried off as booty', captures the sense of proprietorial assertion conveyed by the word in the critical text.

Hebrews achieves what eluded Philo. The author reintegrates the language of exile, stranger, foreign land, and so on, into a religious and realizable world view. He acknowledges the reality of the adverse experience of disenfranchisement engineered through the same language deployed by the Romans. His achievement, contrary to the weight of later Christian esoteric spiritualization, promotes no disconnection from or despising of Earth. Earth in fact is given a value and mutuality of relationship with humanity that defies Roman imperial efforts to ground a hierarchical layered structure in land.

The Roman linguistic framework operated exclusively in terms of, and only recognized, political and legal constraints. Philo's attachment to his own linguistic field was compromised. Hebrews therefore provides on the one hand a strategy of resistance to a Roman hegemony that would dictate the way Earth is to be understood and engaged with, and by which might determine or deny humanity's relationship with its own power.[34] On the other hand, the author resolves the conflict besetting Philo's embrace of, and resistance to, the terminology.

A Retrieved Vision of Earth and its Relationship to Humanity

This explains why the line of Jewish history ends with Rahab. She is the liminal dweller par excellence, given her ethnic, gendered, occupational and geopolitical fragility. Right at the point of conquest and settlement, the refrain of 'by faith' ends. Further, Hebrews breaks the narrative order of the book of Joshua by placing the notice of her faith *after* the fall of Jericho. Rahab therefore holds the apex of his rendition of (new) history and (new?) faith. This is not to accent arrival at some landed goal, for Hebrews goes into a rhapsodic peroration of his argument about the reality of being on Earth as a 'guest' (Heb. 11.32-38). Rather, as Moses leaves the scene in Heb. 11.28, attention is already turning towards the verge of the promised land. Hebrews works this into the text by introducing a word for the water crossing which, in the Septuagint, is reserved for the transgress of the Jordan, not the Red Sea (*diabainw*),[35] and gives it in the plural not the singular verb form centring on Moses (Heb. 11.25-28; Cosby 1988: 48). The final three verses of the

---

34. In this sense, Hebrews is akin to those Gnostic and apocalyptic writings with counter-dominant ideologies which have disenfranchised certain groups from their historical and sociopolitical connections with the land. These writings are efforts to provide different connections, ones that lie outside the control of the ruling powers (Green 1985).

35. Hebrews thus collapses the two crossings and bypasses the faithless wilderness wanderings (cf. Heb. 3.16-19).

'faith' refrain underscore a different relationship with Earth and a different view of Earth's hospitality. Rahab, like Earth, 'welcomes' the wanderers. Her liminal status and place provide the key.

The liminal is a place of passage. But here it is not about a temporary transition *to* a (greater) integration, one to be endured with grim determination and fixed gaze on what is beyond. This liminal zone is *itself* the place of revelation and engagement.

Hebrews 11.29 awakens this understanding by a subtle adjustment to the story of the Red Sea crossing lost on contemporary commentators. Early scribes were, however, alert to the problem. They brought the Hebrews text into conformity with the exact wording of the Septuagint, prizing the virtue of consistency above hermeneutics (Cadwallader 1992). The omission of *ge*, 'earth/land', in the majority of manuscripts brings the Hebrews rendition into line with the Exodus narrative and song (Exod. 14.16, 29; 15.19). The adjective *xera*, 'dry', is used as a substantive: 'dry stuff' in Exodus 14.

When we turn to the Jordan crossing, *ge* is also omitted (Josh. 3.17: *bis*; 4.22). In fact, throughout the septuagint, *xera* occurs alone when 'earth' or 'land' is meant (e.g. Ps. 65.6 [66.6 Heb.]; Gen. 1.9: *bis*; 7.22; Exod. 4.9: *bis*; Ps. 94.5 [95.5 Heb.]; Jn 2.11; Sir. 39.22). It functions as a substantive (Sir. 37.3; Dan.[Th] 2.10; 1 Macc. 8.23, 32). This usage is followed in extrabiblical writings (*1 En.* 97.7; Artapanus *apud* Eusebius, *Preparatio Evangelica* 9.27.36 [1.8]; Hermas; *Visions* 3.2.7, 3.5.3) and in the Christian Scriptures (Mt. 23.15).[36]

Accordingly, the addition of *ge* is noteworthy. Only two parallels occur in the septuagint. The first would not invite notice but for its significance for the second. The formal name *ge*, 'Earth', is given to the *xera*, 'dry land' (Gen. 1.10), by God. 'Dry land' acquires its special significance not only because of its creation but because of its *naming* by God.

The *Wisdom of Solomon* adopts this extended appellation (*xeras...ges*) but applies it in a strikingly novel manner. Here, the Red Sea story is interwoven with creation imagery (Winston 1979: 324-25; Reese 1983: 196-97). For this Solomonic author, the Exodus crossing *was* a new creation found *in the midst of* the threatening waves (Wis. 19.7, cf. Ps. 65.5-6 [66.5-6 Heb.]). Lexically and with the use of motifs, creation and liberation are united. The people of God have no ownership here; they are totally dependent on the mutual cooperation of God and Earth for their salvation.

---

36. The capacity to act as a substantive occurs in such frequency, that by the time of the Christian Scriptures and other early Christian writings, it qualifies as a noun. Hence it scores a separate entry in Lampe's *Patristic Greek Lexicon*, s.v.

Thus, Earth is not to be escaped but rather entered as the new creation. Faith (Heb. 11.1) perceives that one's place does not lie at the end of the journey but at the heart of it. Salvation is found on land *outside* Canaan — indeed, within the waves of adversity. Earth as a whole, not one special allotment, is the province and the providence of God. It can only be properly valued when human grasping is withdrawn, when legal and political reinforcements of ownership are themselves marginalized, and when Earth is free to act as host. Through the liminal experience, Earth enters into a new relationship with human beings.

This is where Rahab becomes so important. She is tolerated and demeaned for her employment and, in Jewish circles, for her Canaanite background. Rahab is a perpetual dweller in the liminal zone: she lives in the walls of the city, neither inside nor outside the city. Even after the fall of Jericho, she remains liminal. This is signified by a telling phrase, hidden from view, but surfacing later as a location of Jesus: she is 'outside the camp *until this day*' (Josh. 6.25, cf. Heb. 13.13).[37]

If Brevard Childs is right, the 'until this day' formula means something like 'this holds true today'. Rahab remained within Israel, but without stable or secure location. Faithful to the pilgrim God, she discovers God's presence and providence in Earth removed from the recognition of political control and legal protections — in the liminal zones. In this sense, Rahab joins Moses, who also dwelt 'outside the camp' (Exod. 33.7), and discovered in that relationship the presence of God.

And this is the place of Jesus. Going outside the camp is not only liberation for one who thereby discovers the God-given value of the whole Earth. It is also liberation for Earth, no longer reified through pieces of paper proclaiming ownership by other than the one who named it 'Earth'. Hence the prostitute participates with the priest (Melchizedek and his order) in the conferring of 'peace' (the last word of the major section, Heb. 11.31) — which confers a welcome, a provision and a place.

Conclusion: Pilgrimage with Earth

Hebrews accepts the identity of pilgrim that is effected by imperial linguistic construction. But Hebrews refuses to be passive before Roman efforts at displacement. Nor does Hebrews retreat into an other-worldly escape that sullenly asserts that it never really liked Earth anyway.

---

37. The notion of voluntary exile is known in the ancient world, sometimes indicating a judgment on the perversity to which a city or country had descended; see Athenaeus, *Deipnosophists* 12.43.7, cf. Lk. 10.10-11.

Rather another (old and new) insight is offered. The whole Earth is God's, and Earth is precious and providential in itself rather than by the ownership of some part of it. The heavenly country is not another place elevated and removed. Rather it is a description of a way of engaging Earth, a way marked by respect for Earth's hospitality and affirmation of Earth's value. Hence, wherever pilgrims are upon Earth, and regardless of whatever recognition may be granted or withheld by an external power, it is there 'upon the Earth' where God's house is.

Hebrews' own linguistic genius is to build a strategy of resistance to Roman removal of political and legal connection with the land. The writing unveils a different relationship with Earth, one built on a greater sense of the value of the whole than on the value of any one place therein as inextricably connected with it. The readiness of centuries of Christian interpreters to choose to read Hebrews with an uncritical adoption of Platonic categories resulted in sacrifice of Earth to an ethereal heavenly other-world, and to ignore the potential of an Earth-reading of this famous chapter, Hebrews 11. Such a reading may not be as forced as the weight of Christian tradition might suggest, for a trace is found in the second-century Christian text, the *Epistle of Diognetius* (5.5): 'Every foreign land is a fatherland, and every fatherland a foreign land.' At the same time, centuries of aggressively pro-heaven interpretations prompt me to ponder the wisdom of continuing to operate with a language field that can so readily be turned against Earth.

There's a New World Coming! Reading the Apocalypse in the Shadow of the Canadian Rockies

Harry O. Maier

Crowchild Trail winds slender like a serpent's tongue through the suburbs of Calgary, Alberta. Skirting the Bow River, it slips westward between speckled brown foothills until it disappears into the white-capped teeth of the Rockies. Along the way it sheds its name and becomes an old highway offering tourists a scenic route to Banff. Two-lane asphalt slices a line through the Treaty Seven reserve of the Stoney Nakoda First Nation (the Bearspaw, Chiniki and Wesley/Goodstoney peoples) situated around the settlement of Morley. Treaty Seven, signed by the Blackfoot Confederacy in 1877, was the means by which the Canadian government gained access to lands necessary for the comple-tion of the Canadian Pacific Railway.[1] Like the railway, our highway is a colonial reminder. On its way it snakes past St Barnabas Residential School and the white picket fences of McDougall Memorial United Church, the Methodist mission church built in 1876 by George Millward McDougall. His son and co-builder of the mission, John McDougall, acted as translator in the Treaty Seven negotiations permanently settling the Stoney First Nation on the Morley Reserve.

I was sixteen when I borrowed the family car, drove onto Crowchild Trail and let it lead me west, not knowing where it would take me. On family trips we had, of course, driven to Banff, but via the swifter Trans-Canada Highway, and I did not know what lay west of the city's boun-daries along this road. Rounding the city limit, high on a hill, a vista of sparkling blue where the Bow River meandered eastward, the golden brown of foothills, and the magnificence of the Rockies invited me to continue driving until swallowed by the mountains.

It was a time of discovery. Recently confirmed as a Lutheran, I was in the full blush of a fervent conversion to Christianity. Even as I ventured beyond the boundaries of familiar city boundaries, I had begun to read

---

1. For a history of the relationship of Treaty Seven to the completion of the Canadian Pacific Railway see Miller (2000: 197-224); Ray (1996: 210-12).

my Bible and so found myself captured by the ancient landscapes of biblical writings — of comfort and temptation in the wilderness, divine appearances on mountains, miraculous feedings in the desert. Both the landscapes of Morley and the biblical stories taught me the importance of what Edward S. Casey calls 'the concreteness of being-in-place, i.e. being in the place-world', and that 'to be in the world, to be situated at all, is to be in place' (1993: xv, 183-270). Once, taking my Bible with me on one of my excursions, on a knoll overlooking the Bow River I stumbled onto the exotic landscapes of the book of Revelation. Here landscape wilderness, that cultural construction of space in apposition to civilization (Schama 1996), gave way to 'wild places' — not that human construct 'nature' so much as the now shrill now comforting voices of Earth.[2] Earth sounded loud and clear through its 'wildscapes' (Casey 1993: 213) of desolation, isolation, dynamism and impenetrable violence. I encountered hail and fire consuming thirds of all forests and grass; seas turned to blood obliterating a third of all sea creatures (Rev. 8.7-8); a river pouring from a serpent's mouth (Rev. 12.15); a two-hundred-mile-long river of blood as high as a horse's bridle (Rev. 14.20); Armageddon filled with the dead flesh of armies (Rev. 16.16; 19.18); four-square heavenly Jerusalem containing the water and tree of life (Rev. 21.1–22.5). Such topographies became surreal when read by the bright light of Alberta skies, sitting on the ancient soil of golden foothills, over-shadowed by timeless mountains. Could God annihilate such beauty? In the apocalyptic tumult to come, in the course of which 'the sky vanished like a scroll that is rolled up and every mountain and island was removed from its place' (Rev. 6.14), would even these majestic Rocky Mountains be levelled?

Confused, I decided I needed a guide help me make sense of these endtime geographies. From a Christian bookshop I hired the orienteering skills of a much-recommended commentator, Hal Lindsey. *There's a New World Coming: 'A Prophetic Odyssey'* (1973), sequel to his best-selling *The Late Great Planet Earth* (1970), was to be my *vademecum* to appreciate the sites, sounds and geographies of what Lindsey interpreted as a map of the imminent end of the world. In the 1970s Lindsey's books were best-sellers. Perhaps more than any other writings of their genre,

---

2.   In what follows I use the term 'Earth' following the Earth Bible Project's definition (Habel 2000d: 27): 'that living system *within* which we humans live in a relationship of interdependence with other members of the Earth community'. Further, I use the term 'earth' (lower-case 'e') to describe 'the ground or land-mass we inhabit... In this context, "earth" does not represent the polar opposite of heaven in a religious sense.'

Lindsey's writings have successfully promoted a reading of the books of Revelation and Daniel as outlining a divinely pre-ordained sequence of political, economic, religious and ecological events of this the alleged last generation living into the Second Coming of Jesus Christ. Coming to me as I was in the heat of new Christian faith, Lindsey's reading of the Apocalypse as tomorrow's news today was a spark that ignited my imagination. Here was proof-positive that we were in living in the last days. Conversion never felt more right.

But there was a cost attached to believing Lindsey was a trustworthy guide to traverse Apocalypse territories. His reading confirmed my fear that the promised end would obliterate these places, becoming sacred to me even as they were holy to the Stoney First Nation for thousands of years before a young white city kid discovered them. In fact, the unavoidable conclusion of Lindsey's apocalyptic surveys was that I was mistaken to be taken up into the wonder of the world that greeted me on my teenage excursions. Instead, his exegesis urged me to turn my attention heavenward from whence Jesus was soon to come, to avert my gaze away from the very Earth that was, in each new trip through Morley, teaching me my place in the web of life. No sooner had I discovered Earth than I was invited to see myself on the eve of a battle pitching heaven against Earth.

Earth, Autobiography and Exegesis

Lindsay's is an invitation whose cost this essay seeks to estimate. The cost is personal, hence the autobiographical beginning. To begin a reading of the book of Revelation autobiographically is to insist upon the centrality of the second ecojustice principle undergirding the work of the Earth Bible Project. 'Earth is a community of interconnected living things that are mutually dependent on each other for life and survival' (Habel 2000d: 24, 44-46). To read the Apocalypse autobiographically is to connect Earth community, exegesis and text. Autobiographical exegesis proceeds from one's own Earth location—one's own concrete 'being-in-place'—as a beginning point of orientation in and among the immediate Earth networks of which one is a part. The metaphor of network is central, for without it autobiographical exegesis quickly becomes anthropocentric, even solipsistic. In the network metaphor, self is only one vertex in a complex series of interconnecting relationships that do not exist for the sake of the interpreter. Though brought to consciousness through interpretation, they are present even without an interpreter reflecting upon them. This contrasts with traditional historical-critical exegesis where the self as interpreter is filtered out from exegesis in order to arrive at an allegedly value-free, objective reading of a text. Such an enterprise becomes docetic if not nuanced by a critical subjectivity that acknowledges the interests every critical investigation brings to its topic of study (the genesis of the interpreter's questions, his/her place in a larger community of scholars, the tradition of interpretation, the relationship of interpretation to politics). It can deny the flesh and blood of real readers approaching a text from a set of not dispassionate interests. It risks Earth — not because its practitioners are not ecologically minded, but because it is the very insistence on objective scientific detachment that belongs to a much larger world view treating the world (of text, of historical backdrop, of author...) as object rather than as partner in exegetical conversation. This is what ecotheologian Sallie McFague (1997: 67-117) contrasts as an arrogant knowing of the world as manipulable object, as opposed to entering into a 'subject–subjects' relationship of encounter, and articulated in the second eco-justice principle invoked above.

For me, Earth *and* Apocalypse came alive in the shadow of the Rockies. But it was only by Earth's cross-examination of the apocalyptic violence against Earth, as an intrinsically worthy partner in exegetical conversation with the text, that a new reading of Apocalypse as pro-Earth text became possible for me. The voices of dissent Earth raised, via the startling beauty of sky, foothills, river and mountain, became voices of dissent and resistance to the easy dispensing of heaven (i.e. sky) (Reid 2000: 240-41) and Earth in dispensationalist apocalyptic interpretation.[3] The Earth voices I heard told me that to dispose of an old creation in favour of a new one was to dispose of *myself.* Again, I do not intend this anthropocentrically: my own being is not the beginning and end of Earth's existence. Rather, I mean that from my perspective as partner in the web of Earth life, to obliterate Earth is to annihilate my own self, for 'if one member suffers, all suffer together' (1 Cor. 10.26). Lindsey's premillennialist voice tempted me to deny my connection with the dust from which I came and to which I one day will return, not to mention the

---

3.   Dispensationalism, alternatively often named premillennialism, coined from and produced for mass consumption in C.I. Scofield's translation of the King James Bible, *The Scofield Reference Bible*, draws its name from Scofield's dividing up of history into seven dispensations or periods, six of which have passed, and the seventh of which is imminent. Premillennialists read the book of Revelation as a prediction of things to happen before the advent of the last, seventh dispensation, the Millennium (Rev. 20.4). The Apocalypse is thus read as predicting an inevitable sequence of calamities before the Second Coming. There is not room here to offer a detailed discussion of the nineteenth-century rise of dispensationalist interpretations of the book of Revelation (see Weber 1987).

memories of and connection with a landscape that continue to define me even though I now live hundreds of miles from the Alberta foothills.

So, in what follows I want to make a counter-offer to those readings of Revelation that outline an imminent future in which God destroys the old creation to replace it with a new heaven and Earth. I am aiming, through a careful listening of Earth's voices, to bring the Apocalypse back down from heaven to this old Earth — which is, in fact, the sacred Earth of Morley and the Stoney First Nation peoples. My overarching aim is to posit an Earth reading of Rev. 22.1-5, the conclusion of the heavenly Jerusalem vision begun at Rev. 21.1. That conclusion, however, must be read against the backdrop of the Apocalypse's representations of its villains and their relationship with the world of nature.

Revelation 22.1-5 offers a vision of Earth creatures living in life-affirming ecological interdependence. To read Revelation privileging Earth means to foreground this vision and interpret the environmental calamities rehearsed in earlier chapters in its light — rather than the other way around, so typical of premillennialist interpretation. Coming at the end of Revelation's vision of the heavenly Jerusalem descended to Earth (Rev. 21.1-27), it urges a renewed relationship of humankind with creation. In the vision, humans bring forth 'their glory' into the heavenly Jerusalem (Rev. 21.24) and receive from the leaves of the tree of life, planted in the city's middle, healing (Rev. 22.2). Revelation 22.1-5 portrays a symbiotic relationship of interdependence between Earth and its inhabitants; it is an Earth text. It models a way of being human in Earth community. This is in sharp contrast with the destructive relationship of Earth and its inhabitants, sketched in earlier chapters of the Apocalypse: rapacious Babylon and its commercial/political allies are its most potent embodiment (Rev. 18.9-24, esp. Rev. 18.11-13), and ecological calamity are its hallmark.

In an Earth reading of Revelation's concluding vision, we do not come to the Apocalypse looking for a snapshot of tomorrow's events. Instead, we read John's visions to see what forms of interdependence they outline, and how they invite us to envision the web of life. Such a reading resists any easy exchange from an apocalyptic discourse into a futurist wager. Instead, it pays attention to what Elisabeth Schüssler Fiorenza (1998: 21-5) names the Apocalypse's literary-aesthetic strategies of persuasion. Put differently, Revelation's apocalyptic language belongs to a genre of literature that depicts calamities of all sorts in order to explore Earth relationships. It offers a mythopoeic retelling of creation to bring into focus the broken and right relationships of Earth community. It paradoxically deploys rhetorical distortion in order to make clear — a distortion whose paradoxical function is lost when woodenly translated into literal descriptions of what must transpire. However shrilly, the Apocalypse (literally, the 'unveiling') offers a revelation not only of 'what is to take place hereafter', but of 'what is' (Rev. 1.19), namely the relationships within Earth community, which at this historical moment are a matter of life and death. While traditional Christian exegesis has interpreted Revelation as offering an unveiling of future events, I want to read it as outlining present realities and possibilities of Earth relationship. The Apocalypse offers two contrasting pictures of Earth relationship, and leaves its listeners with what Barbara Rossing (Rossing 1999) calls 'the choice between two cities', Babylon or Jerusalem, each of which embodies a characteristic relation to creation. As an unveiling, the Apocalypse brings into relief contrasting topographies that are not so much pictures of what is to come as revelations of social relationships that already are, and invitations to a wholeness that may yet be.

The Geography of Nowhere

While critical scholars not formed in premillennialist schools of apocalyptic scholarship tend to dismiss dispensationalist readings as products of a Protestant fringe, it is nevertheless important to identify what socio-political, economic and ultimately environmental agendas such interpretations serve, even if unwittingly. Such an analysis is culturally timely because no biblical text has captured the Western First World imagination more than the Apocalypse, as witnessed by the film, music and popular culture it continues to inspire.[4] Given the hold of premillennialist interpretation on American culture, it should come as no surprise that former President Ronald Reagan and his Secretary of the Environment, James Watt, invoked, respectively, the imminent arrival of a new heaven and Earth to justify their policies; Reagan used it to defend the largest build-up of nuclear weapons in history, and Watt cited it to justify legislation permitting corporations to mine and log national parks.[5] Being premillennialists themselves, both mirrored a popular preoccupation—the imminent end of the planet.

It is *politically* timely to discuss such views because of the lack of critique of the socio-economic function of premillennialist readings of the Apocalypse in silencing Earth voices in the Bible. If premillennialism

---

4.   For a survey of the Apocalypse in popular culture, see Kingswell (1996); for the Apocalypse as furnishing a self-fulfilling script of annihilation in the Christian First World West see Keller (1998).

5.   For a discussion of Dispensationalism in the White House, see O'Leary (1994: 172-93); for Reagan and Watt, see O'Leary (1994: 182).

continues to fascinate and enthral the consumers of Western popular culture and their leaders, then it is a matter of great urgency to return that reading with a critical evaluation that seconds Earth's voices of resistance to its inevitable destruction. This is all the more urgent if, as I argue below, one place where that voice of resistance is loudest is in the Apocalypse itself. Critical exegetical re-evaluation enacts the sixth principle of the Earth Bible Project, 'the principle of resistance', to side with 'Earth and its components' and its 'differ[ing] from injustices at the hands of humans', and to go further by assisting in its 'actively resist[ing] them in the struggle for justice' (Habel 2000d: 24, 52-53). The need to second Earth's voices of resistance becomes all the more pressing once it is recognized that premillennialist dispensationalism arises out of and expresses the economics and politics that makes the majority of Earth's inhabitants slaves to greed and Earth-destroying ambition.[6]

It was a colonizer's road that led me westward from Calgary into Morley, and a colonializer's interpretation of Revelation that tempted me with an Earth-renouncing interpretation of the Apocalypse. Hal Lindsey's *The Late Great Planet Earth* and *There's a New World Coming* are fruitfully interpreted against a backdrop of increasing industrialized removal from and objectification of our planet. David Harvey's *The Condition of Postmodernity* socio-economically critiques modern and post-modern understandings of place and time since the Enlightenment. He coins the phrase 'time–space compression' to describe the result on cultural notions of time and place when Earth is transformed into a field of forever increasing capital via economic development. Development to achieve capital levels place (a distinct geography with its own animal and plant life, time cycles, histories…) into time–space containers that are calculated to win economic profit (see Harvey 1996: 201-207; for 'time–space compression', 260-307). The expansion of capital throughout the globe leads to a globalizing reduction of place into a grand, homogenous time–space field for economic production. Consider, for example, what happens to place in assembly-line production: it is an opening for a space mechanized to yield a certain rate of production. Place gives way to space, which in turn is in the service of assembly-line time governed by future speculation. Finally, on Harvey's analysis, even

6.   This is not to deny that post-1945 premillennialist dispensationalists have been critical of all political ideologies, including capitalism (e.g. see Boyer 1992: 250-53, 263-67), only to point to the irony of how unwittingly premillennialists play into the very sociopolitical order and consumerism they descry as they look forward towards a new heaven and Earth. However, even in these last days, Lindsey (1981: 132, 149, 157-58) champions democratic capitalism over against its detractors.

space is swallowed by time: technology increases the pace of economic development. It shrinks the world through communication and transportation networks created to facilitate an ever-increasing exchange of goods. The virtual space of the Internet delivered at ever faster rates of baud is all the place required to make money. On this analysis 'the worldwide web' is a metaphor which renounces its ecological etymology. On 'the web' one world is replaced by another in the time it takes to click a mouse.

It is useful to consider Lindsey's Apocalypse commentaries with Harvey's analysis as backdrop. Consider the degree to which in Lindsey's books place has given way to a wholly shrunken time–space field of production. *The Late Great Planet Earth* offers by means of its title a dramatic instance of time–space compression. The signifiers refer, of course, to a future event, but offered as a retrospective. Its title describes a time so compressed that the future is already past. Similarly the space the title describes is simultaneously the physical space of the globe and what a book jacket envelops. Here, between two covers, is the end of the world that can be bought, consumed and disposed of. Further, the places named in First Testament and Second Testament apocalyptic texts are little more than spaces for production the reader is hungry to consume as she or he seeks insight into the end of the world. Place names such as the Euphrates River (Rev. 9.14; 16.12) and Gog and Magog (Rev. 20.8) become code words for world powers (the People's Republic of China; the former Soviet Union), which in turn become signifiers of imminent calamity. Reading Lindsey's interpretations of Chinese and Russian Soviets attacking Jerusalem and the nuclear holocaust that follows, one would never guess that in these apocalyptic spaces there are flesh and blood people. Nor in his rehearsal of the ecological disasters used by God to smite enemies is there any thought given to the extermination of myriad plants and animals: God is, in Lindsey's reading of the Apocalypse, an outside observer of nature's travail, a power who cannot take *all* the blame for nature's cruelty towards humankind.

> To be sure, God is the ultimate source of the judgements [those described in Rev. 8.6-12], but He has a willing ally in the fallen natures of men. Ecologists tell us that man's selfishness threaten to pollute him off the planet, so God can't take all the blame when man finally succeeds in doing the job! (Lindsey 1973: 134).

Lindsey compresses places, persons and events into apocalyptic time–space configurations. Like its capitalist analogue, geography only serves as token for the ever hastening clock ticking towards a global production — in this case, calamity. Thus he inadvertently plays into a cultural production of reality in which the planet is no longer a network of interdependent Earth relationships, but a space for apocalyptic productions eagerly consumed at the news-stand. Ecological disasters are little more than signs of the times (Boyer 1992: 331-39).

This is a colonizer's voice interpreting the Apocalypse—a religious expression of an economic reduction of the diverse Earth relations and inhabitants to conform to a pre-arranged time–space script. It is not unlike a kind of venture capitalism, wherein one invests now hoping for a healthy future return. Lindsey's books end with appeals to convert before it is too late (Lindsey 1973: 301-308; 1970: 186-88). If his books produce anything other than dismay at the sorry state of the world, they harvest souls for heaven. Souls that must, like the place names in biblical apocalyptic texts, give up their identity and become colonized by the interpreter's vision of time and space—invested like money in the bank for the inevitable rainy day. Intriguingly, the implied readers of Lindsey's books are urban American middle and upper-middle class college students (Lindsey was active in Campus Crusade for Christ before becoming a best-selling author; see O'Leary 1994: 143-46). His treatments of geography as container for inevitable events reflect the urban flight from place (usually via the automobile) which American culture has undertaken since the Second World War. Lindsey's readers, already having renounced the idiosyncrasies of place to live in more or less homogenous suburban spaces—paved over with strip-malls, freeway turnpikes and fast-food chains—live in what James Howard Kunstler (1993) aptly calls 'the geography of nowhere'. Fitting, then, that they should be invited to look towards a future that is a Utopia. As the etymology suggests, the place they are looking towards is not that much different from where they are: 'no where'. Reading Lindsey's interpretations socializes one to become a heaven-fixed premillennialist renouncing the particularities of time and place except as a form of investment that will pay off in the life to come. Where there is no longer place, there is no longer Earth, and certainly not Earth worth caring about.

Broken and Right Earth Relations in the Apocalypse

Nevertheless, there *is* Earth in the Apocalypse—Earth whose voices never tire of expressing themselves, whether quite literally in voices of thunder (Rev. 10.3-4) and the eagle (Rev. 8.13), or which speak in imitation of Earth noises, with voices likened to the sound of 'many waters' (Rev. 1.15; 14.2; 19.6), the lion (Rev. 10.3), and thunder (Rev. 6.1; 19.6). Revelation is the New Testament's noisiest book. But even when not sounding, Earth makes its voices heard. Indeed, it is voices John paradoxically 'sees' (Rev. 1.10) as apocalyptic visions unfold before him. They are voices of woe and blessing, signalling — visually — contrasting studies in idolatry and faithfulness, broken and right relationship.

In Revelation, ecological disaster portrays broken relations between humans and with God. This is one of its chief literary–aesthetic strategies of persuasion, and it draws heavily upon Older Testament pictures of creation at enmity with humankind to express divine punishment and alienation. In Rev. 8.7-12 there is a 'de-creation story' that reverses the creation story of Gen. 1.1–2.4a: thirds of plant life (Rev. 8.7), then sea creatures and waters (Rev. 8.8-10), and finally of sun, moon and stars (Rev. 8.12) are destroyed. In Rev. 9.3-10, fantastic locusts sweep across Earth, tormenting humankind. These visions of ecological destruction lead up to Rev. 9.20-21, a narrative summation that outlines the result of all this calamity on an idolatrous humankind.

> The rest of humankind, who were not killed by these plagues did not repent of the works of their hands nor give up worshipping demons and idols of gold and silver and bronze and stone and wood, which cannot either see or hear or walk, nor did they repent of their murders or their sorceries or their immorality or their thefts.[7]

Following a narrative hiatus (Rev. 10.1–15.20 — the little scroll), at Rev. 16.1-21 (parallel with Rev. 8 thematically) John again witnesses ecological calamity, this time borrowed from the epic narrative of the Exodus. Disasters reminiscent of the Exodus plague narratives (sores, Rev. 16.2; sea and rivers turned to blood, Rev. 16.3-4; scorching heat, Rev. 16.8-9; darkness, Rev. 16.10-11) fall in quick succession upon those who bear the mark of the Beast and worship its image (Rev. 16.2). The result rehearses and intensifies the outcome of Revelation 8: not only do the victims not repent, they curse God (Rev. 16.9, 11, 21).

In Revelation 17–18 the Apocalypse climaxes in the vision of the destruction of the whore of Babylon and the laments of her allies. Again, John invokes Earth themes. He sees the whore of Babylon riding a seven-headed beast, seated upon many waters (Rev. 17.3), the latter being 'peoples and multitudes and nations and tongues' (Rev. 17.15), that is, the peoples of the Mediterranean Basin under Roman domination. The beast she rides was introduced in Rev. 13.1 and, like its land cousin (Rev. 13.11-12) is a pointed socio-economic caricature of Roman tyranny dominating land and sea for economic gain (see Bauckham 1998: 338-83; Kraybill 1996). Both express an economic relationship of unbridled greed at Earth's expense.

---

7.   In what follows I cite the NRSV, sometimes with slight modification.

In Rev. 18.9-19, the laments by kings, merchants and sea-traders over Babylon's passing and the loss of their wealth continue the caricature. This parody was already forecasted in Rev. 6.6 with an appeal even amid the ecological chaos of the four apocalyptic riders (Rev. 6.2-8) to sell food for inflated prices and to avoid harming the oil and wine. The detailed listing of merchant cargo (Rev. 18.11-14, 16) describes the way Earth is mined, slaughtered, logged, spun and sold for the sake of profit. With good reason does John name these powers in an earlier vision as 'the destroyers of Earth' (Rev. 11.18). If John has anyone in particular in mind when he describes the 'small and great, both rich and poor, both free and slave' who bear the mark of the Beast (Rev. 13.16) in order to 'buy or sell' (Rev. 13.17), it is surely the lamenting merchants and sea-traders of Revelation 18. The Roman Empire was notorious for its extinction of animals and exhausting of Earth resources to feed its hunger for entertainment and luxury (Rossing 1998: 491-94). The *mise-en-scène* for the laments in Revelation 18 is the desolate and abandoned Babylon whose ecological desolation (Rev. 18.2) becomes the potent symbol of the broken Earth relationships between peoples, plants, animals and natural resources that imperial greed lets loose upon the world. A dark eternally, smoking ruin (Rev. 18.9, 23; 19.3), Babylon is all that is death and destruction. It is in anticipation of this scene that the 'de-creation' themes of Rev. 8.7-12 are to be read. The vision of the destruction of Earth is a hallmark of the ancient apocalypse genre's rhetorical–literary strategies of persuasion. In Revelation, divine agents announce the destruction of Earth, but it is debatable whether the destruction originates with God. The angelic trumpet-blowers unveil through mythopoeic visions of cosmic and ecological disaster the broken relations embodied more concretely in the laments of Babylon's mercantile allies.

The Apocalypse uses narratives of ecological disaster and desolation in order to express broken relationship. John also deploys narratives of ecological harmony as a literary–aesthetic strategy of persuasion to win his listeners' allegiance. Like the destruction narratives, these too are steeped in First Testament symbols. When the pregnant woman of Rev. 12.4 (already a potent Earth symbol because of mythic associations with fertility, wisdom and abundance; see Collins 1976: 57-100) flees into the wilderness 'to be nourished' (Rev. 12.6, 14), and Earth comes to help the woman, saving her from the dragon's attack (Rev. 12.16), John invites us once again into the Hebrew epic of Exodus wilderness traditions. Here wilderness signals right Earth relationship—a wholeness indicated by granting the woman 'the two wings of the great eagle' (Rev. 12.14) for escape. Whereas earlier an eagle spoke destruction as summation of ecological violence (Rev. 8.13), now an eagle's wings signal ecological protection. And if the enmity of Earth and humankind expresses First Testament traditions of creation at odds with the children of Adam and Eve (Gen. 3.17-18; 7.1–8.22), the wholeness of Earth relationship recalls a primeval state of blessing: 'To those who conquer I will grant to eat of the tree of life, which is in the paradise of God' (Rev. 2.7). Originary time and endtime meet in the Apocalypse (see Gunkel 1895). Both express whole Earth relationships. The promise of Rev. 2.7, of course, foreshadows the Apocalypse's final vision (Rev. 21.1–22.5). Whereas Revelation 12 takes up a wilderness tradition, John's concluding vision rehearses more urban themes, drawn especially from Ezek. 40.1–48.35, but mixed with rural-looking metaphors. John's development of Ezekiel's urban ideal is politically pointed, as we shall see presently.

As many have noticed, John's depiction of the heavenly Jerusalem offers a reverse picture of Babylon (see Deutsch 1987: 123; Howard-Brook and Gwyther 1999: 157-96). Further, John's final vision represents what Deutsch names a transformation of symbols deployed by Second Temple Jewish texts to describe the restoration of Israel/Zion (see also Rissi 1966). Fewer have noticed the way John's depiction of heavenly Jerusalem expresses hope couched in ancient utopian symbol, and how it outlines a politics designed to stand in sharp relief to the earlier depiction of Babylon (see Royalty 1998: 211-40). John's apocalyptic resources include not only Jewish ideals, but pagan utopian ones as well. As Georgi suggests, the Apocalypse's descended heavenly Jerusalem, with its picture of the garden city, draws upon a Greco-Roman utopian ideal, never realized, of the harmonization of town and country (see Georgi 1980: 351-72). Whereas, in the imperial city, there would be forum and temple, in the new Jerusalem there is a garden with a stream and tree of life. John's city is a political counter to the kind of pro-imperial ideology represented by Virgil's fourth *Eclogue*, where the Augustan order is likened to an idyllic garden. Virgil's depiction is the political application of a century-long hope (see Demandt 2000: 165-94). But John knows a crueller reality of nature at enmity with, or abused by, Empire. When he sees 'a new heaven and a new Earth; for the first heaven and the first Earth had passed away, and the sea was no more' (Rev. 21.1), we see a transformation of First Testament symbol—we also see a transformation of politics. For the sea refers not only to the mythology of chaos and order of Gen. 1.1-2, but the imperial dominion of the Mediterranean much celebrated by pagan authors and exploited by the merchants and sea traders lamenting in Revelation 18 (see Wengst 1987: 7-37).

The *new* heaven and Earth John beholds signal, spatially, a new set of relationships in which Earth—as Isa. 65.17-25 the *locus classicus* for this vision suggests—plays not a role of enmity with humankind, but enjoys one of mutual blessing. Whereas abandoned, smoking Babylon is the final slogan of Earth at odds with a Roman Empire-loving human creation, John's Jerusalem vision expresses one of harmony. A transparent cube, it represents right Earth–divine relationship, even as oriental mythology associated quadrate cities with divinely arranged order (Müller 1961). With its preference for the number 12 (Rev. 21.12), it embodies a numerology hallowed by Hebrew tradition. It *also* embodies an astrological—the ark's cosmic—perfection. Like the twelve signs of the zodiac—each, in pagan astrology, with its own precious stone—Jerusalem is the place where Earth and God dwell together in peace (see Malina and Pilch 2000: 250).

So it is that 'the kings of Earth' (Rev. 21.24), who just three chapters earlier were fornicating with the whore of Babylon (Rev. 17.2) and gathering to battle against Jesus/God (Rev. 19.19), now 'bring their glory' into open-gated Jerusalem. John draws the motif from Isa. 60.5, 11; 61.6, but, as Royalty notes, with a subtle change: whereas in the Isaiah text it is wealth that the nations bring to Jerusalem/Zion, John replaces wealth with 'glory'. This is due to the Apocalypse's literary–aesthetic associations with wealth and Babylon/the Beast in earlier chapters (see Royalty 1998: 232). Earlier in the Apocalypse these powers only took from Earth (Rev. 18.11-13); now they bring, and in bringing, they in turn receive the life and healing of the water and tree of life (Rev. 22.1-2). In any case, there is no need for money. If earlier no one could buy or sell without the economic marker of the Beast (Rev. 13.17), now John insists (twice: in Rev. 21.6; 22.17) that the water of life is free. The 12 fruit trees bearing through each of 12 months a different fruit (Rev. 22.2) echoes the numerology, both Hebrew and astrological, discussed above. Here Earth heals. Just as in Revelation 12 Earth came to rescue the fleeing woman, now John adapts Ezekiel's temple-as-city vision to include healing landscape, and so weds First Testament wilderness and temple traditions.[8]

The city without night (Rev. 22.5) also belongs to a rhetorically charged picture where the danger of social relations symbolized in the whore of Babylon's bloodthirstiness (Rev. 19.6) and her destroyed city's darkness (Rev. 18.23) gives way to a portrait of safety and security. No longer is there any need to close the gates of the city (Rev. 21.25), for the dangers of broken relations represented by the potent biblical metaphor of night and darkness have given way to a more peaceable Earth community. Right relation takes back the night from those who would use it as a cloak for destruction and violence. The vision sets out a renewed heaven and Earth made new through right relationship.

---

8.   The theme of healing landscape is also present in Ezek. 47.1-12, but there the landscape surrounds the city–temple; in Revelation the landscape is inside the city.

Revelation 22.1-5 as Giveaway

The counter-economy of the Apocalypse replaces conspicuous accumulation with conspicuous generosity. Its final vision outlines an Earth relationship not unlike what one finds among North American First Nations peoples. Read, for example, from the First Nations perspective of the Nakoda people of the sacred Earth of the Stoney Nation, the 'kings of Earth' who bring their glory to Jerusalem and receive healing could be interpreted as what the Nakhota/Stoney call 'the Giveaway' (see Grobsmith 1979: 123-31; Kehoe 1980: 17-26). The Giveaway describes a ritual practised by several Plains First Nations in which wealth or objects of value are ritually given away in order to acknowledge dependence on others for success. Through Giveaway, wealthier members celebrate their social location and publicly affirm social obligations in using their wealth to promote an equitable distribution of goods. Giveaway dramatizes the interdependence of tribal members with one another and with Earth. Among Plains First Nations, the Giveaway often takes place in the context of the powwow or tribal gathering in order to mark rites of passage, social honours and, most importantly, to acknowledge the First Nation's relationship with Earth and the Creator.

The Sundance, central especially to Lakoda and Nakoda peoples, also known as the Medicine or Thirst Dance, connects Giveaway with a sacred dance around a specially erected tree symbolizing the interconnection of heaven and Earth and the sacred character of all life. Here the interdependence of Earth was traditionally represented with activities requiring great physical endurance (see Mails 1978; Spier 1921; Lowie 1954: 197-79; Peelman 1995: 209-17). The dance and Giveaway around the sacred tree furnish a provocative way of interpreting that other tree at the centre, this time of the heavenly Jerusalem: 'the tree of life' (Rev. 22.2). Indeed, the metaphor is already cross-cultural in the Hebrew Bible: it originates in Mesopotamian culture where it similarly functions to represent a web of life (Parpola 1993: 161-208).

To read Apocalypse as Giveaway is to listen for Earth voices of resistance and blessing in the literary–aesthetic profiles of ecological destruction and wholeness in Revelation's apocalyptic stories. It is also to situate its vision of a new heaven and new Earth in *this-worldly* living. Earth's voices in Revelation tell us there is indeed a new world coming whenever and wherever there are those courageous enough to live and express the Giveaway of the tree and water of life.

Alas for Earth! Lament and Resistance in Revelation 12

Barbara R. Rossing

Introduction

Earth plays a central and complex role in Revelation 12. On the one hand, the 'woe' of Rev. 12.12 appears to pronounce a curse upon Earth, 'Woe (*ouai*) to Earth and the sea, for the devil has come down to you with great wrath' (NRSV). On the other hand, Earth undertakes a heroic rescue of the heavenly woman from the dragon's pursuit in Rev. 12.16. Just when the woman is about to be drowned, Earth 'opened its mouth and swallowed the river that the dragon had poured from his mouth'.

Is Earth's heroic action in Rev. 12.16 an anomaly? Is Revelation's overall perspective towards Earth negative? Most readers of biblical apocalyptic literature think that Revelation predicts disaster for Earth. The best-selling *Left Behind: A Novel of the Earth's Last Days* expands on Revelation's tribulations with eight novels, an Internet site, a movie and even a board game. Premillennialist Christians take comfort in their anticipated 'rapture' into heaven as an escape from Earth's grim fate. In *The Rapture* Hal Lindsey writes, 'Although I grieve over the lost world that is headed toward catastrophe, the hope of the Rapture keeps me from despair in the midst of ever-worsening world conditions' (1983: 210). Lindsey draws on Rev. 12.12 as proof that he and other Christians will not be left among 'those who dwell on earth' during the woes and tribulation but rather will be 'part of another special group called those who dwell in heaven' (1983: 121). Only non-Christians will suffer the fate of being 'left behind' on Earth.

Even scholars who do not subscribe to such rapture theology wonder whether 'the death of Earth [may be] considered inevitable in a book such as Revelation' (Earth Bible Team 2000b: 49). Ted Hiebert critiques the tendency of apocalypses to deny that Earth is our home, in contrast to more Earth-centered biblical writers such as the Yahwist (J): 'The apocalyptic worldview, whose clearest expression in the Hebrew Scriptures is the book of Daniel, despaired of life in this world... The earth was no longer the true human home' (1996: 153).

Rosemary Radford Ruether warns of the anti-ecological and even genocidal dualism of apocalyptic writings, 'based on the fantasy of escape from mortality... The very nature of the life of the biosphere...is denied' (1992: 82-83).

A few recent biblical scholars have attempted to retrieve more positive strands in Revelation and apocalyptic literature. A dissertation by David Russell surveys biblical and intertestamental apocalyptic texts in order to demonstrate that the 'apocalyptic motif of the "new heavens and a new earth" preserves an important and positive role for the present creation' (see Russell 1996: 6). Nonetheless, the perception remains that apocalyptic literature is anti-Earth. Revelation's pronouncement of 'woe' upon Earth in Rev. 12.12, echoing the 'Woe, woe, woe to the inhabitants of Earth' of Rev. 8.13, could be read as supporting such a negative reading of Earth.

In my view, however, Rev. 12.12 declares not a curse or woe upon Earth but a lament for Earth. This essay will argue that the Greek word *ouai* should be translated not as 'woe' but rather as 'Alas', so that the verse becomes God's cry of mourning or lamentation over Earth, 'Alas for Earth'. In the lament of Rev. 12.12 God gives voice to Earth (the third Earth Bible principle), lamenting Rome's unjust domination over the whole Earth as a manifestation of Satan's presence.

In this essay I will argue that one can read Rev. 12.12 and other apocalyptic texts in a more liberating, ecologically positive way by situating them within the anti-imperial political critique of the book. Revelation's primary polemic is against Rome. Even while Rome claims to reign over the entire Earth, as illustrated by its own imperial propaganda, Rev. 12.16 furnishes a glimpse of an Earth that is not a compliant subject of imperial domination. Earth's heroic swallowing of the dragon's river in Rev. 12.16 is an action that models the sixth Earth Bible principle, the principle of resistance.

Woe or Lament?

The Greek word *ouai* is frequent in Revelation, beginning between the fourth and fifth trumpets in Rev. 8.13. The word is invoked both as an exclamation—its usage in Rev. 12.12 and 8.13[1]—and also somewhat peculiarly as a noun, bearing the definite article: 'the first *ouai*' (Rev. 9.12) and 'the second *ouai*' (Rev. 11.14).[2]

1. See also Rev. 18.10, 16, 19.
2. Within the argument of Revelation these numbered *ouai*'s refer to the last three trumpet blasts and their resulting plagues, reminiscent of the Exodus plagues.

Most English translators render the word *ouai* as "woe". Bruce Malina and John Pilch (2000: 128) follow this translation, explaining that 'a 'woe' is the opposite of a "beatitude"'. Such a woe/beatitude parallel is seen in Jesus' Sermon on the Plain, for example, where Jesus pronounces a series of 'woes' (*ouai* plus an indirect object in the dative case: 'Woe to') following a series of beatitudes (*makarios*, 'Blessed are'; Lk. 6.20-26). If Revelation's pronouncement of *ouai* in Rev. 12.12 parallels the usage of *ouai* of Luke 6, the meaning would be cursing or woe, from the Hebrew Bible covenantal tradition of blessings and curses (see Deut. 28).

But Revelation's usage of *ouai* differs grammatically from Luke 6 and from that of other texts where *ouai* is typically translated as 'woe'. Revelation's references to *ouai* do not have the indirect object 'to', expressed by the dative case in Greek.[3] In order to translate *ouai* as 'woe' in Rev. 12.12 the translator is forced to add a word—'to' ('woe to')— which is not present in any of the references to *ouai* in Revelation. The references to *ouai* in Rev. 12.12 and 8.13 are followed rather by an accusative-case direct object, probably an accusative of reference. For this reason I suggest the translation 'Alas, Earth!' or 'Alas for Earth' (that is, 'Alas with reference to Earth').

Moreover, Rev. 12.12 juxtaposes the cry of *ouai* ('Alas') not with beatitudes, as in the woe/beatitude parallel of Luke 6, but with rejoicing. A summons for heaven to rejoice precedes the *ouai* on Earth in Rev. 12.12, 'Rejoice then, you heavens and those who dwell in them!' A similar *ouai*/rejoice juxtaposition is seen in Revelation 18, where a call to 'rejoice' follows immediately upon the repeated expressions of *ouai* ('alas!') in Rev. 18.10, 16 and 19. The lament of 'Alas, alas, alas!' pronounced by the kings, merchants, and mariners over their city of Babylon/Rome, contrasts sharply with the angelic invitation to rejoice in Rev. 18.20, 'Rejoice over her, O heaven, O saints and apostles and prophets, for God has given judgment for you against her'. There is a dualism between Earth and heaven in Revelation, as critics point out, but in Rev. 12.12 and 18.20 it is the dualism not of curse versus blessing but of lament versus rejoicing.

Ouai is a cry or sound in Greek that can be used to express lamentation or mourning. The standard New Testament Greek lexicon defines the term as an 'interjection denoting pain or displeasure, woe, alas'. Classical and modern Greek lament texts sometimes employ a related word, *aiai*,

---

3.   Some manuscripts of Rev. 12.12 (such as the third-century papyrus P47) add 'to those who dwell on Earth' in the dative case, or put 'Earth' and 'sea' in the dative case. The accusative case is better attested in the manuscript evidence, but such textual variants for Rev. 12.12 show an awareness of the grammatical problem.

to express the sound of mourning (Alexiou 1974).[4] Lamentation or 'Alas' is the sense in Revelation 18, in the series of threefold formulaic *ouai* pronounced by the rulers, merchants and mariners. The object of their expressions of *ouai* is 'the city', in the nominative case. Translators correctly render their expression as 'Alas, alas, alas, the city' (Rev. 18.10, 16, 19). I argue that this standard translation of *ouai* as 'Alas' in Revelation 18 should be followed for the other references to *ouai* in Revelation as well.

Part of the issue for translating Rev. 12.12 is the question of which Hebrew Scriptures traditions lie behind Revelation's references to *ouai*. The word *ouai* is rare in classical Greek literature but widespread in the Greek translation of the Hebrew Scriptures — The Septuagint, LXX — it is used to translate both the Hebrew words *hoy* and *oy*.[5] In his form-critical analysis of what he calls the 'alas-oracles' of Amos, Isaiah, and Micah, James G. Williams draws a distinction between *hoy* and *oy*. In his view *oy*, which is usually followed by a lamedh (the Hebrew indirect object 'to'), is correctly translated as 'woe to' in the sense of cursing. But *hoy* ('alas') is 'in origin a cry of lamentation', rarely followed by a preposition or indirect object ('to'). The *hoy*-oracles of the Hebrew prophets should be read as 'Alas-oracles' (see Janzen 1972). Building on the argument of Williams, I suggest Revelation's use of *ouai* may relate most closely to the prophetic *hoy*, a prophetic cry of lament or 'Alas'.

Does it matter whether we translate the uses of *ouai* in Revelation as 'Alas' or 'woe to'? Although no English word is the exact equivalent for the Greek, there is a subtle but important difference between 'alas' and 'woe to'. 'Alas' conveys a level of sympathy or concern for Earth that the English word 'woe' does not. 'Woe to' suggests that God stands over against Earth, pronouncing judgment or a curse onto Earth. This has been the predominant interpretation in the book of Revelation, despite the fact that none of the references in the best attested manuscripts of the book of Revelation have the dative direct object 'to'. If we translate *ouai* as 'Alas', God can be understood as sympathizing in mourning and lament over Earth's pain, even while sending plagues to bring about Earth's liberation from injustice. Such a translation as 'alas' or 'lament' would be similar to Terry Fretheim's claim for Jer. 12.7-13, in volume 1 of the Earth Bible Series, 'these verses are a divine lament, not an announcement of judgment' (Fretheim 2000: 105).

4.   Spanish translations of Revelation render *ouai* as *aie*, which is more of a sound or a cry than a true word (Jose Irizarry, personal conversation).

5.   Revelation does not follow the Septuagint when quoting the Hebrew prophets, however, and may be translating directly from Hebrew or employing another Greek translation.

Interpreting Rev. 12.12 as a lament rather than a curse also opens up possibilities for employing the third Earth Bible principle, the principle of voice. Pastoral care literature on grief and laments suggests that one function of laments is to give voice to sufferers. Creation's voice is prominent in many apocalyptic texts, both as a sufferer of the effects of injustice and also as an active participant in redemption and salvation. Earth, animals, waters and other elements of creation speak in apocalypses. In Rev. 16.5-6, for example, after the pouring of the fourth bowl, the angel of the waters voices the water's praise to God for judging injustice, 'You are just, O Holy one, who are and were, for you have judged these things'. The 'Alas' (*ouai*) of Rev. 12.12 gives voice to the grief that Earth and sea and other elements of creation will suffer, along with humans, as Satan stalks Earth in the second half of the book.

Earth as Captive to Rome

Why should Revelation lament over Earth? In my view, Rev. 12.12 and other negative references to 'Earth' (*Ge*) in Revelation can be understood as part of the book's political critique against Roman imperial exploitation. Revelation's 'alas' does not proclaim that Earth is cursed by God, but rather laments the fact that Earth has been subjugated by Satan's emissary, Rome, and has fallen under Rome's domain.

Crucial to such a political reading is Rev 11.18, the proclamation that 'the time has come...for destroying the destroyers of Earth'. This statement attributes responsibility for the destruction of Earth not to God but to unjust 'destroyers' who must be destroyed—that is, to Rome. Revelation 11.18 comes at a turning point in the central section of the book. Following the blowing of the seventh trumpet (Rev. 11.15) all heaven breaks into singing. Whereas the seventh trumpet might have been expected to bring more calamities, since 'the third *ouai* is about to come' (Rev. 11.14), instead a heavenly choir announces that 'The kingdom of the world has become the kingdom of our Lord and of his Messiah' (Rev. 11.15). This proclamation that God has taken power and has begun to reign means also that the time has now come for 'destroying the destroyers of Earth' (Rev. 11.18).

But first, a key plot development in Revelation 12 explains why Earth's fate will get worse before it gets better. Revelation 12 takes the form of an 'inclusio', with the central story of the war waged in heaven (Rev. 12.7-12) inserted between two stories about the cosmic woman and the dragon (Schüssler Fiorenza 1998: 224). As Adela Yarbro Collins has demonstrated, Revelation 12 depicts Rome's Satanic power in highly mythological terms, drawn from both Near Eastern combat traditions and from Greco-Roman myths of a monster seeking to destroy the divine child after the child's mother gives birth (Collins 1976). Such myths also carried political overtones—for example, Roman emperors' self-identification as Apollo, the divine child in the Greek version of the myth.

The key plot development at the center of Revelation 12 is Satan's expulsion from heaven, the result of a great cosmic battle between the archangel Michael and Satan. In Rev. 12.9 Satan loses the battle and is thrown down from heaven to Earth. Ultimately, the goal is for Satan to be thrown all the way down into the abyss, an event that will not happen until Revelation 20. With his expulsion from heaven in Revelation 12 Satan is now halfway down. Heaven reacts with rejoicing. God's people, too, can rejoice because their accuser no longer has a place in the heavenly courtroom from which to bring accusations against them (Rev. 12.10).

But Earth cannot yet rejoice. In contrast to the rejoicing in heaven, the cry of 'Alas' (*ouai*) in Rev. 12.12 laments the fact that the situation on Earth will temporarily become worse now that Satan has been thrown down to Earth and is angry. Throughout the second half of the book, Satan will now stalk Earth. Earth and God's people are currently living in this middle time and space, the 'in-between period, between Satan's ejection from heaven and his final defeat' (Murphy 1998: 292). Heaven has already become a 'Satan-free zone' (Smith 2000: 65), but Earth is still held captive until Rev. 20.3.

How is Satan's presence manifested on Earth? Revelation 13 spells it out as Rome, in the form of the two beasts who represent the Roman Empire and the local aristocracy in Asia Minor (Friesen 1993; see also Friesen 2001).[6] Imperial cult worship is the primary topic of concern in Revelation 13, with the exhortation that Christians must not worship or 'pledge allegiance' (*proskynesis*; Rev. 13.4, 8, 15; trans. Schüssler Fiorenza 1991: 103) to Rome. Revelation 13 makes the bold claim that the emperor is not divine but rather is an emissary of Satan. There is also a dimension of economic critique in the observation that no one can buy or sell unless they participate in the imperial cult (Rev. 13.17). This economic critique of Rome is expanded in Revelation 18 with an indictment of Rome as a world trade center whose unjust cargoes from Earth and sea enrich the elites while exploiting the rest of the world (Bauckham 1991; Rossing 1999). Roman slave trade, for which Ephesus had become a hub city (Harris 1999: 74) caps the list of Rome's evils in the cargo list of Rev. 18.12-13).

6.   Rev. 17.10 makes the Rome/dragon/Satan/Beast identification explicit by identifying the 'seven heads' of the dragon (Rev. 12.3) and the Beast (Rev. 13.1; 17.3) as Rome's 'seven hills'.

Roman Imperial Propaganda about the Conquest of Earth

Revelation is not the only ancient text to describe Earth in captivity to Rome. As recent studies have underscored, Rome's own propaganda is replete with such claims (Georgi 1986; Zanker 1988; Nicolet 1991). Victory processions after the conquest of each new land paraded statues of nations, enslaved captives, temple spoils, trophies and other conquered objects through the streets of Rome, proclaiming the ever-widening geographical reach of Roman dominion. Already in 167 BCE the procession of Antiochus IV at Daphne had included two statues Earth and Heaven, Day and Night (Polybius 31.3; Athenaeus 5.195b). The funeral of Augustus included an image of Pompey and 'all the nations he had acquired, each represented by a likeness which bore some local characteristic' (Dio Cassius 56.34.3; LCL trans. E. Cary). Pliny the Elder describes the parading of Judea's balsam tree in captivity:

> Ever since the time of Pompey the Great even trees have figured among the captives in our triumphal processions. The balsam-tree is now a subject of Rome, and pays tribute together with the race to which it belongs (Pliny, *Natural History* 12.111-12; LCL trans. H. Rackham).

Numismatic and archaeological evidence similarly demonstrates Rome's rhetoric of conquest extending to the entire *oikoumene*, the ends of Earth. Statues and coins depict conquering emperors as holding the orb or globe of the world in their hands. Beginning with Augustus, a series of coins depicted the emperor (*Caesar Divi*) standing triumphantly with his foot on the globe of the world, with the goddess Nike (Victory) pictured on the reverse of the coin. As Claude Nicolet notes in tracing the development of this iconography of the globe: 'The ever-more-frequent appearance of the globe on Roman coins from about 76 B.C. or 75 B.C. leaves little room for doubt concerning the meaning of its pretensions...the globe symbolizes a universal domination' (1991: 36).

A coin from the time of Hadrian, about 20 years after the writing of Revelation, bears the inscription *Orbis Terrarum* and shows the entire Earth kneeling at the feet of the Emperor Hadrian, holding the globe in her left hand.[7]

The most poignant advertisements of Roman conquests of lands are the *capta* ('captive') coins, minted in celebration of military victories. Coins celebrating the Jewish War from the reign of Vespasian bear the inscription *Iudaea Capta* ('Captive Judea') and portray Judea as a feminine prisoner seated with hands bound behind her back at the foot

---

7.   British Museum Coins of the Roman Empire, 3.418, no. 1211).

of a palm tree (the symbol of Judea). Other coins with the *Iudaea Capta* inscription show Judea as a mourning woman seated next to a bound prisoner (Calo Levi 1952: 10). Similar *Germania Capta* coins celebrating Domitian's triumph over Germany in 83 CE portray Germania as a mourning woman seated at the foot of a trophy. Trajan's *Dacia Capta* coins continue the same iconography following his conquest of Dacia (Romania), a conquest proclaimed also on the sculptural reliefs on Trajan's column in Rome. Such coins and monuments served as public proclamations of Rome's victories and its humiliation of captive lands.

Monuments celebrating Rome's conquests were frequent also in Asia Minor, including Ephesus and other cities mentioned in Revelation. In the nearby city of Aphrodisias, spectacular sculptures from a recently excavated imperial temple complex, the Sebasteion, extend Rome's ideology of conquest explicitly to the whole Earth (*Ge*). While Aphrodisias is not one of the seven cities specifically mentioned in Revelation, its imperial-cult temple is significant both because of its close proximity to the cities listed in Revelation (only a few miles from Laodicea; less than two hundred miles from Ephesus) and because of its mid first-century date. The Sebasteion's sculptural program typifies the kind of imperial theology prevalent throughout Asia Minor at the time of the writing of the book of Revelation.

The Sebasteion of Aphrodisias was built by wealthy families for the worship of the emperors. Its construction consists of two parallel three-storey porticoes of fifteen rooms each on the north and south sides that were covered with marble relief panels, leading up to the temple on the east. More than one-third of the original 90 relief panels have been found, some with inscriptions. On the north side, a striking set of geographical reliefs with inscriptions personifies the conquered nations or *ethne* that had become part of the Roman Empire, some shown with their hands bound behind their backs. The panels on the south portico depict emperors and imperial family from the first century as well as scenes from nature and Greco-Roman and local myths. Numerous representations of the winged goddess Nike underscore the theme of Roman military victory.

Representations of the figure of Earth (*Ge*) appear in two of the Sebastieon's south portico panels from the top storey, in contexts celebrating imperial victories.[8] The panels from rooms 2 and 3, as reconstructed by R.R.R. Smith, bear special attention. In room 3, a central panel of Victory (*Nike Sebaston*) carrying a trophy is flanked by two

---

8.   A third panel of Earth (*Ge*) is presumed to have also been part of the south portico, paralleling the relief of Oceanos, but it has not been found (see Smith 1988: 53).

'panels of overt conquest', Nero's conquest of Armenia and the conquest of Britain by Claudius (Smith 1987: 132). These panels depict Nero and Claudius in poses reminiscent of Greek conquests of the Amazons, subduing semi-naked female figures at their feet who are identified in inscriptions as the two conquered provinces of Britannia and Armenia. Claudius drags Britannia by her hair, his knee in her back, with his hand raised to strike her in the head; Nero grasps a sagging Armenia by her upper arm. Nearby, in room 2, the central sculptural relief depicts the goddess Roma standing over the figure of *Ge* (Earth). Since only the inscription '*Rhome–Ge*' has been published to date for this panel, not a photograph, I rely on the epigrapher's descriptions of the relief as a reclining figure of 'Earth with hand outstretched to Rome'. This pose suggests that 'Rome conquers an earth which welcomes her dominance' (Reynolds 1981: 323; see also Smith 1987: n. 30 for a description of the relief).

There is a second representation of Earth—also in a subservient position—in room 10, in a scene that Smith entitles 'Augustus by Land and Sea'. In this relief the two personified figures of Earth and Sea are depicted reclining below Emperor Augustus. As Smith describes the scene: 'the naked figure of Augustus striding forward dominates the middle of the panel. He receives a cornucopia from an earth figure to the left and a ship's steering oar from a sea figure on the right'. There is no inscription, but Smith notes that the iconography of *Ge* (Earth) would have been familiar to first-century viewers from the cornucopia. Earth and Sea offer their tribute to the emperor, celebrating Rome's imperial victories (Nicolet 1991: 46). In the same room, another relief shows Germanicus leading a blindfolded captive figure. In his hand Germanicus holds an orb, a sign of the conquest of the world. As in the other reliefs, the rhetoric of the world or Earth is closely linked to that of Roman military conquest and subjugation.

Not all Roman monuments that depict Earth and its bounty are so blatantly imperialistic. Others such as the *Ara Pacis* ('Altar of Peace') in Rome show Earth at peace, dispensing its fertility under the glorious peace of the *Pax Romana*. Even such positive portrayals of Earth, however, assume a backdrop of sovereignty and dominion made possible by Roman military victories. On the opposite side of the *Ara Pacis*, Rome sits enthroned on a pile of weapons. Earth's blessing is part of the cosmological myth of *Roma Aeterna*, the empire 'without end'.

Earth's Resistance to Rome

Revelation's lament, 'Alas for Earth' (Rev. 12.12) concedes that Roman imperial claims, as manifested in the reliefs from Aphrodisias and on the *capta* coins and monuments, have temporarily come to pass. Now that Satan has been thrown down to Earth in Rev. 12.9 Earth has become an arena in which Satan's emissary, Rome, 'makes war' on Earth and on God's saints (Rev. 12.17). Like the feminine geographical figures of Armenia and Britannia and the weeping figure of Captive Judea, Earth (*Ge*) itself has been taken captive by Rome.

Earth's captivity is only temporary, until Satan is cast down to the abyss and a 'new heaven and new Earth' dawns (Rev. 21.1). The strong sense of eschatology in Revelation promises that Rome will not last forever. The book is not so much about the end of the world as about the end of Rome. The present Earth—that is, Earth subject to Rome—will flee away at the last judgment when no place is found for it (Rev. 20.11). The future 'new Earth' of Revelation 21.1 will be an Earth free from Roman domination, an Earth to which God's holy city and God's tabernacling presence will descend. The *doxa* or glory of new Earth and new Jerusalem will be a restoration of the originally intended glory of creation. Robert Jewitt's ecological interpretation of Romans 8 captures this sense of ecological liberation from imperial exploitation, that 'creation itself will also be freed from slavery' and will obtain the 'liberation consisting of the glory for the children of God' (Rom. 8.21, trans. Jewitt, forthcoming).

According to Revelation 12 Earth is not a willing captive, even temporarily. The Earth Bible seeks to identify 'resistance stories that relate to Earth' (Habel 2000c: 52-53). Resistance to Rome has been the subject of considerable recent scholarship by classicists and archaeologists, drawing both on models of peasant resistance to modern colonialism as well as on archaeological surveys that indicate strong persistence of local culture under Roman rule (Alcock 1997; Dyson 2000). The most famous resistance was that of the Jewish Revolt in 67–70 CE, but indigenous populations also resisted Roman rule in Northern Africa (Benabou 1976), Northern Italy, Sardinia, Corsica, Spain, Gaul, Britain, and Macedonia-Thrace (Dyson 1975). Susan Alcock expands the definition of 'resistance' to include a variety of responses by subject peoples. She suggests that Greece under Roman rule can be called a 'landscape of resistance' (Alcock 1997). Dyson's work on Sardinia identifies similar patterns of anti-Roman resistance (Dyson 2000).

Earth's heroic swallowing of the dragon's river in Rev. 12.16 exemplifies such resistance, with its sabotage action against Rome's (the serpent's) domination:

> From his mouth the serpent poured water like a river after the woman, to sweep her away with the flood. But Earth came to the help of the woman; it opened its mouth and swallowed the river that the dragon had poured from his mouth (Rev. 12.16-17).

To be sure, Revelation casts this story of resistance in highly mythological terms, just as Rome cast its own stories of conquest and victory in
highly mythological terms. In order to counter mythological depictions
of Roman emperors as gods and heroes, Revelation draws on its own
biblical palette of mythological imagery. The mythic dimension of
Revelation 12 does not detract from the political critique.

A heroic swallowing by Earth is narrated in another anti-Roman
apocalypse, Second Baruch, written around the same time as Revelation.
In *2 Baruch*, Earth opens its mouth to swallow the temple vessels from
Jerusalem for safe keeping, thus preventing their capture by the Roman
army. Baruch watches as the angel descends into the Holy of Holies and
removes the veil, the mercy seat, the two tables, the priest's garments,
and the temple vessels and gives them to Earth to swallow:

> [The angel] said to Earth with a loud voice:
> Earth, Earth, Earth, hear the word of the mighty God,
> and receive the things which I commit to you,
> and guard them until the last times,
> so that you may restore them when you are ordered,
> so that strangers may not get possession of them.
> For the time has arrived when Jerusalem will also be delivered for a time,
> until the moment that it will be said that it will be restored forever.
> And Earth opened its mouth and swallowed them up (*2 Bar.* 6.6-10; *OTP*
> I, 623).

Earth's swallowing action in *2 Baruch*, like that in Revelation 12, is an
act of resistance against Roman conquest. In *2 Baruch* Earth swallows
something good—the temple vessels—whereas in Revelation Earth
swallows the evil dragon's destructive river. These scenes of Earth's
swallowing may be modeled on a similar anti-Egyptian action by Earth
in Exod. 15.12, when 'Earth swallowed' Pharaoh's chariots, thus rescuing
the Israelites. Other Exodus allusions in Revelation, such as the parallel
between the song of the Lamb and the song of Moses (Rev. 15.3), the
marking of God's saints with a seal (Rev. 7.3-4; Exod. 12.7-13), and the
call to 'come out' (Rev. 18.4), link the situation of John's first-century
readers to that of Israel in Egypt. As Pablo Richard suggests, the book of
Revelation offers a 'rereading of the Exodus, now being experienced not
in Egypt but in the heart of the Roman empire' (Richard 1995: 77; see
also Schüssler Fiorenza 1991).

An Exodus link can also help us interpret one of the most ecologically
difficult aspects of Revelation: the plagues inflicted on Earth with the
seven trumpets and bowls. The destruction of rivers, burning of one-
third of Earth and trees, and other calamities (Rev. 8.7-12) can give the
impression that the book of Revelation is anti-Earth. But Revelation's

plagues are modeled on the Exodus plagues. They should be read not as vindictive punishments but as 'ecological signs' of God's liberating action (Fretheim 1991: 387). Pablo Richard links the plagues also to the assault on the poor, arguing that it is inaccurate even to call the plagues of Revelation 'natural' disasters:

> In earthquakes and hurricanes the poor lose their flimsy houses because they are poor and cannot build better ones; plagues, such as cholera and tuberculosis, fall primarily on the poor who are malnourished... Hence the plagues of the trumpets and bowls in Revelation refer not to 'natural' disasters, but to the agonies of history that the empire itself causes (1995: 86).

Richard draws an analogy to contemporary imperial situations: 'Today the plagues of Revelation are rather the disastrous results of ecological destruction, the arms race, irrational consumerism, the idolatrous logic of the market' (1995: 86).

Conclusion

With its critique of Roman injustice, the book of Revelation laments Rome's exploitation of the entire world, its enslavement of both humans and nature by violent military conquest. While most interpreters of Revelation have focused on the book's critique of injustice against humans, I am suggesting that the cry of Rev. 12.12, 'Alas (*ouai*) for Earth', can be read as a cosmic cry for an Earth free from Roman exploitation and domination.

For us, the issue is to understand how Revelation's ecological lament takes shape in our own global situation. Escapist scenarios of a 'rapture' can only serve to deflect attention away from Earth and away from the book's critique of imperialism. There is no rapture of people up to heaven in Revelation. If anything, it is God who is 'raptured' down to Earth to dwell with people in a wondrous urban paradise (Rev. 21.3; 22.3). The plot of Revelation ends on Earth, not heaven, with the throne of God and the Lamb located in the center of the city (Rev. 22.3) that has come down to Earth. There is no mention of heaven after Rev. 21.10.

We need to seek a historical reading of Revelation that takes seriously its prophetic critique of the Roman Empire as well as its vision for renewal of Earth.[9] The author of Revelation is no ecologist, but he is a critique of imperialism. Revelation sets God's vision for a renewed

9.   I am intrigued, for example, with the Roman Catholic Bishops' *Pastoral Letter of the Columbia River Basin*, using the 'river of life' imagery from Revelation's New Jerusalem vision.

Earth—New Jerusalem—within an overall anti-imperial political context. This can provide a model for linking the discourse of ecology to that of liberation. As Brazilian theologian Leonardo Boff exhorts more generally:

> Both lines of reflection and practice [ecology and liberation] have as their starting point a cry: the cry of the poor for life, freedom and beauty (cf. Exod. 3.7) and the cry of the Earth groaning under oppression (cf. Rom. 8.22-23)… Now is the time to bring these two discourses together (1997: 104).

The book of Revelation is a biblical text that brings the two discourses together, setting its vision for Earth within an overall anti-imperial political context. Revelation gives voice to two parallel cries of lament: the cry of the poor and the cry of Earth.[10]

10.   I am grateful for a Summer 2000 seminar at the American Academy of Rome on 'Representing Geography and Community in Imperial Rome', sponsored by the National Endowment for the Humanities, and to the Wabash Institute for a Summer 2001 research grant.

Bibliography

Adams, E.
    2000   *Constructing the World: A Study in Paul's Cosmological Language*
                (Studies in New Testament and its World; Edinburgh: T. & T. Clark).
Adams, J.N.
    1982   *The Latin Sexual Vocabulary* (Baltimore: The Johns Hopkins University
                Press).
Aland, B. *et al.* (eds.)
    1993   *The Greek New Testament* (United Bible Societies, 4th edn).
Alcock, Susan E.
    1993   Grecia Capta: *The Landscapes of Roman Greece* (Cambridge: Cambridge
                University Press).
    1997   'Greece, a landscape of resistance?', in D.J. Mattingly and S.E. Alcock
                (eds.), *Dialogues in Roman Imperialism* (Journal of Roman Archaeology,
                Supplementary Series 23; Portsmouth R.I.: Journal of Roman
                Archaeology): 103-15.
Alexiou, Margaret
    1974   *The Ritual Lament in Greek Tradition* (Cambridge: Cambridge
                University Press).
Allison, D.C.
    1985   *The End of the Ages Has Come: An Early Interpretation of the Passion and
                Resurrection of Jesus* (Philadelphia: Fortress Press).
Attridge, H.
    1989   *Hebrews* (Hermeneia; Philadelphia: Fortress Press).
Balabanski, V.
    1997   *Eschatology in the Making: Mark, Matthew and the Didache* (SNTSMS, 97;
                Cambridge: Cambridge University Press).
Barclay, J.
    1996   *Jews in the Mediterranean Diaspora* (Edinburgh: T. & T. Clark).
Barrett, C.K.
    1978   *The Gospel According to John* (London: SPCK, 2nd edn).
Batten, A.
    1994   'More Queries for Q: Women and Christian Origins', *BTB* 24: 44-51.
Bauckham, Richard
    1991   'Economic Critique of Rome in Revelation 18', in Loveday Alexander
                (ed.), *Images of Empire* (JSOTSup, 22; Sheffield: JSOT Press): 47-90.
    1998   'The Economic Critique of Rome in Revelation 18', in *The Climax of
                Prophecy: Studies on the Book of Revelation* (Edinburgh: T. & T. Clark):
                338-83.

Bauckham, R., and T. Hart
    1999   *Hope Against Hope: Christian Eschatology at the Turn of the Millennium* (Grand Rapids: William B. Eerdmans).

Beasley-Murray, G.R.
    1993   *Jesus and the Last Days* (Peabody, MA: Hendrickson).

Becker, Itala
    1999   *O Índio Kaingáng do Paraná* (São Leopoldo: Editora Unisinos).

Beier, U.
    1980   *Yoruba Myths* (Cambridge: Cambridge University Press).

Beinart, W., P. Delius, and S. Trapido (eds.)
    1986   *Putting a Plough to the Ground: Accumulation and Dispossession in Rural South Africa 1850–1930* (Johannesburg: Ravan Press).

Benabou, Marcel
    1976   *La Resistance Africaine a la Romanisation* (Paris: Francois Maspero).

Betz, Hans Dieter
    1985   *Essays on the Sermon on the Mount* (Philadelphia: Fortress Press).
    1995   *The Sermon on the Mount: A Commentary on the Sermon on the Mount, Including the Sermon on the Plain (Matthew 5.3–7.27 and Luke 6.20-49)* (Hermeneia; Philadelphia: Fortress Press).

Bilde, P.
    1992   *Ethnicity in Hellenistic Egypt* (Aarhus, Denmark: Aarhus University Press).

Birch, Charles
    1990   *On Purpose* (Kensington, NSW: University of New South Wales Press).
    1993   *Confronting the Future – Australia and the World: The Next Hundred Years* (Ringwood, Vic: Penguin Books).

Bishop, C.W.
    1936   'Origin and Diffusion of the Traction Plough', *Antiquity* 10: 261-81.

Black, M. (ed.)
    1962   *Peake's Commentary on the Bible* (London: Nelson).

Boff, Leonard
    1997   *Ecology and Liberation: A New Paradigm* (Maryknoll, NY: Orbis Books).

Boice, J.M.
    1999   *The Gospel of John* (Grand Rapids: Baker Books).

Boisseau, M.
    2000   'Parchment', *Poetry* 175/3 (January): 177.

Bouma-Prediger, Steven
    1995   *The Greening of Theology* (Atlanta: Scholars Press).

Boyd, G.
    1995   *Cynic Sage or Son of God/Recovering the Real Jesus in an Age of Revisionist Replies* (Victor: Wheaton).

Boyer, Paul
    1992   *When Time Shall Be No More: Prophecy Belief in Modern American Culture* (Cambridge, MA: Belknap).

Brown, William P.
    1999   *The Ethos of the Cosmos: The Genesis of Moral Imagination in the Bible* (Grand Rapids: Eerdmans).

Buchanan, G.W.
1985   *To the Hebrews: Translation Comment and Conclusion* (New York: Doubleday, 2nd edn).

Burney, C.F.
1920   *The Book of Judges* (London: Rivingtons, 2nd edn).

Byrne, B.
2000   *The Hospitality of God: A Reading of Luke's Gospel* (Strathfield: St Pauls Publications; Collegeville, MN: Liturgical Press).

Cadwallader, A.H.
1992   'The Conformity of the Text of Hebrews to the Septuagint', *NovT* 34: 257-92.
1994   'Enscribing Peter as Follower, Listener and Friend (John 21)', in Cadwallader 1994-6: 321-41.

Cadwallader A.H (ed.),
1994b   *Episcopacy: Views from the Antipodes* (North Adelaide, SA: Anglican Board of Christian Education).

Calo Levi, Annalina
1952   *Barbarians on Roman Imperial Coins and Sculpture* (American Numismatic Society Notes and Monographs, 123; New York: American Numismatic Society).

Calvin, Jean
1972   *A Harmony of the Gospel: Matthew, Mark and Luke and the Epistles of James and Jude* (trans. A.W. Morrison; Edinburgh: St Andrew Press).

Carley, Keith
2001   'Ezekiel's Formula of Desolation: Harsh Justice for the Land/Earth', in Habel 2001b: 143-57.

Carmichael, C.M.
1996   *The Story of Creation: Its Origin and Its Interpretation in Philo and the Fourth Gospel* (Ithaca, NY: Cornell University Press).

Casey, Edward S.
1993   *Getting Back into Place: Towards a Renewed Understanding of the Place-World* (Bloomington: Indiana University Press).

Castelli, E.A., and H. Taussig
1996   'Drawing Large and Startling Figures: Reimagining Christian Origins', in *idem* (eds.), *Reimagining Christian Origins* (Valley Forge, PA: Trinity Press International): 3-20.

Cerfaux, L.
1955   'Variantes de Lk. 9.62', *ETL* 12: 326-28.

Chardin, P. Teilhard de
1970   *Let Me Explain* (New York: Harper & Row).

Childs, B.S.
1963   'A Study of the Formula "Until this Day"', *JBL* 82: 179-92.

Cohen, S.J.O., and E.S. Frerichs (eds.)
1993   *Diasporas in Antiquity* (Atlanta: Scholars Press).

Collins, Adela Yarbro
1976   *The Combat Myth in the Book of Revelation* (HTR Dissertations in Religion, 9; Missoula, MT: Scholars Press).
1988   'Narrative, History and Gospel', *Semeia* 43: 145-53.

Collins, J.J. (ed.)
    1999   *The Encyclopedia of Apocalypticism*, I (New York: Continuum).
Collins, J.J., and Adela Yarbro Collins
    1979   ' "Jewish Apocalypses" and "Christian Apocalypses" ', *Semeia* 14: 21-
                121.
Collins, Paul
    1995   *God's Earth: Religion as it really mattered* (Melbourne: HarperCollins).
Corley, K.
    1993   *Private Women, Public Meals: Social Conflict in the Synoptic Tradition*
                (Peabody, MA: Hendrickson).
Cosby, M.R.
    1988   *The Rhetorical Composition and Function of Hebrews 11* (Macon, GA:
                Mercer University Press).
Cosgrove, C.H.
    1984   'The Divine *Dei* in Luke–Acts', *NovT* 26: 168-90.
Creede, Moira
    1977   'Logos and Lord: A Study of the Cosmic Christology of Joseph Sittler'
                (PhD dissertation, Louvain University).
Crespy, G.
    1968   *From Science to Theology: An Essay on Teilhard de Chardin* (Nashville:
                Abingdon Press).
Crossan, J.D.
    1998   *The Birth of Christianity* (SanFrancisco: HarperSanFrancisco).
Cunanan, Jose Pepz M.
    1995   'The Prophet of Environment and Development', in Hallman 1994:
                13-17.
Cuomo, C.J.
    1998   *Feminism and Ecological Communities: An Ethic of Flourishing* (London:
                Routledge).
d'Angelo, M.
    1990   'Women in Luke–Acts', *JBL* 109: 441-61.
Dahood, M.
    1980   'Can One Plow without Oxen? (Amos 6.12): A Study of *BA*- and *'AL'*,
                in G. Rendsburg *et al.* (eds.), *The Bible World: Essays in Honor of Cyrus
                H. Gordon* (NY: KTAV): 13-23.
Dailey, F.F.
    1999   'Non-linear Time in Apocalyptic Texts: The Spiral Model', *Society of
                Biblical Literature Seminar Papers* (Atlanta: Society of Biblical Literature):
                231-45.
Danker, F.W.
    1983   'Graeco-Roman Cultural Accommodation in the Christology of Luke-
                Acts', SBLSP, 13: 391-414.
Davies, W.D., and Dale Allison
    1988   *A Critical and Exegetical Commentary on the Gospel According to Saint
                Matthew* (ICC, 1; Edinburgh: T. & T. Clark).
Delobel, J.
    1989   'Extra-Canonical Sayings of Jesus', in W.L. Peterson (ed.), *Gospel*

Traditions in the Second Century (Notre Dame: Notre Dame University Press): 105-16.

Demandt, Alexander
2000   *Der Idealstaat: Die politischen Theorien der Antike* (Cologne: Böhlau).

Deutsch, Celia
1987   'Transformation of Symbols: The New Jerusalem in Rev 21.1–22.5', *Zeitschrift für die neutestamentliche Wissenschaft und die Kunde der älteren Kirche* 78: 106-26.

Dockery D.S.
1990   'Acts 6–12: The Christian Mission Beyond Jerusalem', *RevExp* 87.3: 423-37.

Donaldson, L.N.
1997   'Postcolonialism and Biblical Reading: An Introduction', *Semeia* 75: 1-13.

Downing, F.G.
1987   *Jesus and the Threat of Freedom* (London: SCM Press).

Dschulnigg, P.
1988   'Die Rede des Stephanus im Rahmen des Berichtes über sein Martyrium (Apg 6, 8-8, 3)', Judaica 44 (4, '88): 195-213.

duBois, P.
1988   *Sowing the Body: Psychoanalysis and Ancient Representations of Women* (Chicago: University of Chicago Press).

Dyer, Keith D.
1998   *The Prophecy on the Mount: Mark 13 and the Gathering of the New Community* (Bern: Peter Lang).
1999   '"But Concerning that Day..." (Mark 13.32): "Prophetic" and "Apocalyptic" Eschatology in Mark 13', *Society of Biblical Literature Seminary Papers* (Atlanta: Society of Biblical Literature): 104-22.

Dyson, Steven J.
1975   'Native Revolt Patterns in the Roman Empire', *ANRW* 2/3: 138-75.
2000   'The Limited Nature of Roman Urbanism in Sardinia', in Elizabeth Fentress (ed.), *Romanization and the City* (Journal of Roman Archaeology, Supplementary Series 38; Portsmouth R.I.: Journal of Roman Archaeology): 189-96.

Earth Bible Team
2000a   *Conversations with Gene Tucker and Other Writers*, in Habel and Wurst 2000: 21-33.
2000b   'Guiding Ecojustice Principles', in Habel 2000d: 38-53.
2001   'The Voice of Earth: More than Metaphor?', in Habel 2001d: 23-28.

Eaton, H.
2000   'Ecofeminist Contributions to an Ecojustice Hermeneutics', in Habel 2000d: 54-71.

Edwards, Denis
1991   *Jesus and the Cosmos* (Homebush, NSW: St Paul Press).
1995   *Jesus the Wisdom of God: An Ecological Theology* (Homebush: St Paul's).

Edwards, Denis (ed.)
2001   *Earth Revealing Earth Healing: Ecology and Christian Theology* (Collegeville: Liturgical Press).

Eisenbaum, P.
    1997a   *The Jewish Heroes of Christian History: Hebrews 11 in Literary Context*
               (Atlanta: Scholars Press).
    1997b   'Heroes and History in Hebrews 11', in C.A. Evans and J.A. Sanders
               (eds.), *Early Christian Interpretation of the Scriptures of Israel* (JSNTSup,
               148; Sheffield: Sheffield Academic Press): 380-96.
Eisenberg, E.
    1998   *The Ecology of Eden* (New York: Alfred A. Knopf).
Eliade, M.
    1958   *Patterns in Comparative Religion* (trans. R. Sheed: New American
               Library).
Ellingworth, P.
    1993   *The Epistle to the Hebrews: A Commentary on the Greek Text* (Grand
               Rapids: Eerdmans).
Ellis, E.E.
    1981   *The Gospel of Luke* (NCBC [pbk]; Grand Rapids: Eerdmans; London:
               Marshall, Morgan & Scott).
Elvey, Anne
    2001   'To Bear the Other: Toward a Passionate Compassion (an Eco-
               logical Feminist Reading of Luke 10.25-37)', *Sea Changes: Journal of
               Women Scholars of Religion and Theology* 1: n.p. www.wsrt.com.au/
               seachanges/volume1/elveyframes.html .
Evans, C.A.
    1993   'The Function of the Elijah/Elisha Narratives in Luke's Ethic of
               Election', in C.A. Evans and J.A. Sanders (eds.), *Luke and Scripture: The
               Function of Sacred Tradition in Luke–Acts* (Minneapolis: Fortress Press):
               70-83.
Farquharson, J.E.
    1976   *The Plough and the Swastika: the NSDAP and Agriculture in Germany
               1928–1945* (London: Sage).
Fejo, Wali
    2000   'The Voice of the Earth: An Indigenous Reading of Genesis 9', in
               Habel and Wurst 2000: 130-39.
Firmage, E.
    1992   'Zoology', *ABD*: vi, 1109-67.
Fitzmyer, J.A.
    1981   *The Gospel According to Luke 1–9: A New Translation with Introduction
               and Commentary* (AB 28; Garden City: Doubleday).
    1985   *The Gospel According to Luke 10–24: A New Translation with Introduction
               and Commentary* (AB 28A; Garden City: Doubleday).
Fledderman, H.T.
    1992   'The Demands of Discipleship: Matthew 8.19-22 par. Luke 9.57-62', in
               F. Van Segbroeck *et al.* (eds.), *The Four Gospels 1992: Festschrift Frans
               Neirynck* (Leuven: Leuven University Press): 541-61.
Flor, Elmer
    1992   'Five Hundred Years of Christianity in South America', *Lutheran
               Theological Journal* 26/3: 150-59.

France, R.T.
　　1990　　*Divine Government: God's Kingship in the Gospel of Mark* (London: SPCK).
Fretheim, Terry
　　1991　　'The Plagues as Ecological Sign of Historical Disaster', *JBL* 110: 385-96.
　　2000　　'The Earth Story in Jeremiah 12', in Habel 2000b: 96-110.
Friesen, Steven J.
　　1993　　'Ephesus: Key to a Vision in Revelation', *BARev* 19: 25-37.
　　2001　　*Imperial Cults and John's Apocalypse: Reading Revelation in the Ruins* (Oxford: Oxford University Press).
Fritsch, A.
　　1994　　'Appropriate Technology and Healing the Earth', in A.J. LaChance and J.E. Carroll (eds.), *Embracing Earth: Catholic Approaches to Ecology* (Maryknoll, NY: Orbis Books): 96-114.
Geddert, T.J.
　　1989　　*Watchwords: Mark 13 in Markan Eschatology* (JSNTSup, 26; Sheffield: JSOT Press).
Gellner, E.
　　1988　　*Plough, Sword and Book: The Structure of Human History* (Chicago: University of Chicago Press).
Georgi, Dieter
　　1980　　'Die Visionen vom himmlischen Jerusalem in Apk 21 und 22', in Dieter Lühremann and Georg Strecker (eds.), *Kirche* (FS Günther Bornkamm; Tübingen: Mohr Siebeck): 351-72.
　　1986　　'Who Is the True Prophet?', *HTR* 79: 100\26.
Gill, W.A.
　　1991　　'Beyond the Boundaries. Marcan Mission Perspectives for Today's Church', in Paul Beasley-Murray (ed.), *Mission to the World*: 35-41.
Glantz, M.H. (ed.)
　　1994　　*Drought Follows the Plow* (Cambridge: Cambridge University Press).
　　1995　　'Drought Follows the Plough: Cultivating Marginal Areas', in J.C. Ribot, A.R. Magalhaes and S.S. Panagides (eds.), *Climate Variability, Climate Change and Social Vulnerability in the Semi-Arid Tropics* (Cambridge: Cambridge University Press).
Goodenough, Ursula
　　1998　　*The Sacred Depths of Nature* (Oxford: Oxford University Press).
Gottwald, N.K.
　　1979　　*The Tribes of Yahweh* (London: SCM Press).
Green, H.A.
　　1985　　*The Economic and Social Origins of Gnosticism* (Atlanta: Scholars Press).
　　1986　　'The Socio-Economic Background of Christianity in Egypt', in B.A. Pearson and J.E. Goehring (eds.), *The Roots of Egyptian Christianity* (Philadelphia: Fortress Press): 100-113.
Green, J.B.
　　1997　　*The Gospel of Luke* (NICNT; Grand Rapids: Eerdmans).

Grobsmith, Elizabeth S.
    1979   'The Lakhota Giveaway: A System of Social Reciprocity', *Plains Anthropologist* 24: 123-31.
Guelich, Robert A.
    1982   *The Sermon on the Mount: A Foundation for Understanding* (Waco, TX: Word Books).
    1989   *Mark 1–8.26* (Dallas: Word Books).
Gundry, Robert H.
    1993   *Mark: A Commentary on his Apology for the Cross* (Grand Rapids: Eerdmans).
Gunkel, Hermann
    1895   *Schöpfung und Chaos in Urzeit und Endzeit: Eine religionsgeschichtliche Untersuchung über Gen 1 und Ap Joh 12* (Göttingen: Vandenhoeck & Ruprecht).
Haas, C.
    1997   *Alexandria in Late Antiquity: Topography and Social Conflict* (Baltimore: The Johns Hopkins University Press).
Habel, Norman C.
    1995   *The Land is Mine: Six Biblical Land Ideologies* (Minneapolis: Fortress Press).
    1998   'The Third Mission of the Church: Good News for the Earth', *Trinity Occasional Papers* 16: 31-43.
    2000a   'The Challenge of Ecojustice Readings for Christian Theology', *Pacifica* 13: 125-41.
    2000b   'Geophany: The Earth Story in Genesis 1', in Habel and Wurst 2000: 34-48.
    2000c   'Introducing the Earth Bible', in Habel 2000d: 25-37.
    2001   ' "Is the Wild Ox Willing to Serve You?" Challenging the Mandate to Dominate', in Habel and Wurst 2001b: 179-89.
Habel, Norman C. (ed.)
    2000d   *Readings from the Perspective of Earth* (Earth Bible, 1; Sheffield: Sheffield Academic Press).
    2001b   *The Earth Story in Psalms and Prophets* (Earth Bible, 4; Sheffield: Sheffield Academic Press).
Habel, N., and S. Wurst (eds.)
    2000   *The Earth Story in Genesis* (Earth Bible, 2; Sheffield: Sheffield Academic Press).
    2001   *The Earth Story in Wisdom Traditions* (Earth Bible, 3; Sheffield: Sheffield Academic Press).
Hagner, Donald A.
    1993   *Matthew 1–13* (WBC, 33a; Dallas: Word Books).
Hallman, David (ed.)
    1994   *Ecotheology: Voices from South and North* (Maryknoll, NY: Orbis Books).
Hamerton-Kelly, R.
    1976   'Some Techniques of Composition in Philo's Allegorical Commentary with Special Reference to *De Agricultura*—A Study in Hellenistic Midrash', in R. Hamerton-Kelly and R. Scroggs (eds.), *Jews, Greeks and Christians: Religious Cultures in Late Antiquity* (Leiden: E.J. Brill): 45-56.

Hardin, G.
    1980   'Ecology and the Death of Providence', *Zygon* 15/1 (March): 57-68.
Harris, W.V.
    1999   'Demography, Geography and the Sources of Roman Slaves', *JRS* 89:
                62-75.
Harvey, David
    1996   *The Condition of Postmodernity* (Oxford: Basil Blackwell).
Hatina, Thomas R.
    1996   'The Focus of Mark 13.24-27: The Parousia, or the Destruction of the
                Temple?', *Bulletin of Biblical Research* 6: 43-66.
Heathcote, R.L.
    1994   'Australia', in M.H. Glantz (ed.), *Drought Follows the Plough* (New
                York: Cambridge University Press): 91-102.
Hefner, P.
    1970   *The Promise of Teilhard* (Philadelphia: Lippincott).
Heidegger, M.
    1993   'The Question Concerning Technology', trans. William Lovitt, in D.F.
                Krell (ed.), *Martin Heidegger: Basic Writings: from Being and Time (1927)
                to The Task of Thinking (1964)* (London: Routledge, rev. and expanded
                edn [German original 1954]): 307-41.
Hendriks, J., and G. Hefferan (eds.)
    1993   *A Spirituality of Catholic Aborigines and the Struggle for Justice* (Brisbane:
                Aboriginal and Torres Strait Islander Apostolate, Catholic Archdio-
                cese of Brisbane).
Herzfeld, M.
    1985   *The Poetics of Manhood: Contest and Identity in a Cretan Mountain Village*
                (Princeton, NJ: Princeton University Press).
Hessel, D.T. (ed.)
    1992   *After Nature's Revolt: Eco-justice and Theology* (Minneapolis: Fortress
                Press).
Hiebert, Theodore
    1996   *The Yahwist's Landscape: Nature and Religion in Early Israel* (Oxford:
                Oxford University Press).
Hill, S.D.
    1998   *Tradition and Redaction in Q* (PhD thesis, Flinders University, Ade-
                laide, SA).
Hobgood-Oster, Laura
    2001   'Wisdom Literature and Ecofeminism', in N. Habel and Shirley Wurst
                (eds.), *The Earth Story in Wisdom Traditions* (Earth Bible, 3; Sheffield:
                Sheffield Academic Press): 35-47.
Honigman, S.
    1993   'The Birth of a Diaspora: The Emergence of a Jewish Self-Definition in
                Ptolemaic Egypt in the Light of Onomastics', in Cohen and Frerichs
                1993: 93-127.
Hooker, M.
    1991   *The Gospel According to St Mark* (BNTC; Peabody, MA: Hendrickson).

Horsley, R.
    1995   *Galilee: History, Politics, People* (Valley Forge, PA: Trinity Press Inter-
                national).
Horton, F.
    1976   *The Melchizedek Tradition* (Cambridge: Cambridge University Press).
Howard-Brook, Wes, and Anthony Gwyther
    1999   *Unveiling Empire: Reading Revelation Then and Now* (Maryknoll: NY:
                Orbis Books).
Hughes, J. Donald
    1994   *Pan's Travail. Environmental Problems of the Ancient Greeks and Romans*
                (Baltimore: The Johns Hopkins University Press).
Iersel, B.M.F. van
    1998   *Mark: A Reader-Response Commentary* (JSNTSup, 164; Sheffield: Sheffield
                Academic Press).
Ilesanmi, T.M.
    1996   'Creation and Environment: The Traditional Perspective' *AAP* 46: ?.
Janzen, Waldemar
    1972   *Mourning Cry and Woe Oracle* (Berlin: W. de Gruyter).
Jeremias, J.
    1965   'Thura', *TDNT* III: 1973-180.
Jewitt, Robert
    forthcoming *The Epistle to the Romans* (Hermeneia; Minneapolis: Fortress Press).
Johnson, L.T.
    1992   *The Acts of the Apostles* (Collegeville, MN: Liturgical Press).
Kaesemann, Ernst
    1968   *The Testament of Jesus. A Study of the Gospel of John in the Light of
                Chapter 17* (London: SCM Press).
    1984 (1938) *The Wandering People of God* (trans. R.A. Harrisville and I.L. Sandberg;
                Minneapolis: Augsburg).
Kasemann, Margot
    1994   'Covenant, Peace and Justice. Five Bible Studies', in Hallman 1994: 28-
                51.
Kehoe, Alice B.
    1980   'The Giveaway Ceremony of Blackfoot and Plains Cree', *Plains
                Anthropologist* 25: 17-26.
Keller, Catherine
    1998   *Apocalypse Now and Then: A Feminist Guide to the End of the World*
                (Boston: Beacon Press).
Kilgallen, J.J.
    1989   'The Function of Stephen's Speech (Acts 7.2-53)', *Bib* 70/2: 173-93.
Kingswell, Mark
    1996   *Dreams of Millennium: Report from a Culture on the Brink* (Toronto:
                Viking).
Kistemaker, S.
    1984   *Hebrews* (New Testament Commentary; Grand Rapids: Baker Book
                House).

Kloppenborg, J.
  1987   *The Formation of Q: Trajectories in Ancient Wisdom Collections* (Phila-
          delphia: Fortress Press).
  1988   *Q Parallels: Synopsis, Critical Notes and Concordance* (Sonoma, CA:
          Polebridge Press).
Koester, C.
  1995   *Symbolism in the Fourth Gospel* (Minneapolis: Fortress Press).
Kraybill, J. Nelson
  1996   *Imperial Cult and Commerce in John's Apocalypse* (JSNTSup, 132;
          Sheffield: Sheffield Academic Press).
Kretzer, A.
  1990   'γῆ, γῆς, ῆ', in H. Butz and G. Schneider (eds.), *Exegetical Dictionary of
          the New Testament*, I (Grand Rapids: Eerdmans): 246-47.
Kunstler, James Howard
  1993   *The Geography of Nowhere: The Rise and Decline of America's Man-Made
          Landscape* (New York: Touchstone).
Lane, W.L.
  1974   *The Gospel of Mark* (NICNT; Grand Rapids: Eerdmans).
Légasse, S.
  1992   *Stephanos. Histoire et discours d'Étienne dans les Actes des Apôtres* (LD,
          147; Paris: Cerf).
Leser, P.
  1974   'No Man, Having Put His Hand to the Plow…', in M. Black and W.A.
          Smalley (eds.), *On Language, Culture and Religion: In Honour of Eugene
          A. Nida* (The Hague: Mouton): 241-58.
Leske, Adrian M.
  1991   'The Beatitudes, Salt and Light in Matthew and Luke', in *SBLSP*,: 816-
          39.
  1998a   'Isaiah and Matthew: The Prophetic Influence in the First Gospel', in
          William H. Bellinger Jr and William R. Farmer (eds.), *Jesus and the
          Suffering Servant: Isaiah 53 and Christian Origins* (Harrisburg, PA:
          Trinity Press International): 152-69.
  1998b   'Matthew', in William R. Farmer (ed.), *The International Bible
          Commentary: A Catholic and Ecumenical Commentary for the Twenty-First
          Century* (Collegeville, MN: Liturgical Press): 1253-1330.
Levinas, E.
  1998   *Of God Who Comes to Mind* (trans. Bettina Bergo; Stanford, CA:
          Stanford University Press [French original 1986]).
Levine, A.-J.
  1994   'Second Temple Judaism, Jesus, and Women: Yeast of Eden', *Biblnt* 2:
          8-33.
Lewis, N.
  1983   *Life in Egypt under Roman Rule* (Oxford: Clarendon Press).
Lieu, J.
  1997   *The Gospel of Luke* (Peterborough: Epworth Press).
Lindsey, Hal
  1970   *The Late Great Planet Earth* (Grand Rapids: Zondervan).

1973   *There's a New World Coming: 'A Prophetic Odyssey'* (Santa Ana, CA:
            Vision House).

1981   *The 1980s: Countdown to Armageddon* (New York: Bantam).

1983   *The Rapture* (New York: Bantam).

Loader, William R.G.

1997   *Jesus' Attitude towards the Law: A Study of the Gospels* (WUNT, 2/97;
            Tübingen: Mohr/Siebeck).

Lowie, Robert H.

1954   *Indians of the Plains* (New York: Natural History Press).

Luther, Martin

1968   'Lectures on Genesis'; 'Lectures on Hebrews', in J. Pelikan *et al.* (eds.),
            Luther's Works (2, 29; St Louis: Concordia).

Luz, Ulrich

1989   *Matthew 1–7: A Commentary* (trans. Wilhelm C. Linss; Minneapolis:
            Augsburg-Fortress).

Mack, B.

1988   *The Myth of Innocence: Mark and Christian Origins* (Philadelphia:
            Fortress Press).

Mails, Thomas E.

1978   *Sundancing at Rosebud and Pine Ridge* (Sioux Falls: Center for Western
            Studies, Augustana College).

Malbon, E.S.

1991   *Narrative Space and Mythic Meaning in Mark* (BibSem, 13; Sheffield:
            JSOT Press).

Malherbe, A.J.

1996   'The Christianization of a *Topos* (Luke 12.13-34)', *NovT* 38/2: 123-35.

Malina, Bruce J. and John J. Pilch

2000   *Social-Science Commentary on the Book of Revelation* (Minneapolis:
            Fortress Press).

Malina, B.J., and R.L. Rohrbaugh

1998   *Social-Science Commentary on the Gospel of John* (Minneapolis: Fortress
            Press).

Maloney, F.J.

1993   *Belief in the Word: Reading John 1–4* (Minneapolis: Augsburg-Fortress).

Marcus, J.

1999   *Mark 1–8* (AB; New York: Doubleday).

Marshall, I.H.

1978   *The Gospel of Luke: A Commentary on the Greek Text* (Exeter: Paternoster
            Press).

McFague, Sallie

1993   *The Body of God: An Ecological Theology* (Minneapolis: Augsburg-
            Fortress).

1997   *Super, Natural Christians: How We Should Love Nature* (Minneapolis:
            Fortress Press).

Merchant, C.

1990   *The Death of Nature: Women, Ecology and the Scientific Revolution* (San
            Francisco: Harper & Row).

Metzger, B.
    1971   *A Textual Commentary on the Greek New Testament* (n.p.p. .UBS).

Miller, J.R.
    2000   *Skyscrapers Hide the Heavens: A History of Indian–White Relations in Canada* (Toronto: University of Toronto Press, 3rd edn).

Modrzejewski, J.M.
    1993   'How To Be a Jew in Hellenistic Egypt', in Cohen and Frerichs 1993: 65-92.

Moltmann, Jurgen
    1985   *God in Creation: An Ecological Doctrine of Creation* (London: SCM Press).

Mooney, Christopher
    1988   *Teilhard de Chardin and the Mystery of Christ* (New York: Harper & Row).

Müller, W.
    1961   *Die heilige Stadt: Roma quadrata, himmlischen Jerusalem, und die Mythe vom Weltnabel* (Stuttgart: W. Kohlhammer).

Murusillo, H.A
    1954   *The Acts of the Pagan Martyrs:* Acta Alexandrinorum (Oxford: Clarendon Press).

Murphy, Frederick
    1998   *Fallen Is Babylon: The Revelation to John* (New Testament in Context; Harrisburg, PA: Trinity Press International).

Myer, B.
    1964   'But Mary Kept All These Things… (Luke 2.19, 21)', *Catholic Biblical Quarterly* 26: 31-49.

Myers, Ched
    1988   *Binding the Strong Man: A Political Reading of Mark's Story of Jesus* (Maryknoll, NY: Orbis Books).

Naess, Arne
    2000   *Ecology, Community and Lifestyle* (Cambridge: Cambridge University Press).

Neyrey, Jerome H.
    1993   *2 Peter, Jude* (AB 37c; New York: Doubleday).

Nicolet, Claude
    1991   *Space, Geography and Politics in the Early Roman Empire* (trans. Helene Leclerc; Ann Arbor: University of Michigan).

Njoroge Wa Ngugi, J.
    1997   'Stephen's Speech as Catechetical Discourse', *Living Light* 33/4: 64-71.

Nweka, A.O.
    1992   'Healing: The Biblical Perspective' *AJBS* 7.2.

Oden, Thomas C., and Christopher A. Hall (eds.)
    1998   *Ancient Christian Commentary on Scripture* (New Testament II, Mark; Downers Grove, IL: InterVarsity Press).

Ogungbile, D.
    1997   'Water Symbolism in African Culture and Afro-Christian Churches', *JRT* 53/2: 21-39.

O'Leary, Stephen
    1994   *Arguing the Apocalypse: A Theory of Millennial Rhetoric* (New York:
                Oxford University Press).
Olley, J.
    2001   'Animals in Heaven and Earth. Attitudes in Ezekiel', *Colloquium* 33:
                47-57.
Painter, John
    1996   'Inclined to God: The Quest for Eternal Life—Bultmannian Her-
                meneutics and the Theology of the Fourth Gospel', in A.A Culpepper
                and C.C. Black (eds.), *Exploring the Gospel of John* (Louisville, KY:
                Westminster/John Knox Press): 327-45.
    1997   *Mark's Gospel: Worlds in Conflict* (London: Routledge).
Palmer, C.
    1998   '"Following the Plough": The Agricultural Environment of Northern
                Jordan', *Levant* 30: 129-65.
Parpola, Simo
    1993   'The Assyrian Tree of Life: Tracing the Origins of Jewish Monotheism
                and Greek Philosophy', *JNES* 52: 161-208.
Peelman, Achiel
    1995   *Christ is a Native American* (Maryknoll, NY: Orbis Books): 209-17.
Pelikan, J. *et al.* (eds.)
    1968   *Luther's Works* 2.29 (St Louis: Concordia).
Plummer, A.
    1922   *The Gospel According to St Luke* (ICC; Edinburgh: T. & T. Clark, 5th
                edn).
Plumwood, V.
    1993   *Feminism and the Mastery of Nature* (London: Routledge).
Porter, S.E.
    1994   *Idioms of the Greek New Testament* (Sheffield: Sheffield Academic Press,
                2nd edn).
Price, J.J.
    1992   *Jerusalem Under Siege: The Collapse of the Jewish State 66–70 CE* (Leiden:
                E.J. Brill).
Rad, Gerhard von
    1972   *Wisdom in Israel* (Nashville: Abingdon Press).
Ravens, D.
    1995   *Luke and the Restoration of Israel* (JSNTSup, 119; Sheffield: Sheffield
                Academic Press).
Ray, Arthur J.
    1996   *I Have Lived Here Since the World Began: An Illustrated History of
                Canada's Native People* (Toronto: Key Porter Books).
Rayan, Samuel
    1994   'The Earth is the Lord's', in David Hallman (ed.), *Ecotheology: Voices
                from South and North* (Maryknoll, NY: Orbis Books): 130-48.
Razak, T.
    1983   *Josephus* (Philadelphia: Fortress Press).
Reese, J.
    1983   *The Book of Wisdom, Song of Songs* (Wilmington, DE: Michael Glazier).

Reid, Duncan
  2000   'Setting aside the Ladder to Heaven: Revelation 21.1–22.5 from the
            Perspective of Earth', in Habel 2000d: 232-45.
Reynolds, Joyce
  1981   'New Evidence for the Imperial Cult in Julio-Claudian Aphrodisias',
            ZPE 43: 317-27.
Richard, Pablo
  1995   *Apocalypse: A People's Commentary* (Maryknoll, NY: Orbis Books).
Ringe, S.H.
  1995   *Luke* (Louisville, KY: Westminster/John Knox Press).
Rissi, Matthias
  1966   *The Future of the World: An Exegetical Study of Revelation 19.11–22.15*
            (SBT Second Series 23; London: SCM Press).
Robbins, V.K.
  1991   'The Social Location of the Implied Author in Luke–Acts', Neyrey, J.
            (ed.), *The Social World of Luke–Acts: Models for Interpretation* (Peabody,
            MA: Hendrickson).
Roberts, Alexander, and James Donaldson
  1981   *Ante-Nicene Christian Library*, I (Grand Rapids: Eerdmans).
Robinson, J.M.
  1999   'A Written Greek Sayings Cluster Older than Q: A Vestige', *HTR* 92:
            61-77.
Robinson, J.M., P. Hoffman and J.S. Kloppenborg
  2000   *The Critical Edition of Q* (Hermeneia; Minneapolis: Fortress Press).
Rossing, Barbara
  1998   'River of Life in God's New Jerusalem: An Ecological Vision for
            Earth's Future', *CurTM* 25: 487-99; reprinted in Rosemary Radford
            Ruether and Dieter Hessel (eds.), *Christianity and Ecology* (Cambridge,
            MA: Harvard University Center for World Religions): 205-226.
  1999   *The Choice between Two Cities: Shore, Bride, and Empire in the Apocalypse*
            (Harvard Theological Studies, 48; Harrisburg, PA: Pilgrim Press).
Rowland, C.
  1982   *The Open Heaven: A Study of Apocalyptic in Judaism and Early Chris-
            tianity* (London: SPCK).
Royalty, Robert M., Jr
  1998   *The Streets of Heaven: The Ideology of Wealth in the Apocalypse of John*
            (Macon, GA: Mercer University Press).
Rudhardt, J.
  1987   'Water', in M. Eliade (ed.), *Encyclopedia of Religion*, XV (New York:
            Macmillan): 351-54.
Ruether, Rosemary Radford
  1992   *Gaia and God: An Ecofeminist Theology of Earth Healing* (San Francisco:
            HarperCollins).
  1996   *Women Healing Earth: Third World Women on Ecology, Feminism, and
            Religion* (Maryknoll, NY: Orbis Books).
Russell, David M.
  1996   *The 'New Heavens and New Earth': Hope for the Creation in Jewish
            Apocalyptic and the New Testament* (Philadelphia: Visionary Press).

Sallares, R.
    1991   *The Ecology of the Ancient Greek World* (Ithaca, NY: Cornell University
                Press).
Sasse, H.
    1964   *ge*, in *TDNT*, 1: 677-81.
    1965   *kosmos*, in Gerhard Kittel and Gerhard Friedrich (eds.), *Theological
                Dictionary of the New Testament*, III (Grand Rapids: Eerdmans): 867-96.
Schaberg, J.
    1992   'Luke', in C.A. Newsom and S.H. Ringe (eds.), *The Women's Bible
                Commentary* (London: SPCK): 275-93.
Schäfer, P.
    1998   *Judeophobia: Attitudes towards the Jews in the Ancient World* (Cambridge,
                MA: Harvard University Press).
Schama, Simon
    1996   *Landscape and Memory* (Toronto: Vintage).
Scheidel, W.
    1990   'Feldarbeit von Frauen in der antiken Landwirtschaft', *Gymnasium* 97:
                405-31.
Schmidt, Thomas
    1992   'The Penetration of Barriers and the Revelation of Christ in the
                Gospels', *NovT* XXXIV, 3: 229-46.
Schnackenburg, Rudolph
    1980   *The Gospel According to John*, I (trans. K. Smyth; London: Burns &
                Oates).
Schneiders, Sandra
    1999   *Written that You May Believe: Encountering Jesus in the Fourth Gospel*
                (New York: Crossroads).
Schottroff, L.
    1991   *Itinerant Prophetesses: A Feminist Analysis of the Sayings Source Q*
                (Claremont, CA: Institute for Antiquity and Christianity).
    1995   *Lydia's Impatient Sisters* (trans. B. Rumscheidt and M. Rumscheidt;
                London: SCM Press).
Schüssler Fiorenza, Elisabeth
    1991   *Revelation: Vision of a Just World* (Minneapolis: Fortress Press).
    1992   *But She Said: Feminist Practices of Biblical Interpretation* (Boston: Beacon
                Press).
    1994   *Jesus: Miriam's Child, Sophia's Prophet: Critical Issues in Feminist
                Christology* (New York: Continuum).
    1998   *The Book of Revelation: Justice and Judgement* (Minneapolis: Fortress
                Press, 2nd edn).
Seim, T.K.
    1994   *The Double Message: Patterns of Gender in Luke and Acts* (Nashville:
                Abingdon Press).
Seow, C.L.
    2000   'Beyond Mortal Grasp: The Usage of *hebel* in Ecclesiastes', *Australian
                Biblical Review* 48: 1-16.

Silva, D. de
 2000 *Perseverance in Gratitude: A Socio-Rhetorical Commentary on the Epistle 'to the Hebrews'* (Grand Rapids: Eerdmans).

Sittler, Joseph
 1972 *Essays on Nature and Grace* (Philadelphia: Fortress Press).

Smallwood, E.M.
 1981 *Jews under Roman Rule: From Pompey to Diocletian* (Leiden: E.J. Brill, 2nd edn).

Smith, R.R.R.
 1987 'The Imperial Reliefs from the Sebasteion at Aphrodisias', *JRS* 77: 88-138.

 1988 '*Simulacra Gentium*: The *Ethne* from the Sebasteion at Aphrodisias', *JRS* 78: 50-77.

Smith, Robert
 2000 *Apocalypse: A Commentary on Revelation in Words and Images* (Collegeville, MN: Liturgical Press).

Soards, M.
 1994 *The Speeches in Acts: Their Content, Context, and Concerns* (Lousiville, KY: Westminster/John Knox Press).

Soggin, J.A.
 1981 *Judges* (London: SCM Press).

Spier, Leslie
 1921 'The Sun Dance of the Plains Indians: Its Development and Diffusion', *Anthropological Papers, American Museum of Natural History* 16/7.

Stanley, A.
 1982 'Daughters of Isis, Daughters of Demeter: When Women Sowed and Reaped', in J. Rothschild (ed.), *Women, Technology and Innovation* (Oxford: Pergamon Press): 289-304.

Stegemann, E.W., and W. Stegemann
 1995 *The Jesus Movement: A Social History of its First Century* (trans. O.C. Dean; Minneapolis: Fortress Press).

Steinhauser, M.G.
 1989 'Putting One's Hand to the Plow: The Authenticity of Q 9.61-62', *Forum* 5: 151-58.

Stevenson, Kalinda Rose
 2001 'If Earth Could Speak: The Case of the Mountains against YHWH in Ezekiel 6.35-36', in Habel 2001b: 158-71.

Stibbe, Mark W.G.
 1993 'The Elusive Christ: A New Reading of the Fourth Gospel', in *idem* (ed.), *The Gospel of John as Literature: An Anthology of Twentieth-Century Perspectives* (Leiden: E.J. Brill): 231-47.

Strecker, Georg
 1988 *The Sermon on the Mount: An Exegetical Commentary* (trans. O.C. Dean Jr; Nashville: Abingdon Press).

Suzuki, David, and Amanda McConnell
 1997 *The Sacred Balance: Rediscovering Our Place in Nature* (Vancouver: Allen & Unwin).

Sylva, D.D.

1987   'The Meaning and Function of Acts 7.46-50', *JBL* 106/2: 261-75.

Talbert, C.H.

1988   *Reading Luke: A Literary and Theological Commentary on the Third Gospel* (New York: Crossroad).

Tannehill, R.

1990   *The Narrative Unity of Luke–Acts: A Literary Interpretation*, II (Minneapolis: Fortress Press).

Tcherikover, V.A., and A. Fuks

1957   *Corpus Papyrorum Judaicarum*, I (Cambridge, MA: Harvard University Press).

1960   *Corpus Papyrorum Judaicarum*, II (Cambridge, MA: Harvard University Press).

Thompson, J.W.

1982   *The Beginnings of Christian Philosophy: The Epistle to the Hebrews* (Washington: Catholic Biblical Association of America).

Tolbert, M.A.

1989   *Sowing the Gospel: Mark's World in Literary-Historical Perspective* (Minneapolis: Fortress Press).

Towns, E.

1990   *The Gospel of John: Believe and Live* (New Jersey: Fleming–Revell).

Trainor, Michael

2000   ' "And on Earth, Peace..." (Luke 2.14): Luke's Perspectives on Earth', in Habel 2000d: 174-92.

Trudinger, Peter

2001   'Friend or Foe: Earth, Sea and *Chaoskampf* in the Psalms', in Habel 2001b: 29-41.

Tuckett, C.M.

1990   'Synoptic Tradition in 1 Thessalonians?', in R.F. Collins (ed.), *The Thessalonian Correspondence* (Leuven: Leuven University Press): 160-82.

1996   *Q and the History of Early Christianity* (Peabody, MA: Hendrickson).

Übelacker, W.D.

1989   *Der Hebräerbrief als Appell* (Stockholm: Almquiest & Wiksell).

Ungunmerr-Baumann, M.R.

1993   'Dadirri', in Hendriks and Hefferan 1993: 34-37.

Urbrock, William

2001   'The Earth Song in Psalms 90–92', in Habel 2001b: 65-83.

Van de Sandt, H.

1991   'Why is Amos 5.25-27 quoted in Acts 7.42f.?', *ZNW* 82/1–2: 67-87.

Verheyden, Joseph

1997   'Describing the Parousia: The Cosmic Phenomena in Mk 13.24-25', in C M. Tuckett (ed.), *The Scriptures in the Gospels* (BETL, 131; Leuven: University Press).

Waetjen, Herman C.

1989   *A Reordering of Power: A Socio-Political Reading of Mark's Gospel* (Minneapolis: Fortress Press).

Wainwright, Elaine M.
　1998　'Jesus Sophia', *BibTod* 36/2: 92-97.
Watts, John D.W.
　1987　*Isaiah 34-66* (WBC; Waco, TX: Word Books).
Weber, Timothy
　1987　*Living in the Shadow of the Second Coming: American Premillennialism, 1875-1982* (New York: Oxford University Press, 2nd edn).
Weinder, F.D.
　1987　'Luke, Stephen, and the Temple in Luke–Acts', *BTB* 17/3: 88-90.
Weinfeld, Moshe
　1995　*Social Justice in Ancient Israel and in the Ancient Near East* (Jerusalem: Magnes Press; Minneapolis: Fortress Press).
Weins, D.L.
　1994　'Luke on Pluralism: Flex with History', *Direction* 23/1: 44-53.
　1996　*Stephen's Sermon and the Structure of Luke–Acts* (N. Richland Hills, TX: Bibal).
Wengst, Klaus
　1987　*Pax Romana and the Peace of Jesus Christ* (trans. John Bowden; London: SCM Press).
Westermann, Claus
　1969　*Isaiah 40-66: A Commentary* (London: SCM Press).
Williams, James G.
　1967　'The Alas-Oracles of the Eighth Century Prophets', *HUCA* 38: 75-81.
Wink, W.
　1984　*Naming the Powers: The Language of Power in the New Testament* (Philadelphia: Fortress Press).
Winston, D.
　1979　*The Wisdom of Solomon* (AB 43; New York: Doubleday)
Witherington, B.
　1998　*The Acts of the Apostles: A Socio-Rhetorical Commentary* (Grand Rapids: Eerdmans).
Wood, C.
　1994　'Anglican Episcopacy and Indigenous Australians', in Cadwallader 1993: 133-43.
Wright, N.T.
　1996　*Jesus and the Victory of God* (London: SPCK).
Wurst, Shirley
　2000a　'"Beloved Come Back to Me': Ground's Theme Song in Genesis 3", in Habel and Wurst 2000: 87-104.
　2000b　'God's Face in the Flood Story', in *BibTod*, 38/4: 218-22.
　2001a　'Retrieving Earth's Voice in Jeremiah: An Annotated Voicing of Jeremiah 4', in Habel (ed.) 2001b: 172-84.
　2001b　'Woman Wisdom's Way: Ecokinship', in Norman C. Habel and Shirley Wurst (eds.), *The Earth Story in Wisdom Traditions* (Sheffield: Sheffield Academic Press): 48-64.
Zanker, Paul
　1988　*The Power of Images in the Age of Augustus* (Ann Arbor: University of Michigan Press).

INDEXES

INDEX OF REFERENCES

BIBLE

OTHER ANCIENT REFERENCES